MANAGING
MULTIMEDIA
LIBRARIES

MANAGING MULTIMEDIA LIBRARIES

by
WARREN B. HICKS
and
ALMA M. TILLIN

R. R. BOWKER COMPANY
New York & London, 1977

Published by R. R. Bowker Co.
1180 Avenue of the Americas, New York, N.Y. 10036

Library of Congress Cataloging in Publication Data

Hicks, Warren B.
   Managing multimedia libraries.

   Bibliography: p.
   Includes index.
   1. Library administration.   2.   Audio-visual library
service.   I.   Tillin, Alma M., joint author.   II.   Title.
Z678.H6   025.1   76-49116
ISBN 0-8352-0628-9

CONTENTS

9. OVERVIEW AND DISCUSSION OF SOME FUTURE CONCERNS

LIST OF FIGURES

LIST OF EXAMPLES

PREFACE

We live in a multimedia world and have now become so accustomed to communication via media that we take it for granted. Not only are we continuously exposed to a variety of media as we go about our daily tasks, but in our homes we enjoy interchangeably and as a matter of course the presence of books, newspapers, periodicals, television, tape and disc recordings, films, and slides. We expect the library also to reflect the resources and services to which we have become accustomed by making man's knowledge readily available in all the formats in which it has been recorded.

Libraries are attempting to satisfy the demands of modern society by expanding their activities to serve the new needs of a more varied clientele. However, the transition from the traditional library to the multimedia library is not easy. Budget needs are greater, but available budget dollars are often less. The sheer bulk of available materials in every type of media poses new challenges of selection, materials control, utilization, and professional skills.

Libraries are not alone in encountering these difficulties and in keeping pace with change. Organizations in business, education, and government are experiencing similar problems. In our complex society, the process of change, which should be evolutionary and natural, seems to be fraught with obstacles and frustration.

In attempting to expand its service, each type of library is adopting a different approach to provision of the resources and activities our multimedia world requires. The typical university library is subscribing to the multimedia concept by building separate collections of nonprint materials for specific departments. Establishing learning centers is the method more often chosen by the community college library. The school library is the forerunner in the implementation of the multimedia concept and is becoming a media center. The public library, although it recognizes the value of the multimedia concept, is slow to break with tradition, except in the very large facility.

Even though all these libraries may implement the multimedia concept differently, their interpretation of it is based on a core of fundamentals that is common to all. Identifying these fundamentals demands a rethinking of the purposes and functions of the library within the framework of the multimedia concept. Successful implementation of multimedia services requires a dynamic management that systematically analyzes, structures, and evaluates, thus perpetuating change and progress.

The purpose of this book is to provide a guide to this kind of management by discussing and demonstrating practical methods for the management of the multimedia library. Discussions and case studies illustrate how these methods have come about as a result of the combination of the theoretical framework and practical implications of two concepts: the methodology of the systems approach to management as evidenced in management-by-objectives (MBO); and the library as a multimedia resource center. The importance of systems analysis as a way of thinking is emphasized in adapting management-by-objectives to the multimedia library. Primary focus is on the need to clearly formulate objectives, understand relationships, and think through an entire process step by step to ascertain that all work produces results that relate to a stated objective. It is assumed that the reader already has some knowledge of the management practices involved in the traditional library, and these are used as a general overall reference framework. The dissimilarities in multimedia materials, however, demand a diversity in management policies and methods which is absent in traditional library administration. A planned approach to processes and procedures is presented which will enable the practicing or prospective librarian to develop skills in managing the modern library conceived as a comprehensive multimedia resource center. The intent of this work is to assist librarians in solving the problems generated by the unique characteristics of multimedia so that the transition from the traditional book-oriented library to the multimedia library may be facilitated.

The book itself is organized in three parts to simulate the building and functioning of a system, namely foundation, structure, and program. This systems approach begins by presenting in Part I, The Foundation, the philosophy of all types of libraries—school, public, college, university, and special. The concepts and principles of professional librarianship must be understood so completely that they permeate every decision and activity. The next step is an analysis which identifies those objectives so that they translate into manageable entities the abstractions of the philosophical statement. The belief that every person should have access to man's knowledge as it is recorded in all types of media is a philosophical position that in practice involves a great number and variety of activities, ranging from procurement to the utilization of resources. In order to carry this out, each activity has to be identified, its purpose has to be established, its relationship to long- and short-range objectives understood, and its production managed to yield the maximum contribution possible.

Thus, philosophy, goals, and objectives are the essential elements on which to begin the building of an MBO system. Part II, The Structure built on this foundation, is comprised of organization and management. In Chapter 2, Multimedia Library Organization, the principles and fundamentals of organization are clarified and the various types of organizational structure are visually illustrated by charts. Organization encompasses all the relationships that ensure the coordination essential to the realization of stated objectives.

With the completion of the organizational structure, management, which is the technique by which the objectives of the multimedia library are effectuated, becomes the major concern. Chapter 3, Multimedia Library Management, gives the principles of management in an easily understood form. This is followed by a discussion of their application in an MBO system.

Since organization and management would be impossible without staff, Chapter 4 deals at length with personnel management. Included are the principles of personnel management and their practical application in designing a personnel management plan.

Once the foundation is laid and the structure is fabricated, activity on the program can occur as described in Part III, The Program. The lifeblood of the library is adequate financing. Funds are obtained through the budget, which is, in essence, a library operating plan translated into dollars and cents. Chapter 5 reviews the entire budgeting process, beginning with the purposes of the budget and progressing through its essentials and criteria to its actual preparation. How a budget is constructed by using the measurable operational objectives method is demonstrated in a practical, step-by-step procedure. Included also are examples of accounting routines for recording and reporting the expenditure of funds.

Attention is next focused on the work that must be performed to achieve management objectives. In Chapter 6 a basic step-by-step procedure is outlined which can be used as a guide in applying management-by-objectives to selection. This basic procedure also is applied in Chapter 7 to the management of technical services: acquisitions, cataloging, and physical processing. In Chapter 8 a similar procedure is outlined and its application to managing circulation and reference is discussed.

In the concluding chapter, the principal topics treated in the various chapters of the book are reviewed. Emphasis is placed on *how the multimedia environment and the uniqueness of different media formats affect management's decisions*, especially with regard to personnel and the planning and operating of processes so that they achieve coordination. The necessity and value of adapting management-by-objectives to multimedia libraries are also discussed. The reader is reminded of the importance of valid objectives, and cautioned against the danger of deriving objectives from results. Other misinterpretations of the MBO method which might occur are also reviewed. In addition, the multimedia manager's view of possible future developments is explored.

For purposes of this book, the term "multimedia manager" is intended to mean the person responsible for the operation on the multimedia library, regardless of size or complexity. The term will be used synonymously with the terms "librarian" or "media specialist" in charge of a school media center, or an administrator referred to as a director or by some other title in charge of a college or university library, or a chief librarian responsible for a large city public library. Questions which are addressed in the book include the following: What can the manager expect his role and decision-making prerogatives to be in coping with changes such as those resulting from library networks and automation? From increased cultural, social, and educational demands, and utilization of multimedia such as television and microfiche? From labor-management relations and the increasing strength of unions and collective bargaining in the library profession? How does the multimedia manager deal with the ever present problem of not only obtaining financing, but also of justifying the budget requested?

To assist the reader in quickly locating the aspects of management in which he or she may be particularly interested, each chapter begins with an abstract of the topics treated in the chapter and concludes with a summary of the key points discussed. An extensive bibliography and index are also included.

The authors wish to express their deepest appreciation to their families for their support and encouragement during the rigorous and lengthy process of writing this book. Thanks are also due beyond the usual expression to the editorial and typing team of Don and Julie Mayo. Professional associates and many others unnamed have provided suggestions, counsel, and guidance. Thank you all.

WARREN B. HICKS

ALMA M. TILLIN

PART I
THE FOUNDATION

CHAPTER 1

PHILOSOPHY AND GOALS

Look to the essence of a thing, whether it be a point of doctrine, of practice, or of interpretation.

The above directive, expounded by Marcus Aurelius Antoninus in the second century, is a fitting way to introduce this book and the exciting business of multimedia library management. The thought suggested by Aurelius has weathered the intervening years and remains applicable in the twentieth century. Beginning where he did in this perceptive statement, we look in this first chapter at the basic concepts which have to do with the foundations of the multimedia library in contemporary society: accountability and the place of the library in today's society; systems theory and the elements of the systems approach as applied to the management of multimedia libraries; the library itself as a system; and the goals and objectives of the library in the areas of information, education, culture, and recreation. We suggest that these concepts are the basis upon which you may build a foundation for systems methodology that will help you understand and apply the principles of systematic management in the multimedia library. Subsequent chapters will look at major aspects and problems in the perspective of these concepts and techniques.

Amid the toppling beliefs and questioned values of our twentieth-century society, we find at every hand growing concern about the need for an understanding of the basic values, goals, and purposes to which our society and its institutions must be dedicated. We seek the insights needed to bridge the distance between individual human goals and those larger purposes of the social order which can enhance both personal satisfaction and social progress.

ACCOUNTABILITY

The literature devoted to this important area of human concern is very large, and a constantly increasing number of books, articles, conference reports, and discussions is devoting itself to this subject. Particularly as individual citizens become more aware of their part in the financing of public institutions do they want to know more about how well the larger social purposes of the institution are being fulfilled. They want to know where money is going, and what impact it has upon the enhancement of human life and community progress. Nowhere is the impact of this growing, insistent need to know being more directly felt than in the library. Nowhere is the public's desire to have an accounting of what its investment in time and taxes is producing more directly visible. Accountability, in other words, has become a prime responsibility for those who manage the library and provide the services that contribute to the enhancement of the public interest through the distribution and management of the resources of human knowledge.

Accountability in itself is not new. Whether expressly formulated or only tacitly understood, it is a built-in part of any activity. What is new is the interpretation of the concept and the breadth of its applicability. Particularly as applied to the multimedia library, it is new that an organization should require an accounting from the various subunits within its own structure; that it must assume the responsibility of providing this same accountability both within its own organizational framework and to the public-at-large. What is new, in other words, is the role that management itself must play in responding to the public's need to know what is happening, while at the same time providing a means for better managing its own affairs. Not easy, this is a challenge that demands reason and practical intelligence, logical thought and experimental procedures. This, in essence, is the process of administration and management, the process in which members of the library profession must become skilled practitioners. Without it libraries cannot satisfactorily comply with account-ability dictums, and consequently, their very survival may be in question.

The fact that accountability broadly interpreted can apply to libraries is only now being widely acknowledged. Once acknowledged as desirable, the question of how to measure a service remains. Those involved in the production of materials formulate principles of scientific management and demonstrate their application. For them accountability is evaluated on the basis of an increase in the number of units produced and a decrease in the per unit production cost. However, libraries have always been viewed as service agencies, and the task of measuring the product of services is more difficult. In general, those involved in providing services do not deal with tangible objects that can be counted but instead, with the effects resulting from their service. In many instances these effects have never actually been clearly identified for they are composed of beliefs and hopes, such as "uplifting all citizens through aesthetic appreciation," that have traditionally been accepted on faith alone. Even in the rare cases where such identification has occurred, the determination of these effects is subject to so many extraneous and uncontrollable factors that business and industrial accountability principles and methods alone cannot be used for adequate appraisal. Thus, service agencies searching for management skills that will be effective in their own particular situations are borrowing techniques not only from industry but also from other fields such as psychology, sociology, cultural anthropology, psychiatry, mathematics, and science. This interdisciplinary approach is particularly evident in education, for example, where the current emphasis on describing behavioral objectives is directly related to the behavioral sciences.

Satisfactory progress in this type of approach has not been rapid. Analysis of the various disciplines is essential. It is, moreover, only the first step. This research must then be synthesized into a useful form that can be applied to the management of service institutions such as libraries and schools, and in turn, into doctrines that are compatible with the specific organization. Guidelines must be fashioned, and their application to situations that are specific to each type of organization must be demonstrated. In many fields of endeavor such as law, medicine, and education, the recognition of management concepts has long been delayed, and the need for management skills only slowly accepted.

Since the services of libraries are, in a sense, cross-disciplinary, their measure-ment becomes even more difficult and confusing. This may account in part for the fact that the personnel of libraries is realizing that a different kind of management is required if library service is to react positively to the modifications that are dictated both by practical limitations currently imposed within the library and by rapidly occurring external changes.

One of the most evident of these external changes is the general acceptance of the concept that knowledge is power. Increasingly the individual in an ever-growing population is recognizing the need to keep up with the accelerating pace of discovery and is demanding the opportunity and the knowledge to do so. A mounting pressure from all sides is challenging the traditional idea that schools are the only places where knowledge and learning can be obtained. Knowledge has always been the business of libraries, yet the majority of the population is not even aware that the library operates a knowledge business. To state the problem in business terminology, the inescapable fact is that the library profession has been only partially successful in marketing its primary product.

To list the various reasons for this only partial success is a fascinating exercise and one that is being increasingly practiced in library literature. However, little has yet appeared that cuts cleanly through the maze of interrelated contributory factors to those basic causes that always carry within them the seeds that propagate failure. Although there are more and more books and articles that treat various aspects of library operations, such as automation and information retrieval systems, there is a sad lack of precise information about the fundamentals that are basic to the overall performance of the library itself. Nor have practical methods which could remedy the situation been suggested. The literature abounds with such statements as "the library must . . ."; "steps must be taken to . . ."; and "methods must be found to . . ." which leave the librarian none the wiser as to how to proceed to rectify the irrelevant legacies of the past and fashion an institution that will efficiently provide a service capable of satisfying the demands of the present and meeting the needs of the future.

It is evident that a methodology is needed to satisfy the growing demand that libraries be rediscovered both in humanistic and economic terms. The essential prerequisite to the design of such a methodology is the recognition that libraries must function as an integral part of our rapidly changing social and technical environment.

The systems management theory which operates successfully under conditions imposed by our modern world can provide the general principles required for such a foundation. The principles that govern systematic processes remain essentially the same even when applied to such diverse fields as industry and education. By using basic systems procedures and supplying data and detail specific to libraries, the translation of management skills into an effective and comprehensive methodology of library planning and developmental functioning can be achieved. By applying a systems approach to their own management, libraries can demonstrate their willingness to be accountable and to function effectively in society on contemporary terms.

THE SYSTEMS APPROACH

The systems approach came into being during the early days of World War II. It was originally developed in designing radar, weapons, combat aircraft, and other hardware, when researchers and designers realized that a weapons system had to function as a whole to achieve the performance expected of it. In designing equipment it also became evident that the importance of the various parts was not in how they operated separately, but how they interacted with other parts to accomplish the goal of the whole system. The success of the systems approach in designing hardware led to its use in designing software—plans for defense and campaigns, for example. Teams of teachers, biologists, mathematicians, physicists, and other professional personnel were mobilized to use the methodology of the systems approach in proving military tactics and strategies, first in the Battle of Britain and then in many major campaigns to follow.

Following World War II, the systems approach evolved rapidly. It continues to be applied in solving many different problems of varying degrees of difficulty and complexity in many different fields of endeavor. Since 1965 it has been used by the U.S. government to evaluate federal programs. The military makes use of it, as do business and industry. Its application is evident in communications systems, space technology, industrial production, information processing and retrieval, management and logistic systems, and in many other areas.

There is no clear-cut set of rules for the systems approach, since it is not a concrete thing but an ongoing process. The systems approach, however, does contain a core of procedures which can be identified, discussed, and used in a step-by-step sequence. The systems approach does not of itself bring order out of chaos or find solutions to problems. It is an attitude, a way of thinking, a methodology which is a tool for management, and its degree of success will depend on how the manager interprets and applies it for a given situation. In the multimedia library, the manager employs the systems approach through the management-by-objectives (MBO) technique, making the interpretations and adaptations necessary to provide better operational efficiency in the organization.

Management-by-objectives, the management process recommended for the multimedia library and explained in detail in subsequent chapters, is considered a phase of the systems approach, just as are program budgeting and management information systems. Therefore, before discussing and demonstrating how the manager practices management-by-objectives, it is important to understand what a system is and to become familiar with the core of procedures embodied in the systems approach.

TERMINOLOGY

Management is now considered a separate discipline. It has its own ever-growing vocabulary, and with it the problem of establishing a standardized terminology. In many instances the interpretation and meaning of a term may differ considerably depending upon the context in which it is used and the point of view expressed. Therefore, in the following discussion of the essentials of a system, terms are defined as they are used in this book.

ESSENTIALS OF A SYSTEM

A system is an organized unity so designed that a predetermined purpose is attained through the interdependence, regular interaction, and integrated functioning of its many diverse parts. The key words that convey the systems concept in this definition are *unity* (the system itself), *purpose*, *parts*, and *functioning*. These may be translated as the major characteristics by which a system can be identified.

PURPOSE

There would be no system if there were no purpose. The design is deliberately created to produce a required output. The purpose is the reason that the system exists. It answers the question "Why?"

PARTS AND CONTENT

Various parts are needed to build a system. The content is the sum of these parts, or components, organized to achieve the stated purpose. The content answers the question "What?"

FUNCTIONING AND PROCESS

To activate the system the parts have to function. The process, or program, is the functioning of the parts manipulated to accomplish the specified purpose. The process answers the question "How?" Both content and process have the same final goal, to achieve the purpose of the system. Therefore, their interrelationship is continuous and their interaction regular. This relationship is illustrated in Figure 1.

The parts that make up the content of a system may, in themselves, be identified as systems with their own content and process. For example, the acquisitions or cataloging departments in a library are both separate systems and parts of a larger system, and in this relationship are designated subsystems. The total system is related to and acted upon by other systems in the environment, called suprasystems. If the total system is studied as a part of a larger outside system, it in turn becomes a subsystem. The media center in the school, for example, is one facet of the school, and the school, in turn, is a part of the larger educational system.

METHODOLOGY

A system, of and by itself, does not produce a better school or a better library. What it does is to demand a way of looking at things so that various segments of thoughts and actions are organized into logical and real relationships. Such a point of view is known as the systems approach. It enables those involved in the system's operation to identify what they want to achieve, how they want to do it, and how they can evaluate the results.

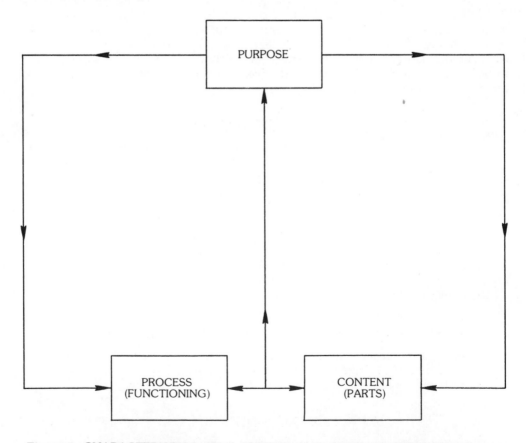

Figure 1. CHARACTERISTICS OF A SYSTEM AND THEIR INTERRELATIONSHIPS

The procedures employed in the systems approach are variously labeled as systems analysis, problem analysis, operations analysis or research, systems planning, and systems design or development. While a different aspect may be emphasized in each of these terms, the strategies associated with all of them are basically the same. They employ a fundamental methodology that consists of six successive major steps. These steps are outlined, with brief explanations, in the following pages. The outline provides the procedural framework that is used in applying the systems approach to the management of multimedia libraries.

Procedures in Systems Methodology

I. *Identify the Purpose*
    A. State the philosophy
       Every system comes into being as a result of certain beliefs and concepts. This is the philosophy from which the purpose of the system is derived, the foundation on which the system is structured. To avoid misinterpretation of the system's real mission, state this philosophy clearly.
    B. Formulate the purpose
       From the statement of philosophy identify the comprehensive purpose of the system. This is the system's rationale, and determines the kinds of processes in which it has to be engaged.

II. *Set the Goals*
    Translate the purpose into a statement of broad goals. These are the desired outcomes expressed in general terms; for example, overall accomplishments, competencies, attitudes, etc., that are expected.

III. *Define the Objectives*
    A. Specify the objectives
       Break down stated goals into objectives which express these goals in specific and operational terms and delineate precisely what needs to be accomplished.
    B. Check the validity of objectives
       A valid objective should have:
       1. A clear definition
       2. Conformity to the system's goals
       3. Feasibility
          The well-constructed objective should be realistic and attainable, but still represent a significant challenge.
       4. Measurability by observation
          The achievement of an objective must come as a result of some kind of observable performance. Observation is a means of acquiring data needed for evaluation.
       5. Standards of expectancy
          To be capable of measurement the properly stated objective must be as specific and quantitative as possible. Many types of activities lend themselves easily to quantification. However, there are many that do not. For these, the measurable factors, such as those for which there are standards that could serve as reasonably reliable indicators of successful performance, should be identified.
       6. Operational capability
          The performance required to accomplish the objective should not engender operational difficulties but should interrelate smoothly with the functioning of all the parts of the system.

IV. *Design the Plan*

Devise processes or programs which convert what is put into each part of the system into the product that contributes to the desired output of the total system.

A. Consider the alternatives

Assess the various alternatives that may be used. Each alternative includes both the components and the different ways of manipulating them to meet other objectives.

1. Gather data

Research, which in this context means data gathering, is an essential prerequisite to the determination of what resources are available, the results of past performance, present conditions and priorities, and possible future ones.

2. Select alternatives

Based on the accumulated and synthesized information gathered, select or reject alternatives.

B. Create the process

1. Integrate alternatives to produce operating procedures that smoothly interact and function as a whole.

2. Build in provision for change resulting from new input.

V. *Implement the Process*

A. Execute and direct the process

1. Operate the process as designed

2. Observe its functioning and output

B. Evaluate the process

1. Measure achievements against specific objectives

2. Modify procedures as needed

VI. *Evaluate the Objectives*

A. Gather feedback information in order to assess the validity of an objective or objectives

B. Determine further program modifications if continuation of objectives as specified is indicated

C. Determine if modification of objectives is needed

The methodology discussed here is visually described in Figure 2.

THE MULTIMEDIA LIBRARY IS A SYSTEM

We have proposed that the library is in fact a system. Certainly, the three aspects that identify a system are present in the library. It is always referred to as "the library," a unity organized for a specific purpose, the communication of knowledge. *Materials resources* (the collection of print and nonprint items in which knowledge is recorded), *human resources* (professional and classified personnel), *facilities*, and *equipment* are its parts. Management is the process through which its reciprocal library-patron relationship is accomplished. The whole, as a process relating patron, materials, and equipment, is the function of the library system within society. It is integrated with society which is its suprasystem, for it is society which influences its purpose, provides its resources and constraints, and evaluates its adequacy. The library also has its subsystems—acquisitions, cataloging, circulation, and the like. Although each has its own specific objectives, the ultimate task of

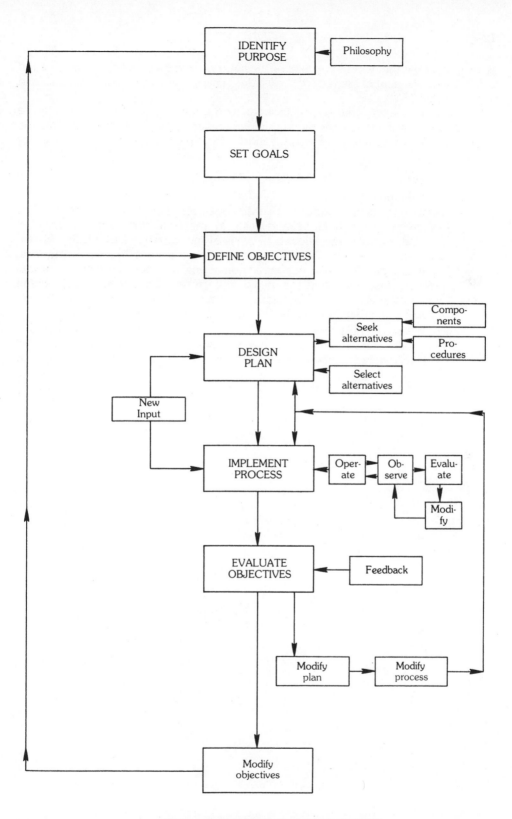

Figure 2. SYSTEMS METHODOLOGY

each is to serve the overall purpose of the library: the dissemination of information and the management of sources of knowledge. This system of relationships is shown in Figure 3.

Let us now apply this line of thought to the multimedia library, utilizing the procedures in systems methodology outlined earlier in the chapter to analyze the characteristics of this type of organization. Consider each step in the order of precedence.

I. *Identify the Purpose of the Multimedia Library*
   A. State the philosophy

      Knowledge is essential for the continuous evolution of human society. The key to progress in civilization rests in the collection and utilization of knowledge as it is recorded in all types of media. Access to this knowledge will result in continuous lifelong education; changes in social attitudes, behavioral patterns, and economic conditions; and development of cultural appreciations, skills, and the meaningful use of leisure time. Every person should have access to this means of enriching life and freedom to choose, according to individual needs, the use to be made of it.

   B. Formulate the purpose

      The modern library is a center that provides comprehensive resources in all those media that will best establish communication with every individual and

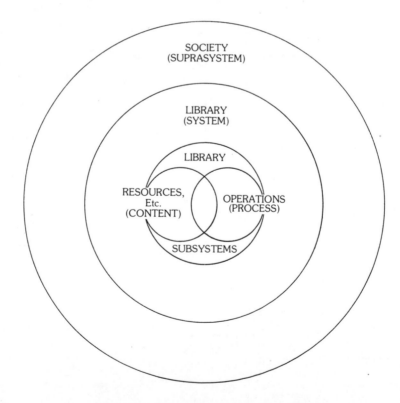

Figure 3. THE LIBRARY AS A SYSTEM

effectively enhance human life. The purpose of the multimedia library is to furnish society with recorded knowledge in such a way that the above results are accomplished.

II. *Set the Goals*

A. Analyze the goals of the traditional library

Traditionally the library has been regarded as a storehouse of knowledge, a point of view that does not necessarily provide for the effective use of mankind's accumulated wisdom. The acquiring, organizing, and preserving of the collection has, in fact, often assumed such priority in traditional library practice that it has become an end in itself rather than a means for implementing the use and application of recorded knowledge to better human life. The exclusion of knowledge in formats other than the book has further reduced the effectiveness of library service.

B. Analyze the need for new goals

The present demands of society necessitate a shift in emphasis that translates with greater validity the concept of the diffusion of knowledge and its consequent effects. This assumes a relationship between the public, the body of knowledge itself, however recorded, and the library, a relationship in which the library is the center of both an inward and outward flow of information that produces effective interaction between the patron and the sources of human knowledge. To assure such a continuous kinetic process the library must abandon the traditional role of passive agent concerned primarily with holdings, and become a dynamic, interactive force which directs its effort toward the creation of situations in which communication can occur.

C. Express goals as functions

The multimedia library performs four basic functions: to inform, to educate, to provide cultural experience and growth, and to provide meaningful recreation for the individual and society. These functions, further, serve the whole of society, including all ethnic, educational, economic, and social strata within society. The whole record of knowledge is the business of the library, and all functions of the library are geared to assemble and organize for access the resources of human knowledge that may contribute to the realization of an enlightened society.

The four functions are inextricably interrelated, not only in their processes but also in their specific goals. It is evident that any one of them relates to all the others. Each, however, in itself, has distinctive characteristics. Let us look, in Example 1, at how these functions work, in practice, as seen from the point of view of goal and process.

EXAMPLE 1
GOALS OF THE MULTIMEDIA LIBRARY
EXPRESSED AS FUNCTIONS

I. *Informational Function*

A. The multimedia library is intended to achieve the following:
1. Communication of ideas
2. Confidence and judgment in the handling of information
3. Utilization of available information to achieve specific ends, change economic, political, and social life conditions
4. Assist in solving problems of society

EXAMPLE 1 (Cont.)

    B. The process by which the multimedia library accomplishes these goals is best exemplified by the role of the library as:
1. A center for reliable information
2. A source of rapid access, retrieval, and transfer of information
3. A locus from which to relate human knowledge to human needs
4. A focal center which emphasizes the importance of information and knowledge toward resolution of human needs

II. *Educational Function*

    A. The multimedia library seeks to implement the following educational goals:
1. To provide for continuous, lifelong education
2. To create and sustain broad academic interests, creativity, and independent intellectual activity, and to support intellectual freedom
3. To encourage perceptual sensitivity and occupational competence
4. To promote positive social attitudes and a democratic society

    B. The processes by which these ends are accomplished by the multimedia library include the following:
1. The provision of educational opportunities and an atmosphere of learning
2. Guidance in the selection and use of materials
3. Training in perceptual and research skills
4. The promotion of intellectual freedom as related to the use and meaning of knowledge and the problems of human survival, emotional balance, and social needs

III. *Cultural Function*

    A. The multimedia library has as its goals the need to work toward the achievement of the following:
1. An improved quality of life
2. Broadened aesthetic interests and artistic appreciations
3. The encouragement of artistic creativity and cultural freedom
4. The development of positive human relations

    B. These goals are supported by processes suggested by the following:
1. The presentation and support of art forms representative of all cultures
2. The support of aesthetic experience
3. Guidance in appreciation of the arts, culturally divergent points of view, and an atmosphere of intercultural understanding
4. The promotion of artistic and cultural expression as related to daily living, sentient needs, and emotional and interpersonal needs

IV. *Recreational Function*

    A. The multimedia library serves the following goals in the area of human recreational needs:
1. To support and enhance a balanced and enriched life
2. To provide for a wide range of recreational interests and the meaningful use of leisure time
3. To support the creative use of entertainment activity
4. To support intercultural understanding

    B. These goals are served by the following processes:
1. The provision of a center for recreational information, the materials for recreation, and programs of recreational value
2. The support of an atmosphere conducive to relaxation and enjoyment
3. Guidance in the use of leisure time
4. The relation of recreation to needs of daily living, education, and culture

Purpose and goals form the conceptual foundation of the multimedia library. By defining these as operational objectives, steps IV through VI of the procedures used in transforming systems methodology into reality may then be implemented: *designing a plan* according to type of library, location, community or institutional environment, and similar factors; *implementing the process*; and *evaluating the objectives*. The technical and human skills of management are needed to specify the conditions required to plan such a program and to put it into practice.

SUMMARY

In this first chapter, concepts have been introduced which are at one and the same time the philosophy and goals of the multimedia library—service to the public, accountability, and the enhancement of human life through the effective management of the resources of human knowledge. Systematic management of the multimedia library is a key to the realization of these goals. Not new, the concept of managing resources has been with us since the first collection of documents was somehow put together and someone took charge.

What is new, and thus demanding of new insights and appreciations, is the way in which accountability is applied in the contemporary library. Management-by-objectives is a recent development of business and industry and can be directly attributed to the development of computer technology and the processing characteristics and capabilities of our new age of science in both learning and human affairs. Now progress toward and accomplishment of goals is measured in terms of preset objectives that are well defined and clearly stated. Knowing where the multimedia library is going makes it easier to decide how far it has gone, and how well the job has been done. It provides the manager with a better sense of "plan," an orderly and progressive action procedure by which to put such a plan into effect, and offers a basis for measuring and evaluating results. It affords the multimedia library manager, in other words, a chance to order professional conduct—to manage the work—on the basis of the values and goals of the total mission, and in terms of the known and carefully stated objectives.

Accountability in this context is an area of professional enterprise which requires special insights and applications. Business and industry deal with production-oriented goods and services, unit production costs, and the like. This is not true of much of the work done in the multimedia library. Here, the professional is dealing largely with intangibles, and with values more difficult to assess and measure. Tradition, highly specialized training and knowledge, and a variety of academic and intellectual values make systemics a more difficult accomplishment in the library environment as compared to business and industry. So, together with insights from computer and related technology and the systems sciences, the contemporary science of multimedia library management has had to look to the social sciences, mathematics, and other areas as well, for the larger conceptual and technical base it needs to establish a science of multimedia library management anchored in the MBO technique.

The first chapter has looked at the basic philosophical concepts which underlie the systems approach and explained the terminology and working applications of management-by-objectives in the multimedia library context. As used in this book, system is *an organized unity so designed that a predetermined purpose is attained through the interdependent, regular interaction,* and *integrated functioning* of its many parts.

The key words in the systems concept are purpose, function, and parts. A system is developed to accomplish a prestated goal, described as an outcome. Functions are those operating procedures by which these outcomes are advanced and accomplished. Parts, in this context, are the separate areas of activity within the total system which contribute to the operation of the whole process. A variety of procedures employed in the systems approach are discussed: systems analysis, planning, design, and the like. Six procedural steps in systems methodology are described in detail: (1) identification of purpose; (2) preparation of a statement of goals; (3) definition of objectives; (4) design of a plan for implementation of the system; (5) implementation—the process step (putting the system into effect); and (6) evaluation and revision.

These steps involve, consecutively, the orderly statement of philosophy and purpose of the intended system, translation of these purposes and values into broad goals and desired outcomes, the definition by breakdown of these goals into measurable objectives in terms of validity, feasibility, measurability, and related factors, and then the design of a plan from carefully reviewed alternatives which can permit effective implementation and evaluation of the process used to get the system into action.

The evaluation step is perhaps the most crucial of these six. On the basis of feedback, new outcomes desired, and observed working characteristics of the system, the process may then be modified as needed to permit better attainment of goals and objectives. The key factor in any system is its self-corrective capability. Based upon prestated objectives, a good system continuously updates and changes itself to realistically and effectively attain its stated goals. The system, in other words, is not an end in itself, but a means toward the attainment of carefully stated outcomes. If it doesn't work, it changes and adjusts.

As applied to the multimedia library, the systems concept is discussed and described in the context of functions and processes. The library is seen as a subsystem of society at large (a suprasystem), in which several internal subsystems, as related to content and process, can be identified: administration and management, budgeting, selection, acquisitions, cataloging and processing, circulation, and the like. The reader is enjoined to recognize, as a starting point in an approach to systematic management of the multimedia library, that purposes and goals form the conceptual foundation of the multimedia library. It is suggested that by defining these purposes and goals as operational objectives, and by designing detailed plans for their implementation, systems methodology transforms them into reality. Understanding of the technical and human skills of management is needed to specify the conditions required to plan such a program and put it into practice. Subsequent chapters will provide the understanding and skills needed to do this.

PART II
THE STRUCTURE

CHAPTER 2

MULTIMEDIA
LIBRARY ORGANIZATION

The math department has provided access for students to calculators on the main floor of the learning center. (Courtesy of Cuesta College.)

Looking at the multimedia library now as a system, we examine the structure of its organization, roles and responsibilities of its staff members, and the relationships, both formal and informal, which exist within that system. In the context of historical perspectives and organizational patterns, concepts, definitions, and applied descriptions are provided as related to organizational formats: centralization versus decentralization, delegation, and policy and management-related concepts and practices. Discussion and examples are provided to enhance the reader's understanding of several principles of organization including the principles of objectives accomplishment, responsibility, authority, accountability, span of control, activities, flexibility, proportion, and communication. Other principles discussed and illustrated with case studies include functionalization, stability, and simplicity. Several linecharts provide visual and quick access to how these principles work in the organizational context. Discussion is given on how these relationships and the organizational structure relate to the challenge of effective management. The chapter points out the essential difference between traditional library management, and the challenges of multimedia management in the contemporary context of management-by-objectives, in the organizational framework of the library.

It has been established that the multimedia library is a system, a unity organized for the specific purpose of communicating knowledge, and that this purpose can best be achieved through management techniques that practice systems methodology. The management process cannot function autonomously in a limitless theoretical vacuum, however. Realistically, it must operate within the parameters of an organization structured to implement the system's goals. Management cannot function without organization.

It is essential, therefore, to structure an organization that is conducive to maximum accomplishment of the multimedia library purpose. Traditional library organization makes its contribution. So also do organizations in business, industry, education, and other fields of endeavor. The changing values of a technological society are a powerful molding force that cannot be disregarded. They generate the demand that knowledge be made available through every kind of medium. The design of the organization, therefore, must be a synthesis of traditional structural elements and those that are unique to multimedia.

A design that is created without a clear understanding of the reason for its creation and the probable effects it will have is nonfunctional, and in all likelihood will be short-lived. A functional design is ensured when analysis of data supplied by research provides basic elements from which the creation can flow. Thus, a necessary prerequisite to devising the structure of the multimedia library organization is a knowledge of organization itself: its purpose, components, and definition; its types and patterns; its operating mode; and its past results, present effects, and future possibilities.

DEFINITION OF ORGANIZATION

Historically, the evolution of organizational theory mirrors the varying concepts and shifting emphases of society. Such reflection is only natural since organization is principally concerned with human relationships in a group activity that, when taken together, equate to the social structure.

Organization is the most effective method yet devised to pool the cooperative efforts of staff and channel them into productive processes. Society sanctions the organization only because it judges the organization to be capable of satisfying some need. If such a need is reasonably well satisfied by a particular device, society passes that device along to future generations as an integral part of its culture. This has been true of the traditional library, which was basically book oriented, and which has been passed on by society as a useful organization. In our changing world of today, however, the traditional library finds itself unable to completely fulfill its historical role. There has been such a knowledge and information explosion and so much new knowledge made available through varied and diversified materials that the traditional book library has had to give way to the multimedia library organization, a unique kind of library development which can better meet the needs of society through the use of diversified materials, techniques, and contemporary technology. At the heart of this role, of course, is the organization of the multimedia library itself.

An organization is made up of people who share an interest in the pursuit of the same objectives. It is characterized by a management or leadership which defines roles and tasks for both the group and its individual members. These members' roles are structured around the activities or functions necessary to the accomplishment of present objectives. Management furnishes them with the needed tools, equipment, and facilities to accomplish the tasks and objectives assigned. The organization creates, through management, adequate policies, procedures, authority, accountability, and responsibility to permit the fulfillment of organizational objectives.

There are many different definitions of organization, depending primarily on background and point of view. The concern of this book is with organization as it affects multimedia libraries. Such organization should be based upon essential elements that are objective oriented, and organizational behavior must be directed toward objectives which are understood by all staff members.

In today's definition of organization there is change from that of the late 1940s and 1950s. Organization's concern at mid-century was related largely to planning, organizing, and controlling the processes of coordinated activity, and on techniques of decision making. In the "now" definition of organization, consideration must be given to the effect of different social systems, goals, and environmental factors upon the management process. In setting up an organizational structure, it is necessary to identify the individuals and groups who achieve the power to give direction to organization, and the conditions under which that power can be made more effective. Power in this usage means responsibility for leadership, direction, and accountability.

SOCIAL SYSTEM

In order to fully carry out managerial functions, one must look at the social systems of an organization. This attention to human interactions identifies one of the basic characteristics of an organization: an organization is a system of structural interpersonal relationships. Individuals are differentiated in terms of authority, status, and role.

Roles must be designed and maintained so people can work together in carrying out action plans and accomplishing objectives. This is the task of organizing; the structuring of roles. It involves grouping the tasks necessary to accomplish plans, assigning activities to departments, areas, or divisions, and providing coordination through delegation of responsibility.

Organizing is a distinctive managerial function and should be distinguished from organization, which is a structure. Organizing is a basic function of managers concerned primarily with formal structure as a means of gaining effective group action. Organization is concerned with the social structure that is associated with human relationships in a group activity.

Tasks and people to accomplish them are the major concerns of organization. The reason that organization exists is the need for specialization of labor. Therefore, the structuring of tasks and assignments is the cornerstone of organizational design. In libraries, the knowledge and skills of professional librarians, paraprofessionals, and clerical personnel are the specialized labors that are utilized in organizational design. Organization structures and integrates activities of the staff so that members work together in interdependent, coordinated relationships. The library organization is objectives oriented, for people work in cooperation to accomplish the library's objectives.

As discussed in Chapter 1, multimedia library organization can be thought of as a subsystem of the broader environment which is the system in which it operates. Whether it is a school, special, academic, or public library, the organization is a subsystem which responds to the needs of the social, cultural, and economic environment of which it is a part. The library organization, therefore, is considered a social system organized for the attainment of certain goals of its larger environment, and the attainment of those goals is accomplished by the performance of specified tasks by the social system of the multimedia library.

TECHNOLOGICAL SYSTEM

Another basic characteristic must be identified in completing the definition of organization as it relates to the multimedia library: technology. The multimedia library is so involved with technology that it must also be regarded as a technological system which utilizes techniques and procedures that are of a specific technical nature.

Technological specialization is based upon tasks to be performed, including the equipment, tools, facilities, and operating techniques needed to accomplish those tasks. Technological specialization is especially evident in the multimedia library where the diversity of materials requires equipment, tools, and facilities considerably different from those of the traditional library. The types of equipment used, such as television, direct access systems, computer terminals, viewing and listening instruments, and the layout of the multimedia library facility itself indicate that the multimedia library is a technological system that requires specialization of knowledge and skills by the professional librarian and other staff members who must be both media oriented and media prepared.

There is a relationship between technology itself and the participants in the organization—that is, there are technological and social subsystems within each of which there is interaction, and between which there is a shared interdependence. Technology utilized in the multimedia library, as in TV and electronic retrieval, for example, affects the kind of input that individuals must feed into the organization and the output that the entire system or organization is able to create and sustain.

It is the people (the social system) who determine the effectiveness and the efficiency which are realized from the utilization of technology. Technological requirements themselves are determined by the task assignments of the organization—that is, the tasks that must be performed to achieve the major objectives of the organization, the multimedia library.

Accordingly, in setting up an organization for the multimedia library, it is necessary to provide for the relationship between technological and social systems. The task requirements of a multimedia library and the technology required to accomplish these tasks influence organizational structure, that structure itself being concerned with the ways in which the tasks of the organization are divided into operating units and coordinated.

To summarize, the reason for organization is to enable people to work together for a common objective. The work necessary to achieve that objective is divided into segments or tasks which are the responsibilities of individuals. The organization is the system that provides a way in which people may effectively interact with one another toward the accomplishment of those shared goals. The organization (the multimedia library) can be defined, therefore, as a *structured sociotechnical system.* It is a *social system* in which people work in groups, and a *technological system* in which assigned tasks must be performed by people with specialized skills.

ORGANIZATIONAL STRUCTURE

Structure can be defined very simply as an established pattern of relationships among the components or parts of an organization. Formal organizational structure is usually set up by development of positions and job descriptions, rules and procedures, and policy to cover authority, responsibility, communications, and work flow.

The organizational chart is a diagram of the formal structure of the organization. Figure 4 is an example of such a chart. It shows, by the job title, who reports to whom, for example. Coupled with job descriptions, samples of which are in the appendix to this book, such a chart makes up a plan of organizational behavior. Together this information shows who is supposed to follow whose direction; what part of the necessary work each person is supposed to do; who coordinates which segments of the organization; and what relationships are to be maintained among these several people. The chart designates official channels of communication from top down and from bottom up, and enables individuals at all levels to determine where the responsibility lies if some part of the work is not completed on time or in the right way.

Certain informal organizations very often exist side by side with the formal organization largely because of the impact of individual personalities. By and large, however, the formal organizational structure represented by a typical chart is likely to determine much of the members' behavior.

A rational approach to organizational theory, as far as the multimedia library is concerned, is to take into consideration the two main approaches to organization: the classical and the behavioral, or human relations approach. The former is based on a number of accepted guides commonly referred to as principles, such as authority, responsibility, and accountability, while the latter takes into consideration the many aspects of human behavior that affect the organization. It is undeniable that all human organizations do have at least one thing in common—they all require division and coordination of the work. Thus, the main difference between the classical and the human relations school is primarily one of emphasis. In defining modern organization we must move away from the strict classicist's view, be concerned with, and give sufficient attention to the human relations aspects of organization. The characteristics, needs, and capabilities of individual members must be considered, along with classical structure, so that good morale may be inspired and motivation encouraged. Increased emphasis on the structure of organization as a social system rather than an authority structure needs to be given.

In summary, the essential components which would be reflected in the organization are these: that it starts with objectives, provides for personnel requirements, indicates task divisions, describes physical assets, sets down policies and procedures, defines authority, accountability, and responsibility, and provides for lines of

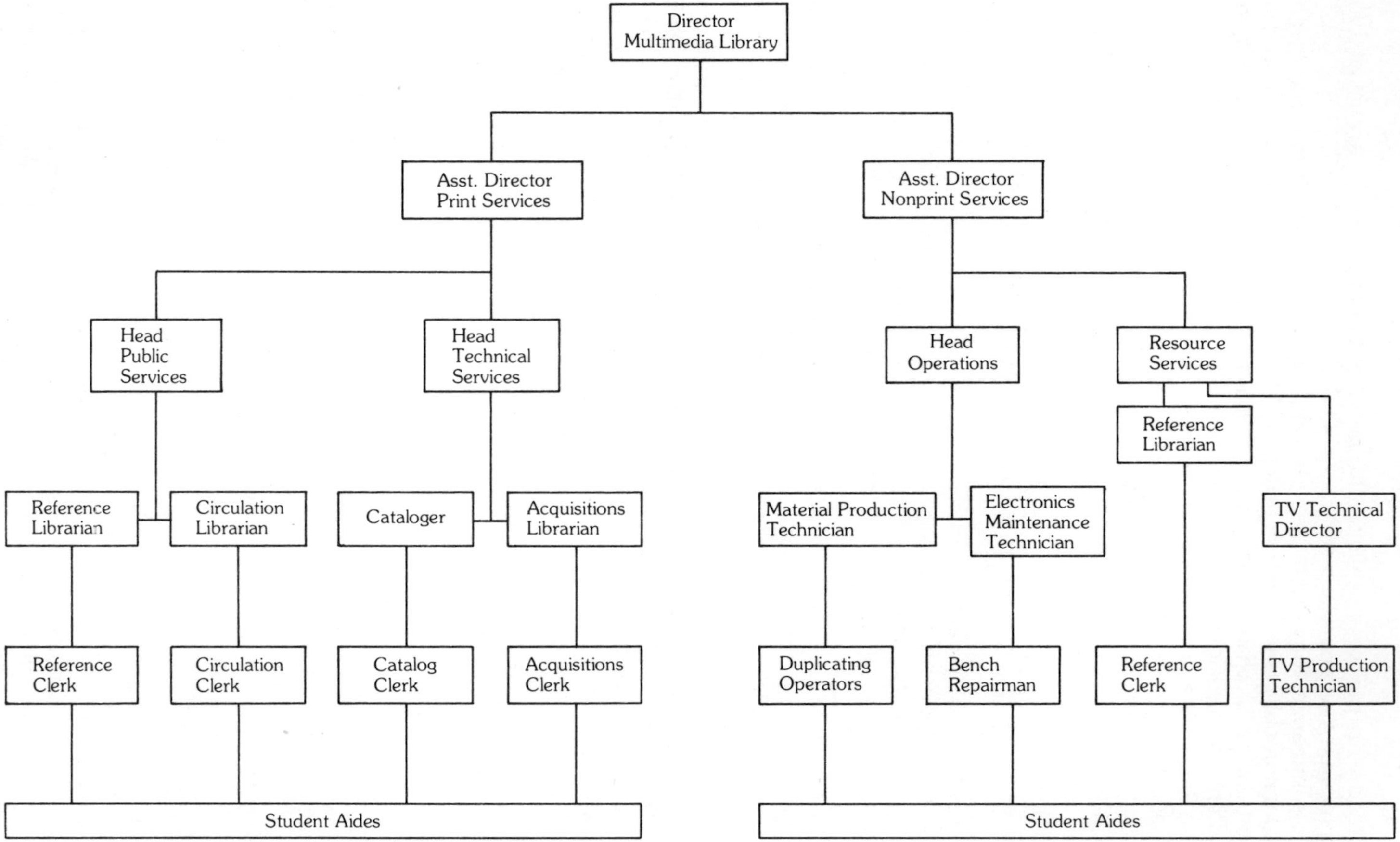

Figure 4. MODEL OF A MULTIMEDIA LIBRARY ORGANIZATION

communication. The combination of these ingredients into the structure should assure the attainment of organizational objectives.

ORGANIZATIONAL ACCOUNTABILITY

It needs to be pointed out that the multimedia library today and in the future must be concerned with setting up an organization that will fulfill objectives relevant to society. And as an instrument of society, the library must provide the value demanded by the population it serves.

Today's public library, for example, is designed to serve the entire public, yet reaches only a part of it. One reason for this may be that the objectives of the public library have not been clearly communicated to society in general. Another is that the public library has not really met the needs of society. This is not in any way an indictment of the public library. Indeed, libraries in the public domain have always provided a valuable and valued service to their communities. What is intended is to dramatize the necessity for the library organization to be developed with the understanding that it will be judged by the extent to which it can achieve its objectives, and that those objectives, based upon the expressed and felt needs of society, must be clearly stated and understood by the society using the library. The ultimate criterion for meaningful library organization is service to society.

NETWORK OF SYSTEMS

Organization may be considered a network of systems. For present purposes a system would mean a pattern of relationships like the assembled pieces of a puzzle within some relevant framework, the picture aimed at the attainment of some specific purpose or objective. To put it another way, in the library, organization can be thought of as a complex of relationships among human, material and equipment resources, and tasks, cemented together in a network of systems. These systems serve as the arteries of communication, carrying the resources of the library through the necessary productive and distributive processes, e.g., cataloging, processing, and reference, to become the means of satisfying the needs of patrons or membership groups. These relationships are illustrated in Figure 5.

The multimedia library organization, then, can be considered as a complete system in that it is a complex of relationships with a relevant structure or framework. It is a dependent system, however, in that it cannot exist without the support of other structures or other systems; for example, the school, college, or university (educational libraries); city or county government (public libraries).

An organization, then, in this context can be defined as a device created by a group for the efficient achievement of mutual, agreed upon objectives. It is made up of people. Its function is to provide the services and values desired by those people and its every action affects and is affected by people. Improvement in organization can be a means, accordingly, of providing more value to more people. If we can create a better library organization, then we can provide better library service.

HISTORICAL PERSPECTIVE

To understand organization, it is necessary to have an historical perspective of organization theory. Accordingly, we have divided our discussion into two sections: classical doctrine, and neoclassical or human relations doctrine.

Classical doctrine deals mainly with formal structure, emphasizing the development of principles which would provide an organization with the ability to function to the maximum benefit of all. The classical doctrine emphasizes the organizational principles of responsibility, authority, and accountability. These three basic principles set up a structure which creates channels formalizing the right of command to plan downward, the duty of the subordinate to obey, and the association of accountability with the flow of authority and responsibility. This formal structure creates a situation where each position is obligated to exercise authority, carry out responsibilities, and is accountable to a superior for the performance of authority and responsibility. Later in this chapter these principles, and many more, are explained in detail.

Later theorists and practitioners have felt that this approach fell short of providing for the human element although an examination of the literature did not show real justification for this statement. Traditional or classical types of organization can best be described as leadership which based its techniques of managing people on the understanding that if the problem was not one of formal organization, it was not an issue in any case. The classical approach overestimated the ability of man to achieve perfection in organization per se. The classicist did not ignore human relations but rather was too optimistic in the application of principles of formal organization as a means of perfecting service to the community. Later thinking, based on research in human personality, learning theory, systems development and management, and other areas, has provided the basis for including more emphasis on human affairs in organizational development.

At the core of all organization theory rests the definition of objectives. There is little argument about the need to define objectives, but there is disagreement about which objectives should receive primary emphasis. Some theorists believe, for

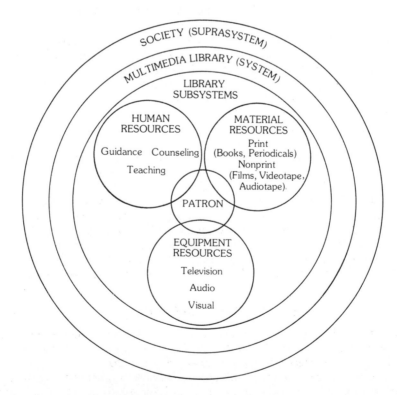

Figure 5. NETWORK OF SYSTEMS

example, that organization's objectives should emphasize the employee, because effective employee performance is essential to the achievement of organizational goals.

Another point of view suggests that the organization's objectives should have primary emphasis, an emphasis justified as a prerequisite of organizational survival; if the organization does not fulfill its goals, it will not survive. Others argue that organization exists for the benefit of all society and that the needs and wants of society should be considered above the objectives of the organization.

In addition to recognizing the importance of objectives, classical doctrine is very much concerned with the division of labor, with functional processes, scalar structure, and span of control.

Division of labor is seen as the assignment of individuals to given activities, generally on the basis of their talent and training, in order to optimize their productivity. The objective of division of labor is to enhance efficiency through specialization. The principle of division of labor is defined as the work of management divided so that each individual, at each level, shall have as few functions as possible to perform. If practical, the work of each individual in the organization should be confined to the performance of a single leading function, in this view.

The scalar and functional processes are concerned with the vertical and horizontal patterns of the organizational structure. Horizontal and vertical patterns are graphically portrayed in Figure 6. They show how the combined tasks of a technical services librarian can be reorganized into a horizontal pattern or a vertical pattern. The scalar process refers to vertical growth and, thus, to the chain of command, delegation of authority, responsibility, unity of authority, and accountability of individuals within the organization.

In Figure 7 it is easy to see that the top person of authority in the organization is 1A who is over 2 and B, and that 2 is over 3, and B is over C, and so on. This is a clear indication of levels of the delegation of authority and responsibility. It also demonstrates the channels by which communication and delegation flow downward, and feedback flows back up to 1A.

Functional process, on the other hand, refers to horizontal growth of the organization's structure through division into specialized parts, and regrouping of these parts into departments, divisions, or compatible units as shown in Figure 8. Structure is the result of the scalar process. The vertical and horizontal lines of responsibility become the vehicles for creating and maintaining relationships among various components of the organization. This structure thus becomes a system or pattern.

The human relations doctrine has evolved out of a recognition for the need to modify classical doctrine to accommodate human factors known to be important in organizational activity. Basically the human relations doctrine is people oriented as contrasted with the work or task oriented emphasis in classical doctrine. Informal organization is also brought to the forefront in the human relations view, and emphasized as a fact with which managers have to cope. The manager, for example, may set production levels or quotas, but it is the informal organization or group which sets the production rates. Thus, modern management theory has modified classical doctrine to a view in which the successful manager incorporates both task and human orientation into the organization, making a harmonious combination of the two. This is recommended as the best organization theory for the contemporary multimedia library.

The work of the neoclassicist has been directed largely toward organizational structure, especially in the area of line and staff relationships, and interpersonnel conflict situations. More employee participation, general committees, better communications, and ad hoc committees are among the prescriptions offered to allow more

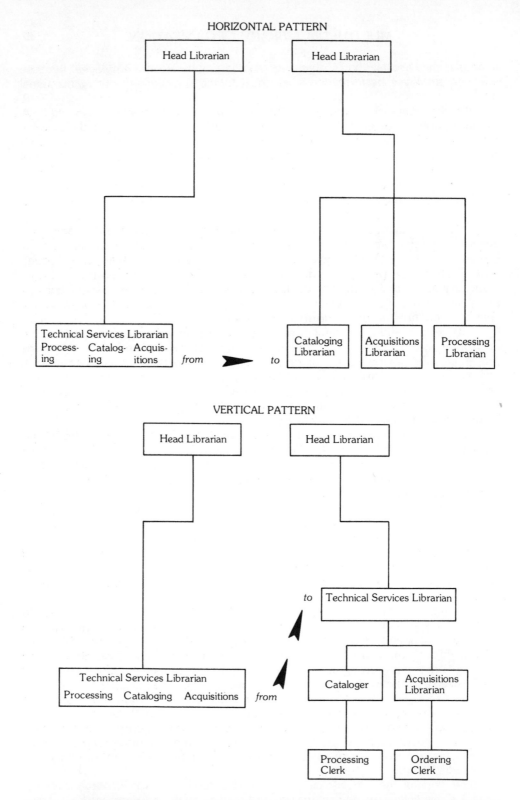

Figure 6. HORIZONTAL AND VERTICAL PATTERNS OF THE ORGANIZATIONAL STRUCTURE

employee involvement and to create more efficiency in library service. It is emphasized that formal organization still needs to be a central concern in order to maintain continuity toward fulfillment of objectives. However, this does not preclude a strong informal organization which would invite employee participation and insure effective communications.

Organization may thus be seen in another perspective: as a pattern or network of relationships among positions and position holders, which bears characteristics of both the formal and informal types. Both formal and informal organizations possess structure, the formal being keyed by decision-making rules, while the informal develops out of interactions and sentiments of position holders.

FORMAL ORGANIZATION

The most common of the organizational structures is represented by a hierarchical model as illustrated in Figure 9. This consists of a vertical dimension, showing levels of authority and responsibility, and a horizontal dimension, showing the functions or units at that level. Department branches or divisions in the hierarchical design assume a pyramid form with successfully higher levels needing fewer persons, for example. Applying this organizational pyramid to the multimedia library situation, we see at the topmost level of the pyramid, the chief executive, whose title might be director of media services, dean or director of learning

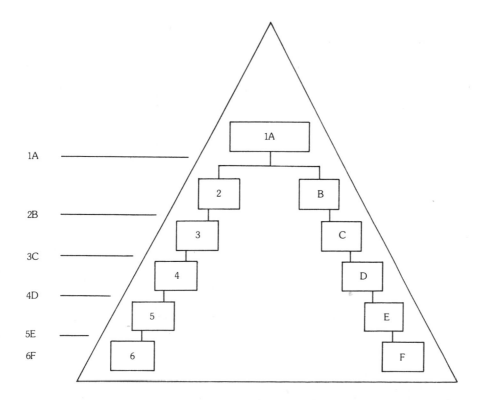

Figure 7. SCALAR PROCESS

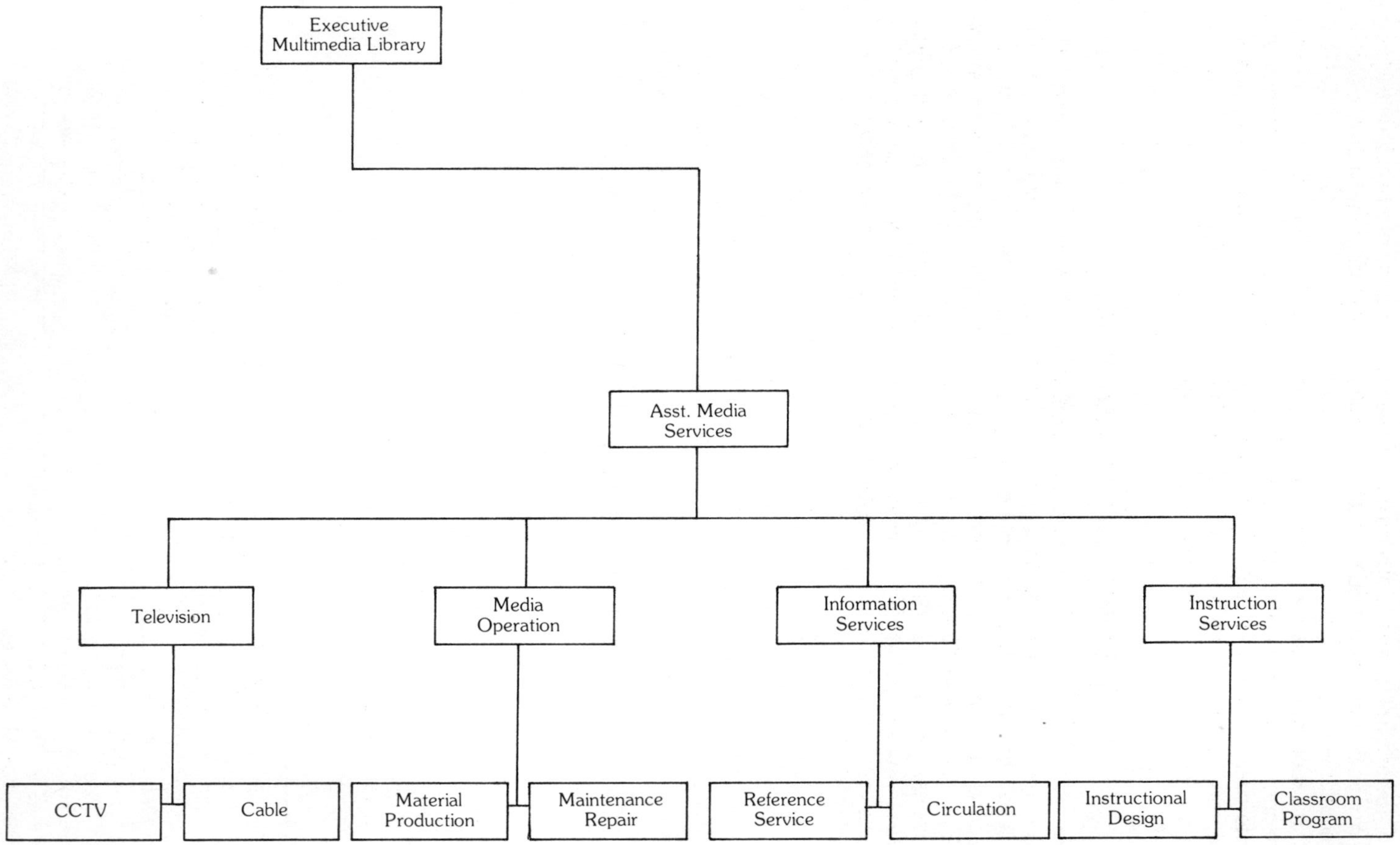

Figure 8. DIVISIONAL STRUCTURE

resources, or some such appropriate label. Directly under this chief executive would be the top management level consisting of the heads of the major activities of the library. This would be the operating management echelon. Directly following operating management would be the operating professional or supervisional level. Paraprofessionals or library technicians who might be placed in an operating supervisory capacity would also have to be considered in the modern media library manpower situation at this level. Following the operating supervision level would be the nonsupervisory clerical and technical employees.

The vertical dimension of this type of organizational structure is concerned with distributing authority in levels ranging from top management to supervision, to clerical and general employees near the bottom of the scale. The different levels also function as a device for transmission of information in the flow of communications and authority within the system.

INFORMAL ORGANIZATION

In seeking to define organization as it relates to the management of the multimedia library, we must consider not only the formal, but the informal organization as well.

Informal organization, as seen in Figure 10, can be defined as that system of relationships which, as opposed to the structured formal organization, includes natural groupings of people in a work situation which emerge in response to the social needs of individuals in their association with others in the work situation. It is well to remember that the informal organization, while it can be described as a structure, would be very difficult to put on paper in the form of an organizational chart. This kind of system is based on people and groups in the larger system or its subsystems, and is very difficult to chart because these relationships are constantly changing.

Formal organization consists of official, authorized relationships prescribed by management. Informal organization, by contrast, consists of many relationships, often unofficial and unauthorized, created by the many individual personalities, groups, and cliques within the formal organization. Without the formal the informal could not exist. And although both formal and informal organization can be discussed separately, it must be understood that, in fact, they are inseparable.

Informal organization is important in a multimedia library because there is a great deal of dependence upon professional media specialists and professional librarians to act as managers within their own areas of responsibility. Particularly in university, academic, college, and school libraries, management responsibility may even be assumed by personnel at lower levels, such as student aides, pages, and volunteers. So the multimedia organization has to be concerned with a number of clearly defined groups. Management needs to be aware of their behavior, and of any linking groups or subgroups that may be created by such informal organization in the form of large groups, cliques, small cliques, friendship groups, and individualized or isolated groups.

Two very important informal organizations in multimedia libraries are those which can be thought of as the print and nonprint groups. The manager must be perceptive as to these groupings and the resultant frictions that they may create.

Cliques which are often observed include those made up of people engaged in the same type of work, such as reference, cataloging, circulation, and other library functions. Smaller cliques may also be seen, based on some specific view or interest which brings them together, such as some special power they are lobbying for, or, in some cases, social reasons. These cliques are often composed of staff members who share the same views and values. Acceptance by individuals among and within them

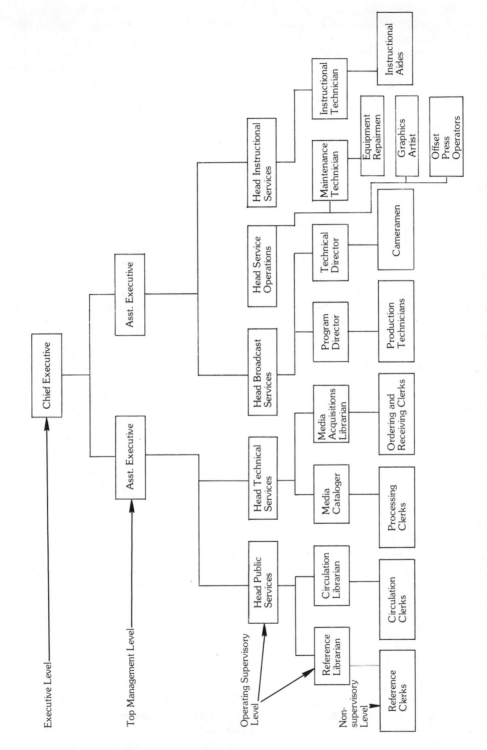

Executive Level

Top Management Level

Operating Supervisory Level

Non-supervisory Level

Chief Executive

Asst. Executive

Asst. Executive

Head Public Services

Head Technical Services

Head Broadcast Services

Head Service Operations

Head Instructional Services

Reference Librarian

Circulation Librarian

Media Cataloger

Media Acquisitions Librarian

Program Director

Technical Director

Maintenance Technician

Instructional Technician

Reference Clerks

Circulation Clerks

Processing Clerks

Ordering and Receiving Clerks

Production Technicians

Cameramen

Equipment Repairmen

Graphics Artist

Offset Press Operators

Instructional Aides

Figure 9. HIERARCHICAL MODEL OF A MULTIMEDIA LIBRARY ORGANIZATION

INFORMAL ORGANIZATION

FORMAL ORGANIZATION

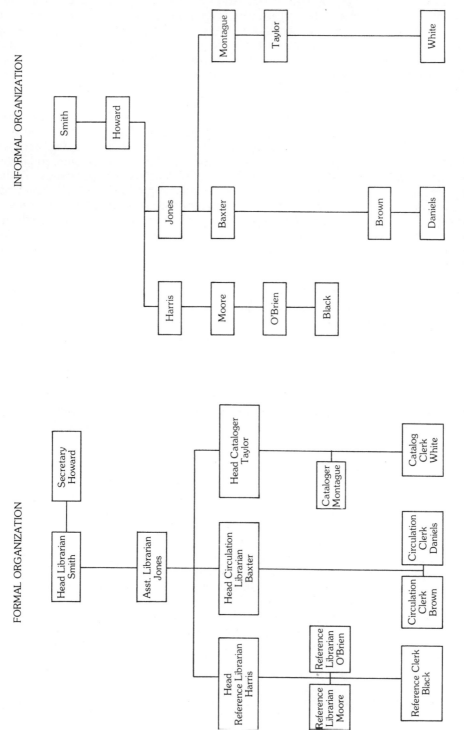

Figure 10. FORMAL AND INFORMAL ORGANIZATION

is only gained through approval of all. And in some cases, cliques become even smaller, but stay related to the primary group nevertheless. Finally, there are individuals, or loners who do not belong to any particular group, but who, depending upon the issue or situation, attach themselves to a particular clique or informal organization for a given time, and for a specific reason, generally self-interest. When either the reason or time for this liaison is no longer of importance to them, they leave the group and go back to their loner status again, or hook onto some other group.

Some of the factors which determine the makeup of informal organization include proximity and self-interest, as suggested above. People who come into physical, face-to-face contact every day or on a regular basis; people who perform similar tasks; and people who have the same or like interests tend to group together. These interests may be within the philosophy or objectives of the organization, or they may not. The latter is especially true of groups of an informal nature who join together when there is a common cause in which everyone has a strong belief and interest. When such an issue becomes paramount, although the basis is informal, it can become a very strong influencing factor in the formal organization and in the manner in which the multimedia library manager operates. When the issue has been solved, such a group is apt to disband.

Informal organizations are very important in the multimedia library because they are created largely by the high degree of specialization among staff workers. Such specialization, in fact, tends to create more informal organization than there might be in other types of organizations. Therefore, the manager must structure the formal organization within a climate of such informal groupings. A lack of clearly delineated accountability, authority, and responsibility in the informal organization makes it difficult for the manager to utilize the organizational structure at hand to create change and reduce resistance to it. Informal groups or organizations have accepted leaders who are not formally appointed, but who have real impact upon the formal organization's objectives. To deal with this kind of situation, the manager needs to use different techniques than would be used in managing a formal organization. The manager would also have a different communications system to deal with, making it more difficult to implement management views within the informal structures of the staff.

The informal organization communication system is sometimes called the grapevine. An example of this is shown in Figure 11. It is necessary for the manager to understand and perceive this communication network and, instead of fighting it, make use of it. It is possible, in fact, to utilize an informal communication network to create rapid response to job, task, and situation requirements. This grapevine factor, however, also emphasizes the necessity for official, formal channels which supply as much communication and information capability as possible because, if the official channel fails to provide full information, the informal grapevine will supply its own, creating gossip and rumor, and sometimes misunderstanding and trouble.

The informal organization and its informational grapevine can also be used to create a better management situation because it has the possibility of exerting very strong pressures upon its members to conform to certain ethical or social controls. These social controls are communicated in the form of standards as reflected by the behavior of the group, for example, verbal or other expressions of attitude. The member of the informal organization finds pressure, many times self-pressure, to conform in order to retain acceptance in the group. The manager needs to know how to use the informal organization to increase performance and not to restrict it. The manager needs to be able to perceive the existence of these groups, find their leaders, and use them to create a more efficient formal organization and to support the fulfillment of overall objectives.

Some discussion is needed here of the important alternatives of centralization and decentralization which relate to these organizational structures.

CENTRALIZATION VS. DECENTRALIZATION

Centralization is the systematic and consistent reservation of authority at central points within the organization. Centralization denotes that the majority of decisions having to do with work being performed are not made by those doing the work but at a point higher in the organization.

If work is reserved for the manager, authority is also reserved. However, the manager may delegate the work but not necessarily the authority to carry it out effectively. When authority is reserved by top management the decisions made should be expressed as largely as possible in the form of policy so that they may be applied to similar problems that come up on the operations level of the organization.

What are some of the factors that favor centralization? Personal leadership is one of the most important, especially in a small organization such as a school media center. Centralization facilitates personal leadership, providing integration and uniformity of action in handling emergencies. As a basic principle, in fact, the more acute the emergency the greater the need for centralized decision making.

Decentralization by contrast refers to the systematic effort to delegate authority to the lowest level possible. A decentralized management organization delegates

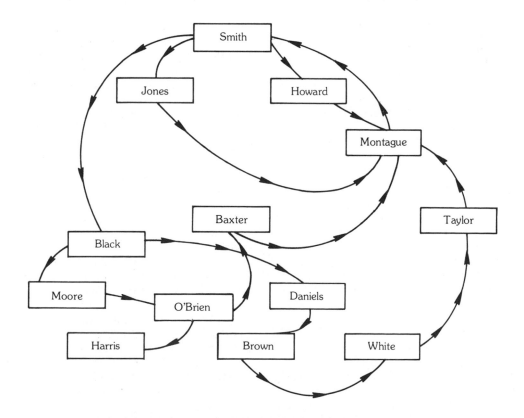

Figure 11. INFORMAL ORGANIZATION: COMMUNICATION GRAPEVINE

authority with reference to responsibility. The key question is: What decisions can be made by the people who are assigned to do the work? The extent of decentralization is determined by what kind of authority is delegated, how far down the organization it is delegated, and how consistently it is delegated.

Different degrees of authority can be delegated in a decentralized organization. A manager may be given authority to make a final decision, for example, without referring to anyone else. A manager may be permitted to make a decision but only after consulting a superior. A manager may be required to refer an alternative to the staff and give consideration to their advice and suggestions before making a decision.

Another method of decentralizing is by control of funds that different levels within the organization are delegated to spend. The key question again is: How much authority is delegated, how far down in the organization is it placed, and how consistently is it delegated? Some areas to be considered for decentralization include the hiring and firing of personnel; approval of wage and salary increases, authorizations of travel expense, origination of purchase orders, and solicitation of price quotations; promotion of personnel; acquisition of capital equipment; and leasing of property or equipment.

In the business world of today, the trend is to recentralize as against the trend toward decentralization that started in mid-century. This trend is not entirely due to the advent of computers. Rather it appears that business was disappointed in the effects of decentralization. Costs were more than expected because of the need for more staff, both at headquarters and at the decentralized units. Further, decentralization resulted in too much loss of control.

Advocates of centralization through computerization have in many instances overlooked the role of staff as a major source of management information, especially of that type of information which cannot be quantified or anticipated. Business has found that executives do not have enough time to use all the information they already have, and often are overwhelmed by the masses of figures and reports created by computers.

What must be done is to insure that the information top management obtains is genuinely relevant to the questions on which it must make decisions. With the computer there is a trend toward what might be called centralization within decentralization, utilizing both the computer and the information it makes available. The systems approach and computer-based information processing offer many new capabilities for organization and management. Centralized computer control can implement decentralized operations.

In a small library organization the librarian or media manager gives orders directly to subordinates. This is absolute centralization. In very large organizations where there is a long scale or chain interposed between the media manager and lower levels of the hierarchy, orders and counterinformation have to go through a series of intermediaries. This, in turn, depends upon the manager's worth, the reliability attributed to subordinates, and the condition of the organization.

One of the best examples of centralization and decentralization in the library organization are the functions that make up technical services, acquisitions, cataloging, and processing of materials. Centralization creates economies and efficiencies because there is economy in cataloging a title once, regardless of the number of copies, and efficiency in the volume of mass production of processing. The centralization of facilities and equipment creates economies and efficiency and reduces needless duplication. Decentralization, while more costly and less efficient, does allow for material to be handled in a nonstandard method which reflects local needs, decisions are made closer to the function or area that must implement them, and results are dependent on decisions made as low in the organization as there are supervisors to make them.

The systems philosophy of organization creates several basic and valuable by-products. The first of these is integration of the many subsystems making up the total organization. Planning tends to put managers in the frame of mind for thinking of the organization as a system. A benefit of the systems philosophy can be the enhancement of decentralization. Advantages of decentralization include greater economies of supervision, improved morale, better development of managers, and, in general, more awareness of the contribution that decentralized units make to the whole.

NEED FOR BALANCE

It is very important that there be a balance between the centralization and decentralization of various functions in the library. Too much decentralization encourages too much freedom of decision making. It is also important to carefully define what is meant by decentralization, and where or how the technique is applied in the wide range of library functions, including administrative, physical, functional, geographic, and, as in business, product areas. Many times decentralization simply means separation of facilities, a type of organizational structure, and the delegation of decision making.

Decentralization as a descriptor for a distinctive type of organization is not necessarily valid either. It is not necessary to change an organization's structure to decentralize. Centralization and decentralization may be seen also as extensions of delegation, the entrustment of responsibility and authority from one individual to another. Decentralization in this context would apply to the systematic delegation of authority throughout an organization-wide context.

The point being made here is that a clear distinction must be made between the organizational structure itself and the focus or distribution of authority within that structure. There must be a balanced distribution between these two factors to provide for both central authority and subordinate operations. Central authority does the work of overall planning, organization, and coordination, and provides motivation, control, and the higher level decision making necessary to cement the operating units of the organization together. Middle management, on the other hand, the multimedia managers in the case of libraries, must be in a position to make decisions also, to keep the organization flexible and responsive to the dynamic, day-to-day needs of the library.

To look at it another way: management must decide on both the quantity and variety of work that each person in the organization should be expected to perform. Once such decisions are made, management at various levels can prescribe work assignments for staff members. Such assignments are carried out by subordinate personnel. The extent to which this assignment of duties and decision-making activity is spread out can then be described as an organizational arrangement which may be termed centralized or decentralized. Decentralization, the concern here, can be defined as a state or organization in which there is considerable delegation of authority and responsibility on several levels or echelons, where decisions are made in terms of work division, provision of adequate personnel to accomplish jobs, and the physical resources required to get those jobs done.

In contrast, an organization is properly referred to as centralized when there is a narrow span of control, relatively few echelons with decision-making capability, and very little delegation of authority and responsibility.

DELEGATION

The design of an organizational structure can materially affect the nature and preciseness of the control factors set up by management.

The program can also be affected by the philosophy of delegation defined in the organizational structure. The more decentralized an organization's structure, the more complex are the problems of coordination and control. The more difficult it is to measure output for an area of responsibility, the more difficult it is to effectively exercise control.

Because decentralized structures permit maximum freedom for the exercise of individual initiative, they depend heavily on cooperation and coordination among members at all levels. Organizations using decentralized structures find a more well-rounded, thoroughly developed employee emerging from the lower echelons than is the case in the centralized structure. Initiative and innovation are frequently stifled in a centralized system. Organization structure, then, can be counted as an important device in helping to resolve the conformity–creativity issue.

NEED FOR POLICY

Decentralization also requires more policy as a means of control. Policy, as described in more detail elsewhere in this book, may be defined as a guide to authority utilization. It can be useful at all levels of an organization's structure, and can be used in conjunction with all types of procedures. Managers must operate within some boundary or framework, and policy provides this framework. Policy is necessary in an organization because delegation is necessary.

When a library is manned by only one professional, formal policy is probably not needed as much. But when individuals are added, some such policy is required to specify authority, responsibility, and accountability. Policy can provide a basis for coordination of decision-making activity by defining conditions affecting the environment in which these decisions are made. Policies limit the recurrence of situations in which a manager must become personally involved in a subordinate's decision-making activity. Ideally, it works this way: an objective is articulated; authority is delegated; a policy is provided; and performance is controlled or supervised by evaluation. A subordinate is held accountable for personal performance under the policy which has provided the guidelines needed for decision making and work at that level.

Delegation is a process whereby a superior divides the total work assignment among subordinate managers or operative personnel and the superior in order to achieve both operative and management specialization. As a result of such specialization, each member in the organization should be able to develop to the maximum the talents needed to perform work assignments effectively. The organization thus takes full advantage of these talents in both managerial and operative tasks.

A final word of emphasis needs to be given to the importance of delegation in this process. In management, delegation cannot be escaped, and the need to delegate tends to increase as the manager's work load increases. Thus as an organization grows its management group must engage in more delegation (i.e., decentralization of responsibility).

A policy, by definition, is a guide; it implies certain flexibility that can be provided only if the policy contains the proper components. It is suggested that a policy, regardless of its classification or use, should contain three basic components: a statement of objectives, a statement of principles, and a statement of implementation.

STATEMENT OF OBJECTIVES.　The objectives should tie-in specifically with the philosophy of the institution and clearly outline the purpose and outcomes expected as a result of implementation of the policy.

STATEMENT OF PRINCIPLES.　A principle may be defined as a basic concept, a basic fact, a truism that, based upon knowledge derived from management philosophy, establishes a framework of flexibility in which the principle can cover recurring situations.

STATEMENT OF IMPLEMENTATION. Implementation can be defined as a practical approach to dealing with a specific set of circumstances. It would contain rules of action which would lend a note of firmness to the policy. These rules, because they are somewhat rigid, provide the right mix in policy to allow both the flexibility and stability to policy control and decision making. No organization can grow beyond a minimal point without formal policy statements acting as guides to action for the decision makers, and directions for subordinates. Policies bring together basic environmental factors of the organization and provide a cohesive support network for managerial decisions. Example 2 illustrates how such a policy should be written.

EXAMPLE 2
MEDIA SERVICES OPERATING POLICY

THE OBJECTIVE

To provide for the instructional program at X College, a comprehensive service which offers direction and assistance in planning, selecting, evaluating, and providing instructional media.

These policies are based on principles which are intended to instill and maintain an instructional climate which fosters improved and increased use of educational media, and on those requirements which are expressed by students, faculty, and administrative staff. Leadership and assistance will be provided toward the effective use of media in instruction. Human resources will serve to help all of those who desire to vary and strengthen their teaching and learning through selective innovation in the use of media.

IMPLEMENTATION

The phrase "media services" is intended to include basic booking and scheduling of audiovisual materials, equipment, and facilities; producing materials in a wide range of audiovisual formats such as slides, filmstrips, displays, models, exhibits, transparencies, motion picture film clips, and instructional kits; planning, producing, and evaluating instructional television activities; and innovations in the field of improved methodology and new technology applied toward the improvement of college instruction.

SERVICES TO BE PROVIDED

Audiovisual and media services will be provided through the media services center of the library. This is a specialized resource center for both students and instructors and provides the following services:

1. Reference service to both students and instructors
2. A central catalog of audiovisual materials owned by the college and/or available to the college via rental or free loan
3. Circulation of all audiovisual materials and equipment
4. Professional consultation to faculty members
5. Notification to the college community of audiovisual/educational media activities on the campus and elsewhere

EXAMPLE 2 (Cont.)

EQUIPMENT AND FACILITIES

The selection, purchase, control, inventory, physical location, scheduling, operation, and maintenance of audiovisual equipment and facilities is the basic responsibility of the assistant dean of instruction, learning resources. Exceptions to this policy will be made in conference with the dean of instruction, the associate dean of instruction, learning resources, and the assistant dean. It is the intention of this section to give central direction to the technical aspects of specifications, maintenance, and operation of the often specialized, delicate, and expensive equipment in use on campus.

1. All audiovisual equipment to be purchased will be discussed in advance with the assistant dean of instruction, learning resources, with regard to specifications, use, maintenance, and operation.
2. The scheduling and control of portable audiovisual equipment used in the instructional program will be done through media services. Instructors are responsible for setting up and operating equipment, rewinding films, and properly packaging equipment in time for pickup.

DIVISIONALIZATION

The best vehicle for decentralization is divisionalization. The need to divisionalize arises when consideration must be given to such factors as easing the burden of authority and decision making of top executives; diversifying; developing more executives and managers; and increasing motivation of middle management by giving them decision-making powers. Centralization does create a situation where the full weight of problems, perplexities, and pressures from every part of the organization is placed upon the chief executive and top management.

The chief executive who has become overly concerned with everyday nitty-gritty decision making suffers a loss in ability to plan and anticipate larger problems. This chief executive becomes obligated to make operating decisions, and to deal with problems of immediate urgency, and finds it almost impossible to take the time to plan and think ahead, to develop a philosophy for work and the organization.

An example that will illustrate divisionalization is presented in Figure 12 (Before and After). Notice in the first part of this figure that the media manager is the sole decision maker. In the second part, a second level has been created. The media manager, who had taken on the management of every detail of the operation in the first design, discovered that in dealing with the rental of films, delivery of audiovisual equipment to the classroom, and fulfillment of production requests, little time was left for decision making and the planning of responsibilities. So a middle management level was set up to which decisions relating to operations could be delegated. Notice how much of the nitty-gritty job is now done by the newly created media operations supervisor.

Notice, also, that this alternative is more workable than, for example, holding on to the decision-making role but adding personal staff to oversee it. An administrative assistant, for example, would not solve the problem, because the executive would still be responsible for the decision process, and for supervision of the assistant as well.

Another alternative is the appointment of a committee. But committees cannot become operational decision makers either. This approach should be used only as a means for developing advisory assistance, which is a good use of committee structure. Bringing together a group of experienced people who are qualified to

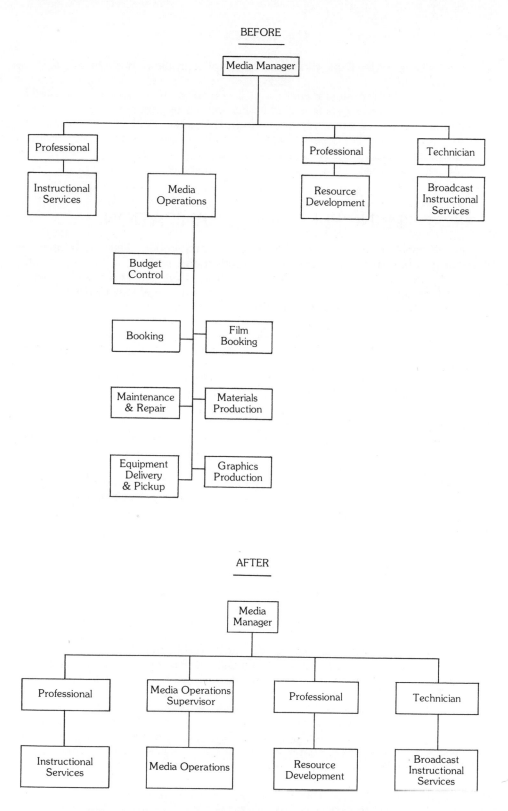

Figure 12. DIVISIONALIZATION—BEFORE AND AFTER

provide real help in developing solutions to complex problems has many advantages for management.

Finally, it needs to be said that the lack of qualified managers and the need for experienced managerial people are additional factors of concern to the profession. Middle management is a training ground for management at higher levels, and if for no other reason than that decentralization provides a training opportunity for future executives, such a structuring is of importance and value. Divisionalization creates the opportunity for aspiring media managers to manage something.

PRINCIPLES OF ORGANIZATION

An organizational approach has been recommended which combines the classical and human relations concepts. To utilize this approach, it is important to consider a number of guides, or principles, which, in the practical world of day-to-day management, have been found to govern the arrangement of organizational structure. These principles can be applied to any organizational structure, irrespective of its purpose.

The premise we are working from is that if basic, proven principles are applied an adequate organization for any type of multimedia situation will result. These principles help create an organization which is both effectively structured and integrated. The basic goal is to create an organization that will fulfill stated objectives. The need is to develop an organization of people working and cooperating together in interdependent relationships. Organizations are, seen in this framework, objective oriented people with a purpose.

Thus is developed a psychosocial system: people working in groups. Organizational principles in this system are concerned with structuring such functions as responsibility, accountability, and span of control.

Technological systems in the multimedia library, which relate to the ability of staff to utilize knowledge, skills, and techniques to accomplish objectives, are a key subsystem in this structure. Integrating these systems and the structured activities at the various levels becomes the organization.

ACCOMPLISHMENT

Organization as a whole exists for the purpose of accomplishing predetermined objectives. All work done in the organization should be dedicated to this end. If it does not contribute to objectives, the work is not necessary and should not be performed.

The same is true of each element or activity within an organization. Each area, department, or division should have clearly defined objectives which are part of and consonant with the larger objectives of the organization. Each position, as well, should have stated objectives logically related to the overall objectives of the larger organization so that, as each task holder meets a goal or objective, the objectives of the entire organization will be met.

This principle is emphasized in the following case study of a situation which involved a central learning center and a number of subject department resource centers. One of these resource centers was not being utilized effectively. There were no predetermined objectives designed to implement one of the basic objectives of the school: to provide specialized learning centers where students could receive remedial help, find materials related to subject matter, and pursue independent study.

To implement this institutional objective, it was decided to organize the center by learning activities based upon the following:

1. To encourage the use of media in the subject area
2. To encourage reading in the subject area
3. To provide programmed materials

After these objectives had been established, it was possible to set up a structure to implement them, to work out a plan of action, define staffing needs, and acquire the materials and equipment needed to make the plan work.

RESPONSIBILITY

The principles of responsibility, authority, and accountability are very important. To create a structure that can be managed by people, it is necessary to have channels providing for these basic functions. This is how management makes an organization operate. The first of these is especially important.

A structure must be based on clearly identified responsibility that is properly defined and clearly allocated. Management must be able to say: "This is the responsibility of a particular activity or function." The manager can then define that responsibility and describe how it will be subdivided and delegated. The creation of an organizational chart will illustrate all the different activities within the organization. The drawing of lines of authority, responsibility, and accountability will show who is responsible, who has authority, and who is accountable to whom.

When charting the organization of the multimedia library, many areas and activities must be given consideration as shown in Figure 9. These include, among others, materials production, receiving and shipping, audiovisual materials, equipment, repair, booking, preview, multimedia lecture, television, electronic and data processing, and microforms. Many areas and functions of both print and nonprint collections and activities must be included.

People who do not understand the nature of their relationships with the total system, and who are uncertain of where their responsibility begins and ends, cannot cooperate effectively toward the achievement of larger objectives. People working and cooperating together are the key to effective organization. It is for this reason that clear statements of responsibility are needed.

A good example of this principle can be found in the previous case cited. In order to establish a good overall organizational structure, it is clearly necessary to develop the lines of responsibility for the central learning center and the different resource centers. The key to how this impacts upon the institution is in the question: Should both the learning and the resource centers be the responsibility of the school media specialist or should the responsibility for each resource center be under a subject department head? The two alternatives are shown diagrammatically in Figure 13.

Obviously, either alternative would work, and both have merit. The important and clearly evident single factor in either case is, however, that whether functions are centralized or decentralized, the principal or manager must clearly define and delegate responsibilities down the line. The examples show clearly defined lines of responsibility in each of the options considered.

AUTHORITY

Authority, like responsibility, must be properly and clearly defined, particularly since responsibility can only be assumed when a commensurate delegation of

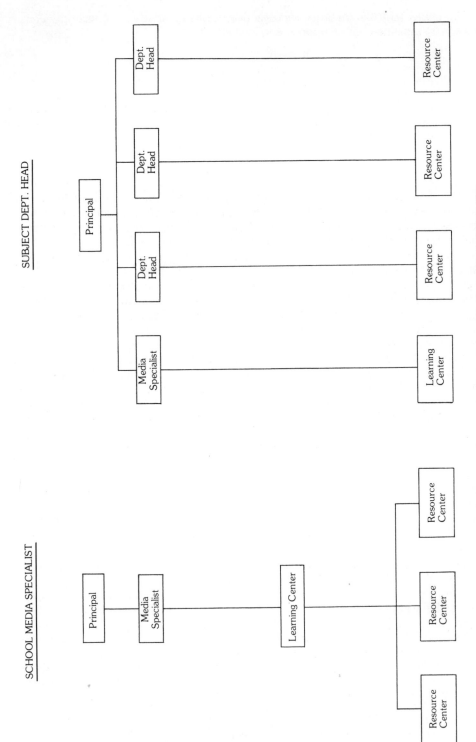

Figure 13. ALTERNATIVES FOR THE PRINCIPLE OF RESPONSIBILITY

authority is made. One basic law of organization and management is that responsibility should not be given without authority. When someone is made responsible for achieving a given objective, enough authority to reach it should be given. Thus, authority and responsibility are tied together. One does not exist without the other.

One point to remember, however, is that when responsibility and authority have been delegated, the media manager has not been relieved of responsibility for the total performance of the tasks. The manager is responsible to a superior for any action delegated in the library, the difference now being that a part of the job has been delegated to a subordinate. The manager must still answer for the total service performed.

Authority and responsibility are tied together as previously stated. The case used to exemplify the principle of responsibility can also be used as an example of the principle of authority. The two organizational models clearly evidence the line of authority from the principal down. Now look at the other side of the coin; an example of responsibility given by management without commensurate authority.

A high school in a large urban city had a somewhat traditional library with no nonprint materials, perimeter shelving, and rows of study tables. The vice-principal, who handled audiovisual equipment and materials, departed. A new vice-principal came in who did not want the audiovisual responsibility, so this task was added to the librarian's job. The librarian, however, was not given any authority over budget, personnel, or facilities to get the job done. That authority was retained by the new vice-principal. Result: frustration on the part of the traditional book librarian toward the vice-principal, and a negative attitude on the librarian's part toward audiovisual and nonprint materials. If authority and responsibility plus the needed staff, budget, and facilities had been provided at the same time, this probably would not have happened. In many institutions the change from traditional library to media centers and media specialists would have transpired much sooner had the principle of authority been recognized and followed.

ACCOUNTABILITY

Each staff member in the multimedia library should be accountable to one superior. Line of authority and responsibility should be so developed that each individual reports to a single superior regarding the work and is accountable solely to that person for proper work performance. Accountability is derived from an organizational structure having predetermined responsibility and authority.

A senior executive cannot require accountability from a subordinate when authority and responsibility have not been clearly defined. Accountability should be based on accurate task assignments, staff selection, adequate facilities and equipment, and appropriate delegation of authority. When the media manager delegates authority and responsibility to a subordinate, the subordinate is directly responsible to that manager for the work assigned. The media manager, in turn, is accountable to a superior both for the discharge of personal responsibilities and for the work which was delegated to subordinates. The media manager is directly accountable for the performance of all work within the individual organizational unit.

A case that exemplifies this principle concerns a college reference department with three professional librarians and a number of assistants. The head reference librarian in this department has delegated the supervision of assistants to the other two librarians without indicating single accountability. Result: a very bad situation; the assistants have two bosses, a clear case of conflict as a result of dual accountability. Miss X, for example, would assign tasks to the assistants who usually worked for her. Miss Z, however, when Miss X left on break, would tell the assistants to stop doing those tasks and to do something else. Clearly, since the head librarian had not applied the principle of accountability, both professional personnel and assistants soon became upset and frustrated. The situation was compounded because Miss Z, who was the more dominant person, was constantly running to the head librarian with stories about the assistants, and otherwise creating further havoc. Several competent assistants simply quit in despair. Poor performance and inefficiency resulted among those who remained, because the assistants really did not know to whom they were accountable. The head librarian should have assigned assistants to both Miss X and Miss Z with clear, single accountability, or placed all of the assistants under one of them only.

SPAN OF CONTROL

This principle refers to the number of people that one manager can effectively supervise. The organization should be structured in such a way so as not to increase the span of supervision beyond the level of management's ability to manage.

In practice, of course, the span of control may vary widely. Because of standardization achieved and similarity in problems among functional areas, it is very important to consider the span of control.

The number of subordinates within the span of control of a given supervisor will vary in terms of the type of management, the organization, the character of the work, the nature and abilities of the staff assistants, and the capabilities of the line subordinates. The number of subordinates a manager can supervise is limited to the same extent that human capacity is limited. A manager has only a specified amount of time during the working day in which to supervise. What the manager does during that time determines the number of people it is possible to contact and personally motivate. The manager who has to arrive at an individual decision for every problem has to have a narrower span of control than the manager who anticipates repetitive problems and can make decisions based upon standard operating procedures already established. Clear and comprehensive policy statements at all levels reduce the volume of personal decision making required, and, hence, increase the manager's span of control.

Definitions of responsibility and authority decide what work is to be done, who is to do it, and what powers are retained. Performance standards predetermine the yardsticks by which a person's work is to be measured. Programs decide what schedule of activities is to be followed. Budgets provide a standing answer to fiscal questions.

The character of the work supervised has a great deal to do with organizational span of control. If the work is uniform, highly standardized, and there are relatively permanent policies and procedures set up, then it is obvious that the manager's span of control can be much broader.

The number of staff assistants made available can increase the span of control of a multimedia library manager. Personal staff can be of help in freeing the manager of detail. With the use of specialized staff, it is possible for the media manager, who has a full range of expert advice and service available, to broaden the span of control in the major technical and administrative areas of the job. These internal consultants can be used to free the manager for those parts of the job which only the manager can perform effectively. This is a very strong point to make in the multimedia library context. It is important for management to have staff assistants available in such areas as television, technical equipment, and materials production, for example, since it is highly unlikely that the manager will be a technical expert in all of these different fields.

The capabilities of both the staff assistants and line managers will be challenged because if the manager is going to increase the span of control, detail and routine decision making will have to be delegated to subordinates. If these line subordinates do not accept the challenge of this delegation and follow through, or are incapable of doing so, it will be difficult for the manager to increase or broaden the span of control.

To put it another way, the principle of span of control is related to the horizontal dimension of the organization. It can be defined as the number of subordinates an executive can effectively supervise. The principle holds that the larger the number of individuals reporting directly to a media manager, the more difficult it is to supervise and coordinate them effectively. The number of persons who can be effectively supervised by a given manager is directly related to the ability of the media manager and the subordinates themselves. Thus, there are two important variables involved in this concept: first, the capacity of the manager to manage; and second, the capacities of the people supervised to respond to that management. Failure to understand the manner in which these variables work has led some authorities to specifically state that the usual number of subordinates a manager can manage effectively is four to eight. Such a rigid application of the principle of span of control is unrealistic, of course. Various spans of control schemata covering fifteen or more individuals or activities have been reported, and these should not be considered exceptions to the basic principle or to disprove the validity of the principle of span of control. A top manager with energy and intelligence can absorb the extra pressures and deal effectively with many relationships. The span of control a manager can be expected to handle is actually limited only by the subordinates who are supervised, their degree of competence and intelligence, energy, ability, and the nature of their tasks.

There is also an important distinction between the actual process of supervision and the degree of access it provides up and down the line. The number of people having access to a manager may be much larger than the number under his close, immediate, and direct supervision. It must be emphasized that in applying the principle of span of control, extreme tallness or extreme flatness in an organizational structure are exceptional cases requiring special justification. The usual practice is to direct the growth of an organization's structure in such a way as to keep these dimensions in reasonable balance, not overly tall or overly flat. If an organization is considerably flat or has an extremely wide span of control there must be some very special justifications. It would not be a normal procedure to develop an organization on this basis.

A situation that illustrates the principle of span of control occurred in a high school media center. The traditional library and the audiovisual area had been centralized under the "media center" label. The head media specialist in charge of the center, however, did not feel that there should be written policy because flexibility was necessary. There were no written procedures for the staff to follow. In addition, the specialist taught an orientation course for freshmen on the use of the center. He trained and supervised all student assistants, directly supervised the other two professional media specialists, and all clerks. As a result, the effectiveness of the media center was low because the span of control exercised by the specialist was overtaxed; too broad. All decisions and judgments came to him without adequate policies and procedures at intermediate levels, and without responsibility and authority delegated down. This was just too broad a span of control. It could be rectified only by delegating responsibility and authority to the two professionals on the specialist's staff, thus narrowing his span of control to more effectively manageable dimensions.

ACTIVITIES

An organization should be built around its main activities, not around individuals. In a good organization, grouping of activities is utilized. Grouping can be defined as the process of arranging work to form positions, functions, and other organizational elements. Closely related tasks should be grouped together. Since grouping is the process of building balanced packages of tasks to accomplish objectives, the best method of deciding what work should be placed in a function is to evaluate its place within the total organization in terms of the purpose of that function.

A case which emphasizes the principle of activities was observed in a large public library branch in a midwestern city. The staff of this library included a supervising librarian, two beginning librarians, a head clerk, and clerks with ratings of I and II.

The problem was with a clerk II. This person was the senior staff member and, as such, had been able to gather the activities which most suited her. She had also been able to get the work schedule geared to her preferences. She did only what she wanted to do and was extremely outspoken. Because of her length of service, she knew a lot of patrons in the community and used this as pressure to get her way. Result: an unhappy and discontented group of fellow clerks.

This situation could have been helped a great deal by having the supervising librarian utilize the principle of activities, organize the assignments into three logical groupings with one II-level clerk in charge of each group, and requiring that all three answer to the head clerk. In this way, activities would have been organized according to the objectives of the organization, and the troublesome clerk would have been restricted to the activities specifically delegated to her. With this reorganization, the staff could have held firm and not allowed the offending clerk to move in on their activities. If the supervising librarian and the head clerk had kept a strong vigil, this could have been accomplished.

FLEXIBILITY

In viewing the organization of the multimedia library, it must be emphasized that the library enjoys a position of mutual interdependence within the larger institution and society itself. Therefore, it is constantly influenced by the dynamic nature of that larger context. If the institution or society changes, as it must, so must the library change. New functions must be performed. Present functions must be changed or eliminated. A greater total volume of effort must be provided for. In such a situation flexibility, or the ability of the organizational structure of the library to change, is readily apparent. Thus, building an organizational structure for the multimedia library must be regarded as a continuous process requiring a constant assessment of the accumulative effects of forces which produce changes, and the continuous evaluation of the effectiveness of the library as an organization.

An example of this principle is in the following case. It happened in an elementary school district in a large urban area. The district had developed media centers in each school, staffed with a professionally trained media specialist. Each of the media centers had a materials collection made up of printed materials only. The nonprint materials had been centralized in the district instructional materials center for some years because most of these materials were reserved for teacher use. Following the principle of flexibility, and in keeping with change in the district's philosophy toward individualization of instruction, it was decided to change the organizational structure of the instructional materials center (IMC) and decentralize its material collection by distributing the IMC materials to the individual media centers. Thus, the organization retained its effectiveness while increasing utilization of the nonprint collection.

PROPORTION

The organization of the multimedia library must be continually revised and evaluated to insure that there is reasonable balance in the size of various areas, divisions, etc.; between standardization of procedures and flexibility; and between centralization and decentralization of decision-making responsibility. Imbalance among these activities occurs because the amount of work to be done by various groups changes as the organization develops new methods, areas, and objectives. Changes and new processes occur. Standardized procedures are necessary, of course, but caution must be given to the tendency to enforce such prescriptions too rigidly.

The same case cited in the previous example can be utilized to describe the principle of proportion. With decentralization of the nonprint collection, the size of the IMC organization changed, and a shift in balance to the individual school media centers occurred.

The IMC changed from a materials center to a control or management unit with the district retaining control by requiring all acquisition requests to clear through the district. Responsibility and authority were redefined and delegated to correlate with the change in proportion of operations. Overall changes required by decentralization resulted in a shift in the balance or size of the units, thus emphasizing the principle of proportion in practice.

COMMUNICATION

In creating an organization, the designer should be aware of the pathways of formal communication. The main thrust of communication is downward, in the form of delegated authority, defined objectives, orders, and information. However, communication is needed in both directions. Upward information flow consists of reports for purposes of control, feedback on objectives, expression of grievances, needs for change, and so on. Informal organization takes care of lateral communication.

The following case is a good example of poor communication. At the center of the situation: a new librarian in a small rural high school. The other characters in this scenario are: Mr. Jones, district business manager; Mr. Harris, administrative assistant to the superintendent; and Mr. Smith, high school principal. The sequence of events was as follows:

The librarian went to Mr. Smith when school started, asked what the library budget was and how to requisition materials and supplies. Mr. Smith explained that a requisition form had to be filled out, submitted to him for signature, and then sent to the district office for signature of the superintendent. Mr. Smith did not know about budget procedures, so he referred the librarian to Mr. Harris. Here is the first instance of failure in communication. Lack of information about the library budget on the part of the principal is, in itself, a failure of communication. A public document such as the school budget should have been communicated in detail to the principal so that he could adequately implement the needs of his school, and work effectively with legitimate staff questions relating to fiscal and budgetary matters.

The librarian, dutiful fellow, did inquire of Mr. Harris regarding the budget. He was told, however, that Mr. Jones did not believe in telling anyone what his budget was—a deliberate failure of communication. So, now totally in the dark, the librarian just put in his requests anyway and resorted to hope, and a prayer. The first requisition was for a black and red typewriter ribbon to be used to type subject headings on catalog cards in red, a practice which the librarian observed.

Months later he still had not received the ribbon. Undaunted, he inquired and was told that the business manager had said there was no typewriter that could use that kind of ribbon, and that he had thrown the requisition away. Again, failure of communication. If there was a question about the appropriateness of the requisition, the business manager should have asked somebody.

Needless to say, the new librarian found this lack of communication a constant problem. He had no idea whether or not he would receive what he had requested. There was never any communication from the district office. To correct this, the librarian should have gone to the principal and explained the situation. He should have asked for a meeting with the business manager. The principal should also have been in attendance, if only to explain that he could not hold the librarian responsible for ordering materials and supplies without adequate communication among all parties concerned.

FUNCTIONALIZATION

When setting up an organization, an early step is to determine the primary function of the organization. Objectives are related to this and other functions. The structure is created by designing from the bottom up and then from the top down. When the basic function is determined, positions can be structured to create effective management to accomplish this function.

This principle is exemplified in a case which occurred in a private high school where the library had acquired a poor image over the years because it was also used as a study hall and a place to send students who were disruptive in class.

The new librarian was appointed with the assignment of redeeming this poor image and creating a new library program for students and faculty. The first step, the principal said, was to determine what the primary function of the library should be: a center for the school, serving curriculum and informational needs of the faculty and students; or a study hall. It was simply not possible to do both in the same facility—this much was clear—so it was necessary to make a decision as to what the primary function of the library was.

The administration decided that the study hall would have to go, and the library's primary function would have to be clearly defined as that of serving as an integral part of the curriculum, supplying information and knowledge to the student and teacher. It was also decided that the library was to be the central facility for materials and equipment. So far, so good. At this point a second basic question arose, however, when one teacher informed the administration that she had no intention of using the central library, and wanted a department library. Here again a decision had to be made as to the primary function of the library. Was it to serve only certain subject matter areas? Should there be a central library, or should each subject division have its own library? In this case it was decided that economically and educationally, the development of materials collections was the function of the central library and that there would be no departmental libraries. The application of the principle of functionalization had clarified the library's role and allowed it to develop stated objectives and to implement an effective program.

STABILITY

Organizational stability must be provided for in the structure of the multimedia library organization so that adequate adjustment can be made for the loss of individual personnel without serious loss of effectiveness. This is another way of saying what is implied in the old adage that there is no such thing as an indispensable person. The organization should not be structured according to individual staff members, but by function and activity. It must be strong enough to withstand any loss of personnel. In school media centers, this can be a problem because many staff members leave in June and entirely different people take over until the following September. A good organization is one that has been developed with enough clearly delineated responsibilities, sufficient areas of accountability and authority, and adequately stated objectives to permit new personnel to step right in and keep the multimedia library operating.

A case illustrating this principle was observed in the reference department of a large university library. One of the lowest clerical positions in the reference area was that of the current periodicals assistant whose main task was to shelve current periodicals and keep them in order. A new person was hired for the position, and after six months a pleasant problem had arisen—he was doing the job much too well. Previous employees in the position had spent so much time reading and leafing through the magazines that the job was never done. The new person completed the tasks as outlined in the job description in half the time, and then did other jobs, such as seeing to the order and neatness of the reference room.

The librarian took advantage of this situation and assigned more and more tasks and projects to this young man. By the end of the year, he had taken on so many tasks and responsibilities that the librarian was completely dependent on him. He was becoming an indispensable person. The librarian, meanwhile, became concerned about losing the assistant. With his experience and knowledge, she feared, he would leave for a better position. So the librarian decided to have the position reclassified to fit the person. Her idea was to create a new position, perhaps an administrative assistant to the librarian. She thought the young man could be convinced to go to library school and perhaps even succeed her when she retired.

Here is a clear case of failure to manage within the framework of a stable organizational pattern, and to attempt to structure the pattern to the special qualifications of a given individual. The personnel director, however, saw that this would not be desirable. He indicated that writing a job classification just to fit one person was not wise. What if the young man left anyway and was replaced with someone who did not have his initiative, motivation, or skill? What new functions were being performed by reference that justified such a budget increase? As an alternative to the librarian's proposal, the personnel director suggested that the assistant should be promoted to an existing position within the library system that was commensurate with his evident capabilities. The point: job descriptions and classifications cannot be written around the people who fill them at a given time; to do this is a clear violation of the principle of stability.

SIMPLICITY

Insofar as is possible, the simplest structural form that will meet adequately the requirements of the particular organizational situation should be utilized. The simplest is the line or scalar organization illustrated in Figure 14. Simplicity must also be emphasized so that objectives can be attained with the lowest possible cost. A line and staff structure would work best in the multimedia context because of the need for specialists who have skills but not line authority. This structure is shown in Figure 15.

The simplest structural form that will work for an organization is the best one. Everything that is not absolutely necessary in the organization should be eliminated.

Organizations have a tendency to progressively add activities and positions; an "addition factor" seems to emerge as they grow. If the principle of simplicity is not kept in mind, an organization can easily become so complex as to be unwieldy. The best means of preventing this is to create a chart of organization and examine its structure from time to time to see if it can be simplified, keeping in mind that the simplest model is the line organization structure.

An example of the application of this principle may be discerned in a situation involving the development of the learning resource center. Learning resource centers have developed from the combination of the traditional print oriented library and the audiovisual center and its nonprint activities. This is shown in Figure 16.

With the development of the learning resource concept, the need for other activities becomes apparent. These include, for example, the career center, independent study center, tutorial center, diagnostic center, television services, materials production laboratory, instructional development services, and the like. Many times these activities are added in a helter-skelter way. The result: an organizational morass so complicated that it is difficult for the staff to understand who is responsible for what and to whom as shown in Figure 17.

In looking at this figure, it is apparent that the helter-skelter addition of activities under both library and media services has complicated the organizational structure. Management of the learning resource center has become very difficult because of dual accountability. A specific example would be TV services. Note that all of the

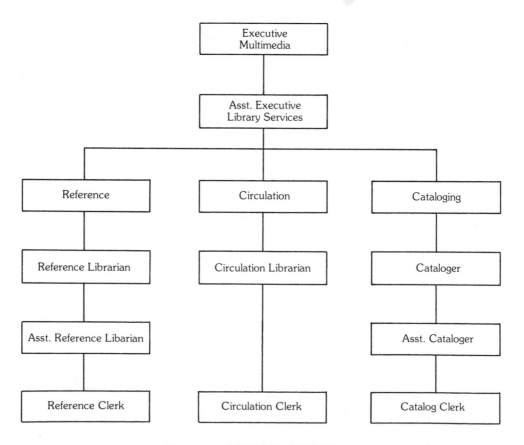

Figure 14. LINE ORGANIZATION

broadcast services are housed in television services area of the learning resource center. Yet the organizational structure is complicated by having separate broadcast services under the office of instruction. This means that the same personnel, equipment, and facilities are used for cable TV, open channel TV, and closed circuit TV. The organizational structure needs to be simplified so as to create more of a line organization with clear and simple lines of responsibility and authority. Figure 18 indicates how this may effectively be accomplished.

MULTIMEDIA FACTORS

In applying these principles to the multimedia library, it is well to consider some of the factors that are unique in this context, and, thus, would affect the structure. One is multiplicity. There are many different kinds of activities in the multimedia library, such as television, audiovisual operations, programmed learning, to name a few, that require a great variety of expertise.

Diversity of materials is another factor. Such diversity creates more specialization, particularly when the equipment necessary to utilize the nonprint materials is considered. With the traditional book, no special equipment is needed to transmit the information to the learner. Television, however, requires individuals who are specialists in the production, editing, and playback of videotapes, and electronic

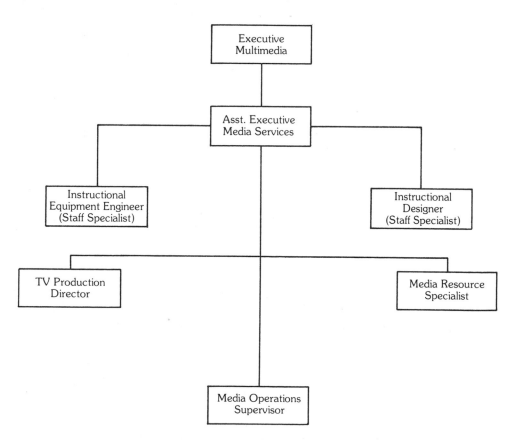

Figure 15. LINE AND STAFF ORGANIZATION

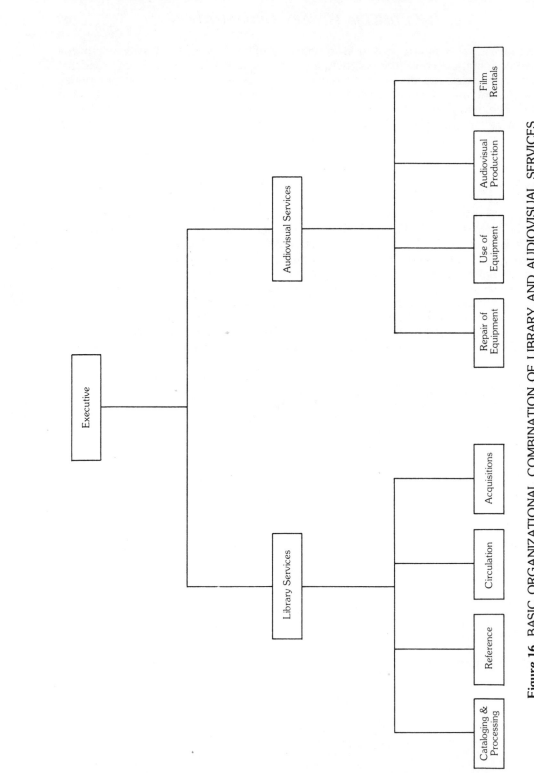

Figure 16. BASIC ORGANIZATIONAL COMBINATION OF LIBRARY AND AUDIOVISUAL SERVICES

specialists to maintain and repair the equipment. Audiotape utilization requires people with sound or audio skills. If a patron wants to obtain information from a 16mm film and cannot thread a projector, someone on the staff must have the skill to assist. In a multimedia library, it is necessary to have a staff of specialists in all of the different media, including books.

Decisions and task assignments are also affected. In handling materials, for example, is acquisition of book and nonbook materials to be centralized, or will books be considered one function, and nonbook materials another? Does the organization decentralize and set up two activity centers to accomplish this task? Centralization versus decentralization, and their degree, is always going to be a factor of particular concern in a multimedia setting. Centralization of authority is always a matter of proportion, and finding the optimum degree necessary for a specific multimedia organization will always be a significant problem for the manager.

Another factor to consider is the development of objectives. Developing objectives for multimedia services is especially difficult not only because they are more complicated and sophisticated, but because of the greater diversity in these services and functions. When dealing with books in the traditional mode, objectives are primarily related to the selection, acquisition, cataloging, processing, and circulation of those books. Multimedia environments expand this spectrum significantly.

By definition, the learning resource concept is concerned with all resources:

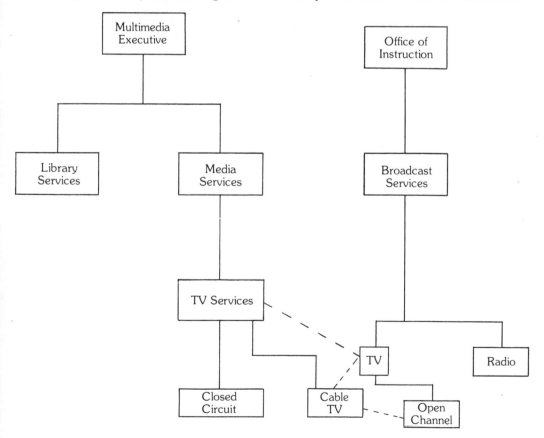

Figure 17. ORGANIZATIONAL MORASS

human, materials, equipment, and facilities. Its primary goal is the efficient use of all these resources to implement learning. It goes beyond the service posture of the traditional print environment, and necessitates direct involvement of the librarian in the learning process itself.

AUTHORITY STRUCTURE

In light of the principles discussed, the multimedia factors considered, and the challenge of management suggested in earlier pages, it is well here to briefly overview the authority structure which must be designed for the multimedia library. Ranging from the top down, authority needs to be distributed, with responsibility, throughout the various levels of the organization. One such design, as shown in Figure 19, resembles the classical hierarchy of management, but provides for a progressively more specialized assignment of working tasks and delegated responsibility as the structure proceeds downward, leaving clearly defined lines of authority and decision making at the higher levels of management.

Within this structure, a variety of informal organizational patterns can be recognized, these being the dynamic, ever-changing and interrelated subsystems of the organization which reflect the day-to-day working relationships that develop among the staff, and which are generated by the coincidence of job clusters, special

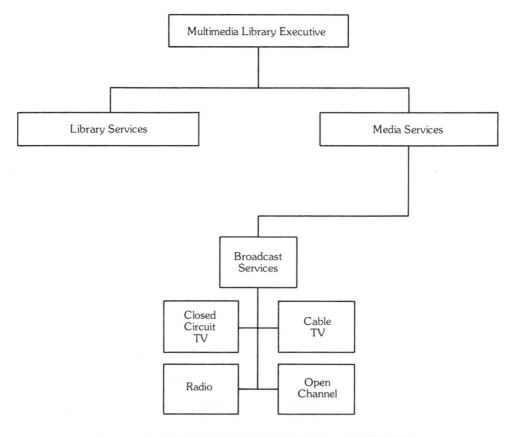

Figure 18. ORGANIZATIONAL MORASS—CORRECTED

interests, areas of pressure or emphasis in library practice, and so on. These kinds of informal substructures are suggested visually in Figure 20. The number and complexity of levels in either the formal or informal designs in these two figures depend upon the size and complexity of the library, the staff, and the working requirements and constraints of the collection itself.

SUMMARY

This chapter has looked at the multimedia library organization as a structured sociotechnological subsystem of the larger system, such as a school or community, within which it operates. The established pattern of relationships by which the organization accomplishes its goals and objectives is its structure. In the multimedia library, this means rules, procedures, policies, guidelines, and the like. The organization is a social system in which people relate to each other, in which they work toward common goals; it is a technological system in that assigned tasks and performance outcomes are obtained by the planned, coordinated, and directed use of specialized skills and insights.

This chapter has discussed organization in the context of these general characteristics, pointing out that the organization of the multimedia library starts

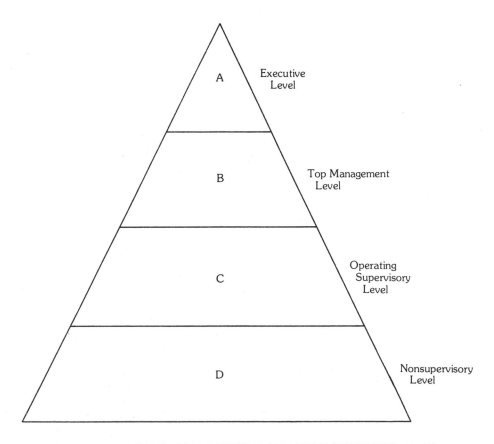

Figure 19. STRUCTURED PATTERN OF AUTHORITY DISTRIBUTION

with objectives, provides for personnel requirements, indicates task divisions, describes physical assets, articulates policies and procedures, defines authority, accountability and responsibility, and provides for lines of communication. This organization is a product of management, on the one hand, and the environment within which management functions, on the other. It is a system within a network of systems, and within it, a network of subsystems functioning together to provide the total effort needed to attain objectives relating to the advancement, through sharing, of the resources of human knowledge.

The chapter looks at organizational theory in an historical perspective, and contrasts the highly formalized classical view with the so-called neoclassical—a downward hierarchy based upon authority in the former, and a people oriented, organizationally structured line and staff effort in the other. It has been suggested that contemporary organization may be seen in a third perspective: a pattern or network of relationships among positions and position holders held together by commonalities of understanding and task orientations and directed by the policies, procedures, and working relationships which lead to the fulfillment of specified objectives. Both formal and informal organizational structures can be discerned in this kind of system, and much of the chapter to follow is given to careful review and discussion of these. Formal organizations remain largely oriented to decision-making rules, while informal organizations develop out of human interactions and sentiments among position holders. Both the formal and the informal organizational

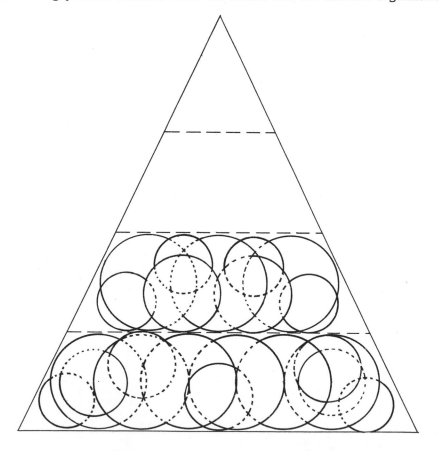

Figure 20. INFORMAL GROUPS IN THE STRUCTURED PATTERN

structures of the multimedia library are important concerns of the media manager in the attainment of the objectives of the library.

Centralization and decentralization are defined and discussed. The centralization concept is looked at as the method of organizational and operational control which systematically reserves authority to central points and people within an organization. Decentralization, by contrast, delegates authority and responsibility to a variety of levels; generally to the lowest level possible within an organization. The chapter recommends a balance between these two structures, and discusses factors relating to attainment of this balance in light of operating policies and procedures.

The chapter concludes with a discussion of the principles of organization which are essential to the combined classical and human relations approach to library organization.

Principles discussed and illustrated with case study examples include: the *principle of accomplishment*, which highlights the need for predetermined objectives; the *principle of responsibility*, which bears upon the relationship between delegated responsibility, authority, and accountability; the *principle of authority*, which extends the previous principle to focus on the importance of authority as an adjunct to delegated responsibility; the *principle of accountability*, which also extends the principle of authority and emphasizes its relationship to span of control; and the *principle of span of control* specifically defined in terms of the practical question—How many people and job assignments can one manager effectively supervise?

Other principles discussed and illustrated include: the *principle of activities*, which emphasizes the need to group activities and job assignments by some logical and task related method; the *principle of flexibility*, which highlights the need for dynamic organizational structure which can respond to change; the *principle of proportion*, which discusses the balance required between and among various activity centers in the multimedia library; the *principle of communication*, as applied both to the formal and informal organizations within the library; the *principle of functionalization*, which relates the structuring of positions in the multimedia library system to the functions for which they are designed; the *principle of stability*, which provides for movement within the structure of the organization to respond to changing needs and opportunities; and the *principle of simplicity*, which suggests that the best organizational structure is the one which does the job best while being least complex. Several organizational structures are illustrated with graphic displays.

These principles, and the organizational patterns discussed earlier in the chapter, are looked at in light of multimedia factors—the special conditions and constraints affecting the organization by the diversity of formats, methods, and materials which are found in the multimedia library context, and these are discussed as they relate to the overall management design of the multimedia library.

CHAPTER 3

MULTIMEDIA
LIBRARY MANAGEMENT

Students receive assistance from trained staff in using media systems in a college learning center. (Courtesy of Learning Center, Los Medanos College.)

In this chapter we look at the purpose, philosophy, goals, and objectives of management. Management is defined, the management-by-objectives (MBO) concept as applied to the multimedia library is discussed, and a perspective is given on the function of management-by-objectives in the context of basic institutional values and philosophy. Definitions and case study examples are provided for the several principles of management-by-objectives, including the principles of delegation, policy making, efficiency, planning, control, scope, decision, and command. Other principles discussed include the principles of accomplishment, measurable results, limitation, and exception. The methodology of management-by-objectives is delineated, and a graphic display is presented to provide direct visualization of the process, through the three stages of planning, designing, and supervising. We note the need to develop objectives from those levels in the organizational structure to which their implementation and effect will apply, and provide insights to the role of the multimedia manager in the process.

Management practices in the traditional library over the past century have proved effective in accomplishing many goals. But these traditional approaches may not be capable of handling the knowledge and information explosion and its consequent tremendous technology. Can today's libraries and those of the future, utilizing their present organizational and management processes, make effective use of the advancing library technology to accomplish their objectives, and satisfy the human and social needs of our system?

The manager of a multimedia library must look at the challenge of the work from this perspective. Human resources are of central importance in balancing technical tasks with objectives in the multimedia library, and in the larger total system.

After studying many different schools of management, the conclusion is, simply stated, that management is the business of getting things done through and with people in formally organized groups. Management is the creation of an environment, the organization of task groups within which people can both perform as individuals and cooperate toward the attainment of group objectives. It is the ability to optimize efficiency toward the attainment of specified objectives.

Management is concerned with planning, designing, supervising, controlling, and revising.

THE MANAGEMENT-BY-OBJECTIVES APPROACH IN RELATION TO OTHER THEORIES

In discussing management theory in the context of the multimedia library, no attempt will be made to treat exhaustively all management theory. Instead the approach of management-by-objectives will be recommended and described in detail. First, however, several other theories will be reviewed to put their contribution to management-by-objectives into reasonable perspective. The MBO approach to management combines contributions from many basic management theories or schools of thought into an approach that best fits the unique character of the multimedia library in the contemporary setting.

MANAGEMENT PROCESS

The traditional or classical management approach can be called the "management process school." This school views management as a process which can best be dissected intellectually by analyzing the functions of the manager. It also contends that the long experience of management in a variety of enterprise situations creates fundamental truths or principles which can be used as yardsticks in clarifying or evaluating management questions and in predictive valuations relating to the understanding and improvement of managing, such as the principles of delegation, policy making, and so on. This approach, to put it another way, is concerned with management as a process of getting things done. It aims to analyze the process, establish a framework for it, identify principles, and build up a theory of management from those principles. It regards management as a universal process regardless of the type of institution or enterprise in which it is functioning.

EMPIRICAL

A second approach to management is the empirical. This position is based on a study of experience. It is founded on the premise that by studying the experiences of successful managers and management situations, it is possible to solve management problems, understand and learn from the application of solutions reached and decisions made, and apply the lessons learned. This view has application in the MBO approach, where objectives certainly are affected by prior experience as well as day-to-day management experiences; they feed back into the decision-making process, and are instrumental in the revision of or selection of new objectives.

BEHAVIORAL

Another school of thought is the human relations or behavioral school. This approach is primarily concerned with getting things done with and through people. It emphasizes that the study of management must be centered on interpersonal relations. It concentrates on the people part of management and rests on the principle of interpersonal understanding—where people work together as groups to accomplish objectives, people should understand people. This view insists that human beings will direct their own efforts, exercise self-control and responsibility, and use their creativity toward the accomplishment of objectives to which they are committed. Leadership becomes an important part of management from this point of view.

SOCIAL SYSTEM

The social system approach to management is another theory which has some application to the multimedia concept of management-by-objectives. In this view, a systems approach is taken, with the library seen as a part of the larger social system. The view of this school is that management is a social system, a system of cultural interrelationships. Advocates of the social system approach see management as a function of the institutional and cultural aspects of society. Certainly it is society which generates the purpose of the multimedia library, provides its resources and constraints, and evaluates its adequacy.

DECISION THEORY

The decision theory approach to management concentrates on the function of rational decision making; the selection from among possible alternates of a course of action, as a management basis. This approach looks carefully at the decision-making process, the process of evaluating alternatives, as a primary focus for management principles and practices. Those who belong to this school of thought contend that future development of management theory will use decision functions as a central focus, and that management theory will develop around this structural center. This view has considerable value in the MBO approach. However, in the seeking and selection of alternatives, and in making decisions, any individual choice will have to be based upon objectives. Consequently, it is the objectives rather than decisions per se that are the important element in the process.

MATHEMATICAL

A final pertinent approach to management theory is what many choose to call the mathematical school. This approach is based on the conviction that management is a system of mathematical models and processes. This school is included among those from which management-by-objectives has evolved simply to recognize that mathematics does belong here, at least as a basis for orderly thinking. Mathematics and mathematical theory are here best seen as a tool, not as a theoretical base for management thinking. They can be useful as the basis for a system of relationships in management for reviewing and working with data, and in ordering and analyzing feedback as objectives are evaluated and modified.

In summary, the multimedia MBO position is based on the precept that many theories or schools of thought do indeed contribute to basic management theory and practice, and the MBO position has been developed by taking different parts from various approaches to management theory and joining them together.

PRINCIPLES OF MANAGEMENT IN MANAGEMENT-BY-OBJECTIVES

In management-by-objectives the manager's duties include establishing objectives, planning programs to accomplish objectives, dividing work, and controlling activities. Certain principles that will assist the manager in the practical daily performance of these duties will be reviewed in the following paragraphs.

DELEGATION

Management must provide for delegation of authority commensurate with responsibility entrusted to members of a staff. The manager has the responsibility of dividing the work and establishing structural relationships. An ability to delegate and assign tasks is the key to this function. The manager's concern is to manage by delegation, not to carry out the work.

The following case is a good example of dividing the work and establishing structural relationships. In a junior high school, a federal project required the addition of a professional librarian to the school staff. The person who had previously worked with the book collection, Miss Brown, was not trained in librarianship, but, because of her length of service, had to be retained in some capacity in the library organization.

The federal project was concerned with converting the library into a full media center and having it become an integral, functioning part of the learning system of the school. The principal thought that, since rapport with faculty was so important, it would be better to send one of his staff teachers to library school than to bring in a completely new person. He was fortunate in having Mrs. Bidle, who had taught English for years and who was interested both in librarianship and new, media-centered instructional techniques. Mrs. Bidle was a friend of Miss Brown. On her return from library school, she was faced with the problem of Miss Brown and what to do with her. It was obvious that since she was the other full-time person on the staff, it would be necessary to delegate specific areas of responsibility to her despite her lack of professional training in librarianship.

Mrs. Bidle decided to retain for herself responsibilities relating to the implementation of learning situations, and to delegate routine technical services to Miss Brown. Accordingly, she delegated the ordering, receiving, preparation, and processing of new materials to her colleague. Miss Brown was comfortable with routine procedures in the workroom, while Mrs. Bidle was free to handle students and faculty in the areas of learning for which she had been professionally trained. Mrs. Bidle had effectively divided the work load by careful delegation, had established an effective structural relationship by making Miss Brown responsible to her, and had provided for the most pleasant and productive division of effort in the new media center environment.

POLICY MAKING

One of the biggest problems in management is the preparation of definite, clear-cut policy statements. Such statements need to be done with clarity if they are to be effective. The manager's task is to articulate these policies so they may be understood and carried out at all levels.

The following case will emphasize the importance of good policy. It is concerned with a common problem in elementary school libraries: volunteers and the lunch break.

On certain days when the librarian was at another school mothers were used in the library as volunteers. These volunteers managed to keep the library operating but had a problem during the lunch break. The children were very noisy, and the mothers were finding it difficult to control them. As winter weather approached, and the youngsters remained inside, the situation worsened. Mothers stopped volunteering for lunch-break duty.

The librarian decided that a definite policy on student use of the library at lunch had to be established. Her first step toward developing such a policy was a workshop for all the volunteers, where the problem was fully discussed and suggestions were solicited. From these, a clear-cut policy was formulated: students entering the library during lunch break must have a written request form signed by a teacher and stating the reason the student would use the library. With such a policy, it was thought that the volunteers could control the number of students coming into the library, and could send them back to the classroom if they were not doing what their request form indicated as their reason for being there.

Since it was necessary to obtain the support of the teachers, the librarian took the policy to a school staff meeting. The problem and proposed policy were presented, asking for the teachers' support and suggestions. The teachers definitely understood the problem and agreed with the policy. Following this, the policy was explained to the students so that everyone understood why it had been established. Children who went to the library after that used the privilege constructively, and the volunteers were able to handle the lunch break.

EFFICIENCY

Management creates efficiency in a work situation when each employee is given a definite job to be completed in a given time and in keeping with clear standards of performance. "Parkinson's Law" suggests that employees will expand work to fit the amount of time they have to complete it. If this is so, the manager who assigns a task without such limits is risking inefficiency. Thus, standards of performance and definite time deadlines on tasks assigned are essential to the efficient performance of staff tasks in the multimedia library.

Standards of performance give management definite measurements by which to gauge efficiency, to evaluate and control performance, and to estimate the plan for the future. A good example of this is seen in the instance of a student assistant or page who shelves books. How many books should this individual be able to shelve within a given time? If the manager does not set a standard there is no way of knowing or measuring accomplishment in this job. A standard of performance by which to measure the work needs to be set; for example, a complete book truck per hour.

In the processing of nonprint materials, what standards of performance should be determined for processing kits? How many audiotapes can be copied in a fifteen minute period? A case involving microfilm illustrates the need for standards of performance and definite deadlines.

A special library housed an important historical file on California artists. It was decided that since the material was so important, and because it was necessary to insure its safety and retention, it should be placed on microfiche. A service bureau was contracted to do the existing files, and a staff member was to keep the microfiche file up-to-date by copying new material on a regular basis.

This task was assigned to the catalog and processing clerk, a responsibility which was added to her already assigned duties. The librarian, however, failed to develop any procedures, set any standards of performance, or establish any deadlines for the job, and what was worse, the accumulating material continued to be circulated to patrons. It finally came to the librarian's attention that some valuable material had been lost before it had been placed on microfiche, and it became apparent that something had to be done.

A procedure was set up by which all material was put on microfiche before it was placed in the vertical file. A standard of performance and deadline were set: all material prepared for the historical file on California artists had to be placed on microfiche and returned for filing in the vertical file within ten days after the librarian had completed her assignment of subject heading and processing for the vertical file. Further loss of material was thus averted, and the microfiche job was under control.

PLANNING

In order to satisfactorily accomplish anything of importance, management must plan in advance. Management-by-objectives is a valuable technique if for no other reason than that it makes planning a necessary part of creating objectives.

The necessity of planning is emphasized by the following personnel situation relating to the development of a new high school media center which was actually a merger of two schools. With the merger, it was necessary to combine the two materials collections. One collection's cataloging had to be redone to coincide with the other. This meant hiring a full-time cataloger and a second professional in the media area.

The present media specialist planned to utilize the person hired in duties other than cataloging after the first year. He spent a great deal of time on interviews and finally selected the best qualified person for the position. The person was hired, signed a contract, and expected to start on the first day of school in the fall. Two days before school was to open, however, the cataloger was informed that he would not be employed after all because of a budget cutback.

It is obvious in this case that management did not plan adequately. There is no excuse for spending interview and selection time without definitely knowing whether or not there are sufficient funds to pay for a position. Nor should a person be promised a job for which funding has not been finalized.

CONTROL

Planning is of little value unless subsequent management control assures that plans are carried out. Here again a neophyte manager can fail. A control mechanism to follow through and measure accomplishment is an essential element of planning itself.

This case, involving a new public librarian, emphasizes the need for control. The librarian was hired to replace one who was retiring. Definite plans were formulated that reflected the objectives of the new librarian. Everyone was happy with him because there was a clear indication, in the beginning, of a well-planned program. However, as the year wore on, the new librarian himself started to feel frustrated because the staff did not seem to be fulfilling his well-thought-out plan. The clerical help was spending too much time getting jobs done; there was wasted time in socializing. Reminders were tried, with praise and appreciation shown when tasks were done well, but still the work was not completed.

The problem was clear: plans were made but controls to assure their completion were not set up. Upon realization of this fact, the new librarian set up techniques and procedures to assure control. Means for evaluation of every employee were set up on a quarterly basis, allowing the librarian to inform each employee, in writing, of the level of performance. Standards of performance and deadlines to control completion of work were also set up. Statistical reports were required to measure changes and relationships to past performances. Job descriptions, which defined specifically what was expected of each position, acted as a control method. By responding to the need for controls to implement planning, the new librarian solved the problem.

SCOPE

A person exercising authority must be held accountable for carrying out all the activities within the scope of his responsibility. When the manager delegates a particular activity, the staff member designated is responsible for carrying it out. One's own accountability has to be clear to the assigned individual. If this is not understood, the scope of both authority and responsibility for a given task or individual may become undefined. A portion of the task may become a vacuum into which someone else can move and take over authority and responsibility not intended or understood.

Understanding the scope of an assignment is absolutely essential to the function of delegation, and to the implementation of accountability in management. Management will find it easier to manage if it keeps this principle in mind because it can create better lines of supervision, and set up more workable control methods in such a context.

This principle is exemplified in the case of an elementary school principal who delegated to a new media specialist the responsibility of setting up a media center and having it accessible to and used by teachers and students. In order to carry out this assignment, it was necessary for the media specialist to obtain an understanding from the principal of the scope of the assignment.

A background fact needs to be noted here. Prior to setting up the media center, teachers had brought their classes to the library once a week. The principal decided, however, that this would no longer be done and that an open policy would be established, with students and teachers coming to the center on a first come, first served basis.

The media specialist, meantime, worked very hard to increase the use of the center. He succeeded so well that a problem relating to the principle of scope was created: There was so much use of the media center that many teachers found they simply could not get their classes in; all space was taken. Some teachers and students just gave up trying to get into the center. It became obvious to the media specialist that a real problem existed, and a solution had to be found.

He indicated a desire to bring up the problem at a faculty meeting, but was told that problems dealing with teaching schedules were not within his scope of responsibility. After explaining to the principal, however, that it was not possible to carry out his delegated responsibilities as assigned, and discussing the principle of scope, the media specialist finally convinced the principal that scheduling of teachers in relation to the media center was indeed within his scope.

The problem was explained to the faculty and a system of priorities was worked out so that all teachers were assured a regular opportunity to bring their classes to the media center, and the center was still available for individual student use on a first come, first served basis.

DECISION

Decisions must be based upon definite policies. Thus, accurate information upon which to make decisions is of paramount importance. Good decisions cannot be based on poor information.

What is the definition of accurate information? To some degree, it depends on management judgment. It often becomes subjective, in fact, because one person may inform the manager of one thing, and another person something entirely different. The manager will have to make a judgment of what is accurate—decide what to believe—or seek further information. In any case, the manager must accept the role of decision maker, making definite decisions based on a timely recognition of the need for decision and the availability of sufficient information for such decision making to occur.

The following is an excellent example of how a manager recognized the need for a decision, moved carefully into the situation, and made the decision.

The school involved was a junior high school in a large urban area. The school had obtained an ESEA (Elementary and Secondary Education Act) grant to convert the library into a media center. The people involved: Miss Jones, librarian; Mr. Harris, part-time AV coordinator; and Mr. Ford, principal. In preparing the grant, the principal had found that both Miss Jones and Mr. Harris, while very enthusiastic about the media center plans, had not been able to supply strong support.

Miss Jones was a traditional book librarian more concerned about the cataloging tasks in the workroom than the needs of the students and faculty in the reading room. Mr. Harris was enthusiastic but did not feel that his training and background as a shop teacher qualified him as a media specialist. So Mr. Ford was faced with a decision as to who would staff the new media center, who would head it, and who would do all the necessary planning. Mr. Ford wisely made the decision to bring in a new media specialist, leave Miss Jones on the staff as cataloger, and assign Mr. Harris to continue to work part time on the production of materials and repair of equipment. Miss Jones and Mr. Harris were both delighted with the decision, and an effective, working media team was created.

COMMAND

Managers must often issue "commands" or orders before anything will happen. No matter how much they adhere to the principle of participation (described in Chapter 4), they will also need to provide arbitrary and forceful directions from time to time. They will have to indicate precisely what they want done before it will be done. In every instance of this kind, they will have to be totally certain of their position, and the various facts and circumstances relating to their decisions, before they act.

If their orders conform to the staff members' understanding of the situation and of the managers' responsibility and authority to act, such an order will be more effective. Staff members need to realize that the situation itself is creating the need for direct control, and that they are not being dictated to by an arbitrary management out of hand. Any directive given under these circumstances should be clear, concise, and not overly detailed.

It is necessary, of course, to give sufficient information in a directive to insure understanding, but not so much as to imply a lack of confidence in the staff members' ability to respond and carry through responsibility. The skilled manager does not flaunt power when issuing commands or orders. Suggestion rather than an outright command is recommended. This approach stimulates better acceptance. Too, the staff member will find it more acceptable and better understand the need for it, if the reasons and goals for an order are known. If the manager is generally open and gives full information when possible, the staff member will move and readily accept an arbitrary directive when the details for management reasons must be withheld.

The following case demonstrates arbitrary and forceful direction by a media manager in the form of a command. The situation took place in a college where portable audiovisual equipment was delivered to classrooms and picked up by paid student assistants. This activity was under the direct control of a supervisor who was acting under the policy that student assistants being paid out of strictly college funds should be full-time students.

Douglas was one of the best AV delivery student assistants, but two weeks before the end of the semester he dropped a class which placed him below the minimum number of units for a full-time student. The supervisor felt that Douglas was vitally needed because there was no time to obtain and adequately train a replacement before the end of the semester. Coupled with this was the uncertainty of other student assistants' schedules for finals. Douglas's continuance on the job was vital to the smooth operation of the AV delivery system. On this basis the supervisor told Douglas that he could stay on until the end of the semester.When it came to the attention of the media manager through a time sheet, it was necessary that a command be given, and that Douglas's job be terminated.

What the supervisor was unaware of was that confusion already existed as to the status of a student assistant who was not a full-time student. The legal implications of the question were already under study by the administration. There was high-level concern that if an employee could not be classed as a student assistant, then he would be classed as a clerical employee at a much higher rate of pay, and with other rights and privileges as related to the classified service. If

Douglas were retained for two weeks while not a full-time student, there was the possibility that he would have some kind of permanent employee status as a clerk. A legal opinion had been requested on this kind of situation. Meantime, until it was cleared up, the media manager had no recourse but to countermand the supervisor's decision and "command" that Douglas's job be terminated.

ACCOMPLISHMENT

Objectives are really a means for carrying management delegation down to a specific period, usually the fiscal year. Management objectives state the specific accomplishment expected of each individual in that time so that the work of the entire management group and the library staff is blended for that period. In terms of the principle of accomplishment, each staff member has a known task to complete which contributes to the overall accomplishment expected of the entire staff for the period. To the extent that management does this well, each staff member knows exactly what is expected, and total production is enhanced. To the extent that management does a poor job, productivity and overall accomplishment will be lowered.

A case study which demonstrates the principle of accomplishment is concerned with a technical services unit in a new community college learning resource center. The primary objective of technical services was to add 10,000 acquisitions to the materials collection, thus implementing a major objective of the learning resource center: to meet established materials standards. Since the cataloger did not work during the summer session, management established a specific, required minimum for acquisitions received, cataloged, processed, and ready for student use each month. The figure was set at 1,000. This meant that the single professional cataloger had a known task of cataloging at least 50 titles per day. Based on a 20-day working month, this resulted in a minimum of 1,000 (20×50) items per month.

MEASURABLE RESULTS

In order to do a good job of management, it is essential that objectives be stated in terms of measurable results. Better understanding on the part of staff members, better overall direction, and therefore, better management in general are obtained when standards for evaluation are known and implemented. Without a means for measuring achievement, staff members may become separated from the central drive or main objectives of the library, and, although working hard, put their efforts in the wrong tasks.

It must be emphasized, however, that extreme accuracy is not critical in such measurement. In many cases, observation and other general evaluations will suffice. The point is that measurement should not become an end in itself but rather a means to an end. Management will find that individual staff members are better stimulated with measurable objectives than without them.

The case used for the previous principle helps to explain this one: the objective of the cataloger was to catalog 1,000 items per month, a measurable objective. The objective can be simply stated as follows:

To catalog 1,000 titles of print and nonprint materials combined, each month of service. The measurable results are statistical records showing an increase of 1,000 items in the accession record each month of service.

LIMITATION

During any set period management must be concerned not only with establishing objectives, but also with limiting the number of objectives to be achieved. Too many objectives tend to take the drive out of the MBO method. It is suggested that as a working rule no individual on the staff should have to achieve more than five specific objectives during a performance period. If there are more than this number, they should be combined in some way. A program or course of action for a specific period having too many objectives tends to highlight the minor ones to the detriment of the major ones. Any objective that is less than 10 percent of a particular task or assignment should probably be combined with another one. Where too many objectives are listed, the staff member finds it difficult to know what the important accomplishments should be and what the less vital supporting objectives are. Many times, also, the individual will find that it is not possible to get satisfactory recognition for a job well done unless there is a means of measuring accomplishment for each objective. Too many objectives make it nearly impossible for the staff member to feel a sense of having accomplished a job well.

Objectives, it must be emphasized, must also be reasonably attainable and within the capability and reach of the staff. Otherwise, drive and motivation are negatively affected. It is well to remember that people derive more motivation and stimulation from success than from failure. There can be little enthusiasm in fulfilling objectives that are too many in number and too high to achieve.

A case which illustrates this principle concerns a new media director in a small community college. Coming in new, she was vitally concerned with making a good impression, so after evaluating the situation, she set sixteen objectives for herself.

The evaluation process included a monthly "Evaluation of Progress." By the end of the second month, it became obvious that all sixteen objectives could not be achieved, and so some were combined with others, and others were put over to the next year, leaving a total of nine. At the end of six months, the director and her immediate superior discussed her progress. She was dismayed to learn that she still had too many objectives—her time was being spread too thin. Some of her valuable time was being spent on minor objectives.

With the help of her superior, the director again reviewed all of the remaining objectives, and culled them down to four. During the remaining six months, the director found these four objectives were attainable, and the year was completed with a sense of satisfaction.

EXCEPTION

Decisions should be made at the lowest level in the organization at which competence exists to make them. The principle of exception suggests that only unusual or significant deviations from expected performance should be brought to the attention of the media manager. Thus, if the manager is selective in delegation of authority and responsibility, carefully spells out the roles of staff members, and provides them with an adequate resource base, the manager can expect the staff, within reason, to make a normal range of decisions associated with those roles. There will always be occasions, of course, which will require consultation between the individual member and the manager.

The principle of exception is also an important concept in terms of control because it underlines the fact that the media manager should be concerned only with matters that are of a nonroutine nature. In making decisions about the division of work and related matters, management should utilize this principle. If it is followed closely by staffers who handle routine matters, the media manager can be free to concentrate on the exceptions and not have to be concerned with matters of routine.

Routine procedures relating to the circulation of materials provide a good example of the principle of exception. In a large high school media center the media specialist had delegated the responsibility of circulation procedures to a full-time clerk with instructions that only exceptional situations were to be brought to his attention for decision. In delegating this responsibility to the circulation clerk, the authority to adjust fines and overdues within guidelines was granted.

This procedure worked very well in that the circulation clerk did make the necessary decisions and the media specialist was not bothered with circulation matters. Then one day an exception occurred. It seems that one of the English teachers required each student in her senior American literature class to read a number of fiction books and give written reports. This was a good assignment for the library, but a problem arose when the teacher required each book to be turned in along with the report. The teacher was holding books so long that they became overdue. The students didn't think they should be responsible for fines—it was the teacher who was to blame.

Since there was no specific routine to handle this situation, it was an exception and the clerk was right in bringing it to the attention of the media specialist. After explaining the problem to the teacher, the media specialist worked out a solution: the teacher would bring the books in and have them checked out to her; thus, the students would no longer be responsible and would not owe any fines.

METHODOLOGY OF
MANAGEMENT-BY-OBJECTIVES

Objectives, and what makes them, vary according to the type of organization for which they are developed. In determining objectives for the different types and levels of multimedia library organization, method or technique affects good management. Where you start, for example, is a case in point. Objectives should originate as far down in the organizational hierarchy as possible. The lowest level of professional—the technician—and certainly the clerical staff member must be included in the development of the rationale for objectives. Doing this provides involvement for all staff members who are going to be affected by, or concerned with, the achievement of objectives. Involvement helps to obtain a firm and active commitment toward common goals.

The development of objectives should follow the MBO procedure diagrammed in Figure 21. Note the steps in this procedure carefully. Examine the questions which are basic to the procedure. What policies and regulations are essential? What is the level of technology? What are the pertinent factors? What resources and staff capabilities are at hand? What constraints will be placed on the use of them? What problems and opportunities will be faced with the establishment of objectives?

The answers to these questions will provide a basis on which objectives can be initially articulated. They may then be examined in the light of alternatives, and further questions may be examined. What are some of the plans of action that will lead to the fulfillment of these objectives, and how do they relate to environment, facilities, resources, other problems, and constraints? What are the alternatives? The examination of alternate plans will reveal whether proposed objectives are pragmatic. Evaluation will become a necessary part of this consideration, and an action plan can finally be developed which will permit specific objectives to be accepted.

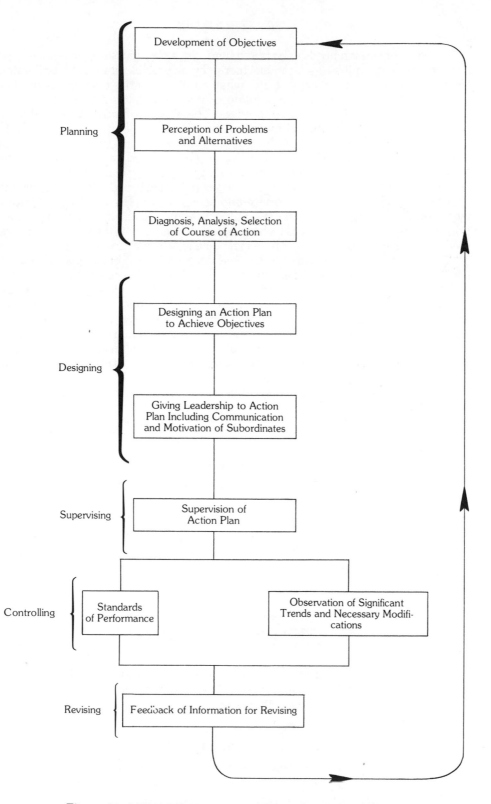

Figure 21. MANAGEMENT-BY-OBJECTIVES PROCEDURE

A word of caution needs to be noted here: since objectives should be developed from as far down in the organizational hierarchy as possible, it must be understood by those involved in management that when an objective has been proposed from any level, it must still stand the scrutiny of middle and top management before actually being accepted and put into effect. This means, in other words, that any objective proposed must be submitted up the line, and that it may be modified at each successively higher level. It is a part of the technique of participatory management, that at each level an objective may be modified, and that the increasing wealth of knowledge and scope of authority at each succeeding level of the organizational hierarchy may result in changes reflecting broader familiarity with the total needs and possibilities for service and achievement. The manager may not be aware of all the factors which affect an objective and may have to accept modifications of proposals by executives higher up, just as the staff must be open to changes made in their proposals by their manager. Finally, it is well to note that this whole process must be done with discussion and communication both up and down the line, so that final objectives reflect the best thinking of all concerned.

With all this discussion of objectives, the word must be defined. The definition of an objective is: an aim or an end of a plan of action, a goal, an object, something toward which effort is directed in achievement. In management-by-objectives, an objective is defined as: a condition that should be achieved or a condition that should exist to implement the concept and philosophy of multimedia utilization; the objectives for any particular multimedia library should cover all of the conditions that management is trying to bring about.

In the chapters to follow, the development of objectives will be made very specific by showing actual examples relating the different functions or activities of a library, such as budgeting, selection, acquisitions, and so on.

EXAMPLE 3
EXAMPLE OF STATED OBJECTIVES

OBJECTIVE

Plan and prepare a series of in-service training programs for the faculty and learning resources center staff in the types of media available and supportive equipment needed to present the media.

METHOD

1. Survey the faculty for those interested in attending specific workshops.
2. Schedule workshops for specific areas of faculty interest.
3. Schedule a series of workshops in the utilization of newly acquired equipment.
4. Make individual contact with instructors who are having difficulty in using certain equipment. Keep aware of these individuals through reports by the media operations supervisor, from personal knowledge, and from observation.

EVALUATION

Keep a log of all workshops and individual contacts made throughout the academic year and prepare a descriptive, written evaluation of progress accomplished.

FUNCTIONS AND ACTIVITIES OF THE MEDIA MANAGER

Before getting into the specifics of setting objectives, some further discussion is needed of the functions and activities of the manager in relation to multimedia library operations and management-by-objectives. Since this concept is new and many people are going into it for the first time, there are those, even among experienced, conventional library people, who do not readily understand its effects and uniqueness. And when these types of people are on the media staff, a continuing watchfulness is needed at the management level. It is strongly recommended that the media manager guard against simply determining objectives and then leaving it up to the staff to fulfill them in any way they deem advisable. The media manager simply cannot leave it up to them. Instead, and particularly in the initial use of the MBO technique, it is imperative for the media manager to work very closely with the staff every step of the way.

Neither can the media manager afford not to carefully review the way in which the staff is operating in the periods between control checks. This does not mean, of course, that the manager should check everything they do. It means to be aware of what is going on and to be available to help when needed. One of the fundamental precepts of management-by-objectives is that it effectively makes all professional library staff members managers. Another point worthy of attention is that high productivity in fulfilling objectives can always be related to the effect of supervisory conduct. Supervisors who check everything that their subordinates do, restrict and cut down on productivity. The media manager must determine how much supervision is necessary to create efficiency and high productivity, and how much self-direction is needed, while still retaining management control.

Middle and top management should also be fully dedicated to the multimedia concept and to the MBO method, to make it work. If top management really wants to get the job done through management-by-objectives, and genuinely accepts the multimedia concept, this success is all but assured. Line authority is, of course, necessary in many instances. No objectives, plans, or techniques will be fully implemented unless staff fully understands that line management is truly committed toward guiding them to that end.

Now, to the question: What does the manager do? The five standard functions of management are planning, designing, supervising, controlling, and revising. These constitute the management process, the activities by which a manager manages; by which the job is done. The manager's functions provide the basic action framework for applying the systems approach to the multimedia library.

FUNCTIONS OF THE MANAGEMENT PROCESS

Among the five functions of the management process, *planning* is the first; it is the function that precedes action. Planning involves the development and selection of objectives, and the determination of alternatives which affect those objectives. Planning is a primary function of every manager.

Designing, the second function, is concerned with delineating the organization, defining the tasks to be performed and how they are going to be distributed among the staff toward the achievement of objectives, including the assignment of responsibility for specific jobs, and the authority to get them done. The media manager groups library activities, assigns them to individuals, and provides a means of coordinating them.

Supervising is concerned with setting up the personnel requirements and necessary avenues for recruitment, selection, placement, and training of staff members. This is the third leadership function, so essential to any management technique. Supervision, properly given, motivates and coordinates all of the staff. It involves dealing with people. It communicates to staff the importance of objectives, and persuades them to bend their utmost efforts toward the achievement of objectives.

Controlling, the fourth function, describes methods used to achieve objectives. Standards of performance have to be set up and measured against actual performance, with provisions made for the correction of deviations from those standards. Control keeps the staff on course and assures action necessary to fulfill the library's objec:.·es.

Looking at these functions from the systems point of view, it can be seen that the management process is in a sense repetitive; that is, a circular process is developed involving planning, designing, supervising and controlling, with *revising* the final step for a continuous cycle, so that the system may function effectively toward the accomplishment of predetermined objectives, and where necessary, change or revise itself to keep going and to improve.

PLANNING

Planning, in the MBO technique, is the foundation of the entire system. It is the basic function of the process because it determines objectives for the media manager. Planning helps the manager to perceive the problems and alternatives involved in the development of objectives and points to a course of action. The manager may then design a program to achieve these objectives.

In planning, the media manager must decide in advance what is to be done and who is going to be involved. Planning bridges the gap between the decision to create an objective and the actual, pragmatic determinations that are necessary to develop a means of achieving it. Planning is one of the important aspects of multimedia management in creating, directing, and organizing which can initiate trends and set its own course rather than merely going along with existing trends or tides.

The media manager must be a planner and an innovator, a person who starts, rather than follows, the trend.

The central functions of management have been discussed briefly, but it is important to look in more detail at the planning process itself. A careful examination of the following seven steps of planning will suggest how management functions, and how the management process relates to the specific task of planning in the multimedia library. The first step is for the media manager to be constantly on the alert to *identify problems and to recognize opportunities* at hand. This awareness must precede any planning or determination of objectives.

The second step is the *setting of objectives*. When objectives have been established and achieved, problems which have been identified should be solved, and desirable opportunities should be incorporated into the system.

The third step, *determining planning premises*, has to do with obtaining data which will affect the determination of objectives, the necessity for alternative objectives, and a course, or courses, of action. In this step the media manager must be concerned with policies, budgets, and prior objectives as well as goals of the larger system of which the library is a part.

The number of these premises may act as constraints. If they are internal to the library, however, they can be handled by the media manager. If external, they may be beyond his control.

The fourth step pertains to *reviewing alternate courses of action*. In any planning process, it is necessary to look at a variety of ways to achieve objectives so that all possible courses of action can be evaluated before one is chosen as the best, or at least the most workable.

Step five is *evaluation*. In deciding upon the best course of action among several alternatives, it is important to evaluate each in the light of the objective to be achieved, and the various planning premises and constraints which are known to the planner. After such an evaluation, it is possible to select a course of action which can reasonably be expected to be the best for the situation in question.

It follows then that step number six is *selection* of the plan of action; a choice which is made after careful review of all premises, constraints, major goals, policies, costs, staff, and material resources available. As a part of this choice, alternative courses of action should also be selected for use at a later time if the primary choice has to be modified.

The last step in this process is the *implementation* of the action plan itself. Here the total management process comes into play, and the media manager uses all the tools and techniques available to construct the necessary support and implementation systems to fulfill the action plan and carry through objectives.

DESIGNING

Designing, as was pointed out in earlier pages, is the second major function in the management process. Designing is concerned with the actual initiation of a plan of action. Leadership is a major element in this undertaking. It is the indispensable organizational action required to put the action plan to work and to carry out the program which has been designed as a result of planning activity. This includes communicating the plan to the staff, and motivating them to work toward its successful achievement.

In management-by-objectives, leadership through positive motivation is recommended. The challenge of leadership in this context is to relate the requirements of the organization to individual and organizational needs and goals, and to do this in a way which is profitable to both.

As a leader the media manager is in a unique position. Many times the manager is caught in the middle between demands made by the organization of which the library is a subsystem, and the needs of his staff and patrons. The choices made, and the leadership exercised, often make the difference between success and failure in the program.

SUPERVISING

Supervising is the third major function of the management process discussed in looking at the concept of management-by-objectives in the multimedia library context. It is a key activity because it is the means by which the manager obtains effective group action. It is the structuring of roles and tasks and the direction of people working together. It is the business of grouping activities, assigning these activities to divisions, departments, or other units, and the provision of necessary coordination through delegation of authority and responsibility to act.

The design of the organization's structure is primarily developed in relation to tasks of people. It involves grouping activities, span of management, and designation of line authority and responsibility. The management challenge in organizing for this is to provide for the achievement of predetermined objectives, using the organization's structure as a vehicle to do so.

CONTROLLING

The fourth basic management function is controlling, and it is of paramount importance because it is the real test of a media manager's ability to keep people on course toward stated objectives. Since plans and operations rarely remain on course, constant vigil and guidance for staff is needed. The ingredients of control are (1) standards of performance; (2) evaluation and measurement of performance against these standards; and (3) modifications or correction of deviations from standards toward performance which will enhance the fulfillment of the action plan.

Setting standards for performance defines for all what is expected of them. Once a standard has been established, performance can be evaluated by several means, including observation and reports. The most used means for measuring performance is by the media manager's personal observation. The manager is right on the scene and can personally check such items as time and cost, for example, as well as qualitative aspects of each task. There is some disadvantage in this manner of measuring performance, however, in that it does lack precision. Increasingly, reports and evaluation of performance are being put in written form. The use of computer-based processing systems and related technologies requires standardized information in a written form. A written report also has the advantage of being a permanent record which can be reviewed periodically by the manager and staff. Statistical reports, as in Example 4, are one of the most common and most useful means of evaluation. Surveys and questionnaires can also be beneficial in collecting and processing patrons' views and comments. The media manager who is aware of significant trends within or without an area can use such data to modify objectives and supporting routines, if they are going to be affected by these trends.

EXAMPLE 4
MONTHLY STATISTICAL REPORT

	1976	1975	Increase or Decrease, %
Circulation—total	5,681	3,526	+ 61.1
Patron attendance	48,760	34,825	+ 40.0
Microfilm use	673	647	+ 4.0
Total reference questions	2,463	1,213	+103.0
Fines collected	$640.80	$367.00	+ 74.6
Lost books	183.22	41.62	+340.2
Microfilm receipts	12.30	6.70	+ 83.5

REVISING

The fifth and final basic management function in the systems approach of management-by-objectives is the development of a means for acquiring feedback and making evaluations based on this information. Trends and measurements of performance are reviewed in this activity, and looked at in terms of the action plan as related to objectives. In feeding back through the system, the data may make it necessary to revise. Revisions may include modifying objectives, reassigning duties, improving motivational techniques and communication, examining the organization itself or the plan for action, improving the training program for staff, and even reassigning people.

THE INFORMAL ORGANIZATION

The media manager in the multimedia organization must remember that it is not possible to control and prescribe every relationship within the staff. Certainly, a manager cannot expect to be able to deal with all the emotions and feelings among the staff, and many are certainly beyond management's control. Nevertheless, it must be recognized that these feelings are real, and that they do affect both the quality of cooperation among staff members, and alignments among and between them. It is these alignments which result in what is termed informal organization. The media manager must perceive and understand such organization and how it affects the objectives, and accept the reality of this phenomenon: there is no choice by the manager as to whether there will be an informal organization. It will exist. The manager can only minimize it where it interferes with general organization, by developing a structured and strong formal organization which will, to some degree, keep such informal relationships under control.

On the other hand, the manager may well recognize that informal organizations sometimes create a basis for teamwork and staff cooperation which can be beneficial to an organization. The manager needs to understand and work with this kind of inner organization, and utilize it to the best advantage. In other words, the manager needs to maintain management control of the situation, while recognizing that informal organization is a fact of life.

Informal organization begins with social groupings within the formal organization. These groupings are formed spontaneously and naturally. They have a tendency to remain small. They are concerned with satisfying members of the group, they develop an unofficial leader, and they create a degree of stability. Many times such groups are formed to create influence and power for or against the formal organization. These groups also have a tendency to resist change from the outside and to exercise functions against their own members to enforce group interests. The stability of informal groups in an organization can be of value to the media manager because it creates support for productive work if utilized correctly.

The informal organization has a tendency to support strong personal ties among people in a group. The media manager can perceive personnel problems and use the informal organization to ferret out grievances and reduce such unfavorable factors as turnover and absenteeism. By making a thorough study of group personalities and differences the manager will be able to make reasonably accurate predictions of group behavior and reactions to authority. Perception of informal organization, and an understanding of the impact that it has, will help the manager do a better job of managing.

One enormous value of informal organization is that it serves as a vehicle for the provision of social satisfaction to the employee. Often it is the informal organization which creates the warmth, acceptance, and understanding that the employee is looking for in a relationship with other members of the organization. Friendship and satisfactory social situations are highly essential to an effective and satisfactory working environment, and it is in the interest of good management that these qualities be encouraged.

A very important function of the informal organization is the traditional communication system or grapevine. This person-to-person, word of mouth phe-nomenon can add to managerial effectiveness if the manager will study, understand, and use it to make sure that truthful and accurate information goes into this system. Of course, there are disadvantages as well, which the manager must guard against. Rumors and false information move as fast as facts.

An additional factor for the media manager to consider is that the more a group learns to work together on their own the larger the number of personnel who can be included in the span of control. A major premise of management-by-objectives is that determined objectives allow the staff to work more on their own. As individuals and informal groups learn to work more effectively together, to interact, and indeed are encouraged to do so, the manager will find that it is possible to devote less time to individual coordination and more to larger concerns. The manager, of course, must make constant judgments as to how well the individuals and groups are able to work together and how little direct supervision must be given.

Another management factor relating to informal organization that can be helpful in areas where the manager may lack technical skills is staff expertise and experi-ence. The manager may be well versed in television, reference, and cataloging but lack skills in graphics, for example. With a strong sympathetic informal organization, however, the manager may find expertise among the staff and a willingness to participate in the decision making and job process; something the manager could not require or expect in the formal staff organization. In this sense, the manager becomes a part of an informal group, and can use its power and talent to accomplish extraordinary tasks.

Management-by-objectives encourages flexibility and puts a great deal of emphasis on innovation. The end result of management is to fulfill objectives, and not simply to make procedures and techniques used to achieve these ends in themselves. So management-by-objectives leaves a great deal of room for individual variation in the management process.

Informal organization is valuable in this setting. By putting faith in informal and group relationships, the manager will find that individuals are more apt to voluntarily adapt to needs and requirements, to the pragmatic demands of their jobs, and to actually work much more effectively as members of a total team.

In looking at the management aspects of informal organization, the media manager must of course recognize those constraints and problems it may also create. Among these is work restriction. In some cases informal organization will create work restrictions in the form of unauthorized actions, insubordination, disinterest, and even disloyalty that may work at cross-purposes to the objectives of the formal organization. A staff member's fear of, or overreaction to, pressures can result in negative effects. The media manager must always be alert to pressures from the group which might emphasize or dictate negative behavior from an employee. Attitudes, beliefs, habits, even customs, of informal groups must be observed and weighed by the manager, and where they have negative impact, in the manager's judgment, immediate action to reduce the effectiveness of such groups must be taken.

A degree of uncertainty in staff posture is without doubt a factor created by the informal organization. However, the MBO approach is concerned with bringing the human factor into management and informal groupings. It is also a simple fact that the degree of uncertainty in management control is increased when a human relations approach is emphasized. It is a gamble worth taking, however, with much to give if the manager utilizes this natural people-to-people factor cautiously and wisely, giving groups time to respond to needs positively, and to form their own directions toward organizational objectives.

SUMMARY

Management is the business of getting things done with and through people in formally organized groups. It is the creation of an environment in which specific goals and objectives can be realized. It is the organization of task groups and the utilization of individual skills and understandings toward the performance of larger organizational goals and carefully planned performance outcomes. It is the optimization of efficiency toward the attainment of specified objectives.

Management's concerns are primarily in the area of planning, designing, supervising, and controlling the operational functions of the multimedia library. Management-by-objectives is the most effective way of accomplishing these functions. Systematic management-by-objectives has evolved from, but is distinct from, several approaches to management. It is a culminating contemporary approach to multimedia library management which reflects the best of other schools and provides the most fruitful and comprehensive model for library management in the new technological age—an age in which technological capabilities join with the best values and practices of traditional experience to provide a whole new and remarkably better foundation for effective management than has previously been known.

In the traditional management process view of the profession, the management function of library administration is seen in terms of intellectual process—fundamental truths and principles—and other qualities of individual and collective professional experience in librarianship. The empirical school of management theory holds a view that relates closely to the traditional or classical basis for management, but goes a step further and suggests that the experience of the profession yields principles and practices from which managers may derive sufficient insights to guide their own practice. Both of these approaches have merit and proven value in the professional experience.

A third school is the human relations position, which emphasizes the "people" part of management and centers upon those aspects of professional conduct which relate primarily to human behavior in the context of library operations. Some discussion is given also to the social system approach to multimedia library management, which is a systems application based upon a view which sees library management in the context of the larger society served by the library.

Other approaches to management of the library include the decision theory position, which asserts that the decision-making process itself is the central function of management and the core activity from which all other management functions and procedures are derived, and the mathematical school, which derives practicing management principles from a system of mathematical models and processes.

There are a number of identifiable principles central to management-by-objectives. These include: (1) the *principle of delegation*, in which the need is stressed to delegate authority with responsibility; (2) the *principle of policy making*, which dramatizes the need for appropriate policy statements to guide library practice; (3) the *principle of efficiency*, which necessitates providing for standards of expectation, measurement, and evaluation in job assignments; (4) the *principle of planning*, an essential feature of management-by-objectives; (5) the *principle of control*, which emphasizes the need to follow through—a principle of particular importance to the planning process itself; (6) the *principle of scope*, which necessitates the careful definition of parameters for all tasks assigned and for all authority and responsibility delegated; (7) the *principle of decision*, which highlights the decision-making function of the manager, and related factors; (8) the *principle of command*, which stresses the responsibility of the manager to think through any directive-type action needed and to take such actions carefully and decisively; (9) the *principle of accomplishment*, which emphasizes the need for careful specification of all work outcomes and performance expectations as related to assigned staff tasks; and (10) the *principle of measurable results*, which reminds the multimedia manager that the whole process of management-by-objectives is keyed to the evaluation of work accomplished, both in progress and at point of completion.

Other principles discussed: (11) the *principle of limitation*, which reminds the media manager that objectives, like other things, must be limited to a number and kind which are realistically attainable; and (12) the *principle of exception*, which stresses the need to have most decisions made at the operational level where delegated responsibility and authority have been specified. Only exceptional matters not covered by normal operating policy or procedures should be taken to higher levels of management. Each of these principles is discussed in an example or case study.

The methodology of management-by-objectives is given further discussion in this chapter. It is stressed that objectives should originate as far down in the organization as possible, and that the involvement of every staff member who will be affected is a desirable and important management procedure. The manager's task, in addition to careful evaluation and handling of such input, is to maintain open and effective communication through all levels of the organization.

The chapter concludes with discussion of the five standard functions of management and their application to both the formal and the informal organizations of the multimedia library staff: planning, designing, supervising, controlling, and revising policies, procedures, and practices in the operation of the unit and related concerns.

CHAPTER 4

THE PERSONNEL MANAGEMENT PLAN

Microform printers have made stored information available in larger quantity and variety than ever before. Instructing the patron in ways of accessing such information is a key technical task of multimedia library staff. (Courtesy of Chabot College, photo by Kandy Arnold.)

Personnel management is seen in this chapter as an interdependent, decision-making subsystem of the larger multimedia library organization. Discussion is given to the philosophy of personnel management, its relationship to the motivation, direction, and effective utilization of time and skill, and its overall function as a tool for effective control of library practice. Objectives are defined in the context of personnel management and the management plan, and the principles of personnel management are discussed and illustrated with examples. These include the principles of appreciation, clarity, fairness, information, initiative, and consideration. Other principles which are important as guiding rules for the personnel manager that are discussed include the principles of participation, praise, pride, security, selection, sociability, teamwork, welcome, and conditions. The student of management is apprised of the need for a carefully developed plan for personnel management, and the process of personnel management is discussed in terms of the acquisition, improvement, and maintenance of personnel. A flowchart of the personnel-planning procedure provides a visual overview of the process, and discussion is given to the application of this process on the basis of the principles outlined in the body of the chapter.

Management of any kind can only function when it has personnel to carry out its organizational objectives. This is especially true of personnel management. Therefore, personnel management must seek to make the staff of the multimedia library effectively contribute to its success by developing a staff whose tasks are fulfilled in an economical and effective way. As seen from the point of view of the systems approach, it is imperative to remember that personnel management is an important function; an interdependent decision-making subsystem within the larger organization of the library.

The major objective of personnel management is to increase the individual employee's effectiveness. Management endeavors to increase individual effectiveness with additional objectives which will give each employee an increased sense of personal satisfaction in the work and the work environment. The most important point that management has to consider in dealing with staff is how they feel about their work, their associates, their supervisor, and the organization for which they work. The principles of personnel management which follow are essential to the fulfillment of this end.

The multimedia manager has the responsibility of meeting the library's needs for personnel with people who have the skills and experience to do the job. The manager must be concerned with setting up the processes necessary to utilize these skills.

The personnel function is also an important aspect of the total management of the multimedia library because the manager has the responsibility for developing coordination among many people. Management must provide the leadership which will create effective coordination and utilization of both human and material resources toward the achievement of the objectives of the multimedia library. Management is not only a process, it is people. Accordingly, the organization and motivation of people becomes one of the central functions of management. Thus it is necessary for the media manager to develop a personnel management plan. This plan in turn should be based upon certain truths or principles. So the first step in the development of such a plan is to thoroughly review the foundation principles of personnel management. These principles relate to the way in which employees are viewed by their superiors, the way in which they are dealt with, the way in which they perceive their own roles, and the way in which they relate to fellow staff members and the users of the multimedia library. In the following paragraphs, discussion is given to these principles.

PRINCIPLES OF PERSONNEL MANAGEMENT

APPRECIATION

Everyone likes to feel important, and this feeling is a significant aspect of motivation. How a person feels about an accomplishment has a great deal to do with efficiency and productivity. Accordingly, it is important for management to emphasize those factors in personnel work which enable the employee to experience recognition for work, attitude, and dedication. The employee who feels appreciated has a positive attitude and can relate this sense of worthiness to the work.

The following case helps to illustrate the negative feeling an employee may experience when appreciation is not shown for worthy effort. The head librarian in the reference area of a large public library found out, via the grapevine, that one of her best assistant librarians wanted to transfer back to branch work. The assistant had been brought to the main library in the first place on the assumption that she would replace the present head librarian upon her retirement. The assistant had worked very hard at creating a good situation, and the head librarian was more than satisfied with the work.

The rumor made the head librarian aware that her handling of the assistant had been remiss. Although she was most satisfied with the work of the assistant, she had never told her so, or communicated her appreciation for the good work the assistant had done.

In order to remedy this situation, Miss Blue, the head librarian, called the assistant to her office and reviewed her performance since coming to the main branch, expressing her appreciation for the assistant's excellent work. Miss Blue followed up on this by expressing continued appreciation at every opportunity. This simple but important change put an end to the negative feelings experienced by the assistant, and she no longer considered transferring back to the branch library. The rumor was undone, and a positive, healthy relationship between the head librarian and her assistant was reestablished.

CLARITY

There should not be any confusion in any staff member's mind as to duties and responsibilities. The person who clearly understands an assignment is most apt to be a productive employee. There are several principles of management which bear upon this problem. They may be summarized as *delegation*, *single accountability*, and *authority*. Each of these supports what we have called the principle of clarity in this paragraph. Delegation clarifies responsibility for doing something. Single accountability provides for clear definition of functional responsibility. Designation of authority removes any question of responsibility and directly assigns decision-making roles among staff members. If management follows through on these principles, it will be very clear to the staff just where their duties and responsibilities lie. Such clarity helps create good morale and eliminates frustration.

The following case study demonstrates what may happen when clarity, for example, fails to be considered in a librarian's professional and managerial conduct.

Bill, a young man, was hired at a public library in a small midwestern city. One of his main objectives, as agreed between himself and his head librarian, was to develop a publicity campaign. For this, he was given a small budget. Bill obtained some specially printed posters advertising the library's services as one of his first expenditures. These posters were placed in the windows of business houses and other agencies serving the public.

An influential patron who did not agree with the idea of "advertising" a library wrote to the head librarian, Miss Taylor, complaining about the money spent on the posters. Highly defensive about the patron's complaints, Miss Taylor in turn wrote a memo to Bill informing him that he no longer had authority to expend publicity budget funds. Miss Taylor did this without consulting Bill personally. Bill felt her action was out-of-hand, that the publicity program idea was still a good one, but that he was now unsure of just what his duties and responsibilities were. The result: frustration and confusion on his part. Miss Taylor had not clarified his assignment; she simply took away the fiscal resources to do it.

FAIRNESS

Fairness is a condition most important in personnel management because it greatly affects the feeling of staff members about management. Employees need to feel that supervisors are playing fair. In the exercise of criticism, decision making, determination of matters relating to compensation and the like, staff members must feel that the media manager is treating them fairly. Without this assurance, morale is adversely affected, and the informal organization, through the grapevine, may create inefficiency, disrupt harmonious relations among employees, and generally lower the performance of all concerned.

A case which emphasizes the need for playing fair in dealing with personnel is one concerning the hiring of a new circulation head in a university library. The basic educational and experience requirements for this position were a master's degree and at least three years of professional library experience. Many librarians on the staff were interested in the job, but did not apply because of the professional experience requirement. One person, however, did apply, although he had only one year of applicable experience. As it turned out, this person was hired for the position on the strength of his record as a retired military senior officer. The selection was made by a five-person committee who apparently thought that command experience had something to do with commanding a circulation department.

A number of librarians on the staff protested immediately. They felt it was an unfair tactic for the committee to change the rules in the middle of the game without telling all the potential players. Fortunately, the selection was reviewed by higher administrative authorities and the appointment withdrawn. Everyone was in agreement that it was unjust to exclude staff members who would have applied for the position if, in the first place, the experience requirement had been stated as one year. The problem would not have arisen, however, had the principle of fairness been taken into consideration at the time of initial selection.

INFORMATION

The manager must understand that employees need to have information on events and actions affecting them or in which they have an interest. Good rapport and high motivation can be assured by making certain that all employees are adequately informed about matters affecting their work and welfare. It is well to remember that it is better to provide correct information than to have the grapevine manufacture gossip and rumor. Sharing information can be an effective means of staff motivation. Secrecy breeds suspicion and frustration.

The circumstances surrounding a staff Christmas party provide an interesting case in point. For many years a large public library had allowed its staff to have a party on the last working day before Christmas. Gifts were exchanged, and refreshments consisting of potluck contributions created a great deal of variety and participation. It was one of the most important social gatherings of the year and did a great deal for morale and rapport.

Early in the Fall a new department head in circulation was approached by one of her staff members with the suggestion that each department should have its own Christmas party. This idea was brought to the director who set up a committee of three to review the Christmas party situation.

Almost before the committee got started, however, misinformation became a problem. The committee had only three members, so all departments were not represented. Neither did they keep minutes or circulate official information. So, as the holiday season grew near, rumors about the Christmas party became such an issue that the staff became polarized into three groups: status quo; Christmas parties by department; and no Christmas party. With the secrecy surrounding the three-man committee meetings, the director had a serious morale problem on his hands.

He solved the situation by requiring a representative from each department to serve on the committee; the minutes of all meetings were sent to everyone, and it was announced that a vote of all staff members would be taken by December 15. The entire staff overwhelmingly voted to keep the all-staff party, and further serious damage to staff morale and rapport was averted.

INITIATIVE

The media manager must encourage and inspire the staff to show initiative in thinking and executing plans. Subordinates should be allowed to exercise initiative within the limits provided by their job assignments, and by normal tenets of respect for authority and discipline within the library.

The case of a new circulation librarian in a small college library exemplifies this principle. In delegating the responsibility of running a circulation desk, the head librarian had included the authority to adjust and forgive fines at the discretion of the circulation librarian. The problem in this case was one of getting the circulation librarian to take the initiative to make the decisions necessary in cases involving fines.

At first, she was conscientious in holding to the rules regarding fines and overdues. However, when she had had a few confrontations with very belligerent students, she began passing the buck and referring the students to the head librarian. The head librarian quickly realized that the circulation librarian would have to be encouraged to use her own initiative in handling these situations. Realizing, however, that this could only be done by example, she called the circulation librarian into her office when student fine problems were discussed. After a few such experiences and with encouragement, the circulation librarian was able to take the initiative and handled these decisions herself.

CONSIDERATION

Management must give careful and thoughtful consideration to the probable effect each rule, notice, and practice established for the library will have on the feelings and performance of staff members. This is especially true when considering changes, especially if management is contemplating an action that may be interpreted as demeaning, for example, by any staff member, or one which will create resistance within the staff. It is best to involve the people affected.

There may be times when a manager is forced into a situation where higher authority has put out a directive that is not within the manager's control—a directive which will be distasteful to the staff. If this happens, the best thing to do is seek reasons for such a change, and explain them to the staff. In this way members become involved. People like to be involved. They like to think that they have something to say about change.

Consideration means that management is considerate of all staff members. The manager should ask, "What do you think?" Each time management implements a change or sets up a new rule, careful, thoughtful consideration as to how the change may be expected to affect the staff should precede such a move.

A case that focuses on this problem occurred in a small public library that had just hired a new library school graduate with a master's degree in library science to head its circulation area. The rest of the circulation staff was made up of clerical assistants who had been on the staff for years.

Almost immediately the new librarian, uncompromisingly putting into effect her professional training, ran into problems. She arbitrarily insisted that each patron show an ID card instead of giving the number verbally, and ordered her staff to insist upon it. Other changes she instituted were also based on what she had learned in library school. The problem: these changes created animosities among the staff who felt they had been dealing with this library's patrons for thirty years and should have been consulted before such changes were made. They could easily ask for ID cards, but the matter was more personal than procedural. They had known many of their patrons for years and felt they could trust the patron to give the correct ID number verbally. Putting them arbitrarily in a position of compromising an accepted trust in this instance was inconsiderate and unworkable. The new circulation librarian should have realized this, and realized that new members of an organization have to be cautious about making changes without being considerate of the staff affected.

PARTICIPATION

Participation can be considered a strong tool of motivation for the manager to use in creating better relationships with and among employees. This principle is concerned essentially with stimulating greater employee participation in decision making and policy development. More information can be brought into the decision-making process by involving more people. People who must follow instructions from higher authority accept them more readily when they have contributed to the decisions and policy statements upon which such instructions are based.

This principle also contributes to a feeling of importance in the employee. Being given an opportunity to help with the decision-making process, and seeing that suggestions are taken, valued, and desired, the staff member is more positively motivated to carry out the related duties as assigned.

A case which has to do with employee participation in decision making and policy development may be cited here. It concerns a high school district and its libraries. The district had recently acquired a computer, and the district librarian thought that perhaps it could make a contribution to many pressing library problems.

The district librarian met with all librarians and presented the idea to them. At this meeting different problems were identified and a committee was established to suggest computer uses. All of the librarians were involved in researching problems and suggesting computer utilization which would help in solving them.

The committee's primary proposal was to develop a centralized, district-wide book catalog produced through the computer. It was felt that knowing what was in all of the collections would create better use of resources through interlibrary loans and student access to all of the district's resources. It would also be a first step in developing centralized bibliographic and acquisition procedures.

When the proposal was presented to the librarians, there was some opposition just out of sentiment and simple hostility to change. This hostility, however, was soon resolved. The heavy participation by all opened the way to discussion and compromise, and the district librarian was able after additional meetings to resolve a majority of the differences and convince the several librarians to support the computer proposal.

PRAISE

Everyone likes to receive recognition for work well done. Praise should be used by management as a tool of motivation. Good work should be rewarded with praise. The manager must learn to use praise judiciously, however, because it is impossible to praise everything and everybody constantly. In handling personnel, when and how to use praise as a motivational tool must be learned.

The case presented here is a simple situation where recognition for work well done was needed. A high school librarian had hired a library technician to handle the classroom AV equipment and the production of transparencies and other materials. The technician had shown a great deal of initiative as well as planning ability. He had organized the different tasks in such a way that after a year the librarian needed to have little concern for this particular operation.

When the technician started the second year, he was doing such a good job that the librarian practically ignored the operation. This continued until after a Christmas vacation when the librarian received a few faculty complaints about the technician's belligerent attitude.

The librarian decided to discuss the situation with the technician to see if the problem could be identified. She started out by praising the technician's work, and then asking if he felt there was a problem. With this approach, the problem surfaced. The technician felt he had worked hard and done well; however, his immediate supervisor had not recognized his work—she had not praised him for it. He interpreted this to mean that the faculty was unhappy with his performance. Thus, his belligerent attitude toward faculty members. The head librarian assured him that she had been remiss in not giving him due praise and recognition. Good relations were again established between the technician and the faculty.

PRIDE

A feeling of at least a reasonable degree of pride in objectives, methods, and accomplishments is certainly a most important component of personnel management. Human beings must have pride in their accomplishments. If employees do not have at least some degree of pride, adequate performance cannot be expected. Management must, therefore, encourage a reasonable degree of dedication among staff members toward doing a good job. The manager implements this principle by clearly defining objectives and outcomes expected, communicating these to the staff, and recognizing achievement when a task is well done.

In the multimedia library organization, this is important because there is more specialization and clear-cut assignment of functions and tasks. Yet there are those who would minimize the principle of pride in today's world because, it is suggested, society has created such mechanization and disregard for individual accomplishment that it is difficult for the manager to create pride in task accomplishment.

Nothing is further from the truth. Most people continue to have a desire to enjoy a sense of pride in their work, and if the job they do can provide this worthwhile feeling, it can be utilized very effectively as a management technique in the accomplishment of library objectives. Management must constantly seek ways to develop and utilize the principle of pride.

The value of this principle is in the worthwhile feeling created by its application. The following case demonstrates this application. The school involved in the case was an elementary one in an urban ghetto area. Under a federal grant, a media center was started with great success. The success was so great, in fact, that after the grant had terminated, the district continued to support the media center, including a full-time media specialist. Clerical help was supplied only on a part-time basis—a clerk who was shared by other elementary libraries. As a result the media specialist had to depend to some degree on volunteers.

The media center facility was very crowded, with poor working conditions, and to keep volunteers motivated and interested in doing a good job, the media specialist had to work especially hard to create pride and dedication. Without this it just wasn't possible to keep or use volunteers as a work force.

Monthly workshops were conducted. The media specialist explained the need and value of the volunteers' work. The need to keep objectives in mind and how to achieve them was emphasized over and over again. With application of the principles of praise and appreciation also, the pride created by this approach kept the volunteers dedicated to their tasks, and their contribution remained a real factor in the continued success of the media center.

SECURITY

All employees need a feeling of security, freedom from uncertainty. Management must provide this feeling. Good morale in a job depends upon such security. Very little efficiency, dedication, or high-level work performance can be expected from someone who is afraid of being fired at any moment.

Fear is far from an effective tool of management despite the fact that it has been used as a means of controlling employees by many managers. Typically with negative management practices, the "boss" creates fear in the employee so that a job will get done. After a time when the threat does not materialize—even though he may have fallen short of doing his best—he rationalizes that it is not going to happen. He slackens up a bit in his performance. So management must create new fear, to "keep him on his toes." This becomes a cycle. The manager keeps building fear until the objective of management becomes one of creating more fear instead of developing positive attitudes in the employees toward the fulfillment of genuine organizational objectives.

It is important that management do its utmost to maximize employee performance. A reasonable sense of job security is mandatory as an incentive in developing such performance. The importance of job security is emphasized by the following example.

For the past ten years, a certain junior high school has been using as a library a considerable collection of books supervised by a clerk, Mrs. Downs. It has been functioning smoothly all of this time, with regular class visits. Now, the principal, vitally interested in individualized learning, and feeling that a well-developed media center is a necessity, discusses this with the district, and puts in for an ESEA Phase II

Project. The project is approved, and as a result, it becomes necessary that the district obtain the services of a professional librarian.

With the addition of a full-time professional librarian, Mrs. Downs becomes very concerned about the security of her position. She feels threatened because a stranger is being brought in to take over "her library." Since Mrs. Downs has been doing a satisfactory job for many years, has excellent rapport with the staff, and is familiar with the school and community, it is important to retain her and to take steps to keep her a happy, productive employee.

In order to give Mrs. Downs security, the librarian decided to entrust her with the specific responsibilities of processing book materials and handling circulation. By giving her these specific responsibilities, along with authority which required supervision of another clerk and student assistants, it is possible to create an adequate sense of security for Mrs. Downs, and at the same time implement the learning center concept.

SELECTION

Careful personnel selection, which makes use of every available device and technique to be sure that, as nearly as possible, each person selected is suited to the work assigned, is one of the first essentials of good personnel management practice. The techniques or devices utilized to accomplish good selection include carefully prepared job descriptions, appropriate tests, thorough interviews, completion of well-developed applications, evaluation of experience information, review of placement papers, recommendations, and educational preparation. If employees selected for a job are suited to their assigned tasks, they will be happier employees and have better morale.

Job descriptions or specifications are an absolute necessity in hiring practice. If the job requires a particular personality or set of psychological traits, such factors must be considered during selection. Careful evaluation of prospective employees is indispensable in making sure that they are physically, mentally, and temperamentally suited to the job they will do.

The following case demonstrates how careful selection may be carried out. It indicates how a mistake in preparing a job description can disrupt an excellent selection procedure. The personnel director of a large school district had the responsibility for the supervision of the selection procedure and the authority to validate the final selection.

When a librarian was due to retire at the end of a school year, the personnel office put into motion the machinery to obtain a replacement. The position was for a traveling elementary school librarian who would cover three schools. The personnel office prepared the job description, screened applicants, and then turned the selected applicants over to an interviewing team made up of a principal and two librarians.

All applicants were screened, the list was reduced to twelve, and the team was informed of the time and place for interviews. On the appointed day the selection team found that the first three applicants did not know that they needed a car. One of them indicated that he was not interested in a traveling job.

The problem was in the language of the job description, which mentioned only that an elementary librarian was needed. No mention was made of the need for a car or that the job required traveling. As a result, the interview team had to first determine if the applicants could travel, and whether they had their own transportation. It was also necessary for the personnel office to rewrite the job description and contact all applicants with a new job description.

SOCIABILITY

One of the responsibilities toward employees most likely to be overlooked by management is that of making each person as compatible as possible with every other person in the activity so that working will prove to be a satisfying social experience. This does not mean that everyone has to be a close friend to everyone else; it does mean, however, that the manager should create an atmosphere in which personnel look forward to an enjoyable experience during the day. It is necessary to create some kind of congeniality, an environment in which people can work together. An example would be to provide a comfortable and pleasant atmosphere for such social opportunity as coffee breaks.

Personality conflicts are another matter of great concern to management. At one time or another all managers must face this problem. Some solve it by either separating the individuals or creating a situation where the problem is minimized.

No matter what approach is used, sociability is a key aspect of individual effectiveness. Most people care about other people and want to get along with them. Management sensitivity to this very real human characteristic is an important key to successful personnel practices.

This principle is emphasized in the following case. In a large university library, a brilliant new beginning librarian had a personality clash with a clerk who had been a staff member for many years. After the new librarian had been on the job for about three months, the problem had come to the point where they were both complaining to the director about each other, and the effectiveness of both employees was being jeopardized.

Instead of accepting the responsibility of trying to create a congenial environment, however, the director told the two parties to settle their differences between themselves. Of course, the differences were not settled and the librarian moved on to another position. The librarian, who had great potential for this library, was lost, and the clerk, who was due for retirement in a few years remained, but was now in a position to have to learn to relate again to a new professional.

The director should have discussed the problem with both parties at the same time. In this way, the differences would have been out in the open and perhaps resolved. If there was still no understanding, the director should have transferred one or the other to a different unit in the library.

TEAMWORK

Teamwork is necessary to insure coordination among the various operating units of the multimedia library as well as within each unit itself. Such coordination and communication provide a basis for a continuity of effort toward the fulfillment of objectives. An accepted teamwork concept among employees will also dramatize the need for overall management controls and direction for the entire organization, making such controls less threatening to the personal feelings and initiative of the individual employee.

The following situation demonstrates the need for teamwork even in the context of a nitty gritty day-to-day management problem. A simple request for a telephone extension caused an involved problem in a large university library. In one of the workrooms at this institution there was only one phone to handle a large number of incoming calls. The person working nearest the phone was constantly interrupted to answer the insistent ring. If this individual and others in the immediate area were away from their desks, as was frequently the case, the phone was often unanswered, and the constant ringing became irritating to everyone.

The problem boiled down to one of adequate phone coverage so that one or two people were not always being interrupted. The manager of the area decided to utilize a teamwork approach, and the problem was presented at a staff meeting.

Staff response was most gratifying. Additional extensions, an intercom system, and the removal or relocation of the phone were considered. After discussion it was agreed that the responsibility of answering the phone would be rotated among the staff members, and a schedule was worked out to facilitate this. Flexibility of this schedule and cooperation among the staff insured teamwork and offered an efficient and workable solution to the problem.

WELCOME

A welcome, especially from someone in authority, will count much toward building the feeling of personal adequacy so essential to efficient work. When a new employee has been through the selection and hiring procedures, it is imperative that management make the new worker feel a member of the team. It takes time for a new employee to become acclimatized and reach a high level of efficiency in performance. The manager must drop around regularly, ask how things are going, and if there are any problems. The manager working directly with a new person can give encouragement, answer the many questions that inevitably arise on a new job, and resolve problems and difficulties which can perplex a new employee.

The value of giving a welcome to new employees is demonstrated in a case involving volunteers in an elementary school district. There were six schools in this district, with only a professional district librarian. This meant that Miss Turner, the district librarian, had to depend on volunteers to staff six libraries.

Being new, Miss Turner wanted to be sure that this system of volunteers would work. An orientation session was set up and a manual of operations developed. A substitute list was prepared and given to the library chairperson of each school.

The system seemed to be working, so Miss Turner turned her attention to other duties. In a short time, however, a high percentage of volunteers had dropped out of the program, and by the end of the school year, library hours were not generally regular, and in some cases, libraries could not even be opened.

Miss Turner decided to get to the bottom of this problem and see if it could be rectified for the next school year.

She selected a sample of the volunteers and contacted them for their views. One item kept coming through in all of her interviews: the volunteers did not feel welcome. They thought the orientation and manual were fine, but when they first appeared on the job no one bothered to give them a welcome, or to acknowledge their presence in the library.

Miss Turner decided to find a way to treat the volunteers as special people. She arranged her schedule so that she saw and welcomed each volunteer personally. She followed this up by either telephoning or personally contacting each of them before the opening of the school year, to be sure they felt welcomed and needed.

Miss Turner followed this up with a show of consideration in the form of brief individual notes to each volunteer on special occasions during the following year. A telephone message system was also set up, messages on special projects were left for the volunteers, and they knew Miss Turner would respond if they called for help. These procedures had good results. The libraries were open during their scheduled hours, staffed by volunteers who felt needed and appreciated, and Miss Turner's problem was resolved.

CONDITIONS

The quality of equipment, physical facilities, and working conditions provided for an employee on the job are highly important factors in achieving efficiency and high production. The better the working conditions the higher the efficiency and production with the same amount of human effort.

How working conditions can affect the production of an employee is demonstrated by the following case which occurred in a large high school where an auditorium was converted into a spacious library. The plan was to have the library and a study hall combined. An office and workroom in one corner were partitioned space, since no walls were put into the room itself. Acquisitioning, cataloging, and processing were done in the partitioned area.

However, typing noise from the office bothered students who were assigned to study hall; an eight-foot high partition provides very little sound protection. Students flipped pennies over the partition to irritate the clerk when she started typing in the office area. The clerk's efficiency and production were seriously impaired, and the problem became a serious matter of concern. Among suggestions considered were to leave the tables next to the partition empty; another, to find an effective way of locating clerical duties elsewhere. This was done, and the improved conditions permitted better work by the clerk, and eliminated interruption of study hall activities.

DEVELOPMENT OF THE PLAN

The principles discussed in the preceding section will not by themselves assure an effective personnel management program. They must be brought together, along with other factors of management, within what may be called a management plan. The following sections will discuss how such a plan may be developed, whether for a large organization where management functions are departmentalized, or in the smaller unit where personnel management is only one of the responsibilities of the multimedia manager.

PREPARATION

In preparing a personnel management plan, the manager must carefully consider in advance every detail required in the development of a successful and adequate program. The manager must understand that all aspects of personnel work interact and have a cause and effect relationship on one another. Particularly with relation to personnel selection the manager needs to be aware of the effect of decisions made at this stage, and the orientation procedures and later in-service training that will be needed. If the people involved in selection of personnel are well trained, and thus able to more carefully employ the appropriate people, there will be less subsequent training required for new employees. This is one of the values of the paraprofessional or library technician programs that are now appearing at community colleges. Selection of new employees out of such programs will often provide better people for library positions from the time of initial hiring.

A personnel management plan designed within the management-by-objectives (MBO) concept starts with the determination of objectives. The objectives for personnel management have been clearly defined in a previous section of this chapter, but the importance of objectives in the personnel management plan cannot be overemphasized. The development of an effective personnel plan absolutely requires that objectives be definite and well understood so that policies and decision making can relate to those objectives.

PERSONNEL MANAGEMENT PROCESS

It is now necessary to develop a personnel management process so that predetermined objectives can be accomplished. There are three functions that are vital in this process: acquisition of personnel, improvement of personnel, and maintenance of personnel.

The first of these, involving the selection of personnel, has been discussed earlier. The second step will be examined here, assuming that the manager, and not a separate personnel department, will have the responsibility for implementing or delegating to staff members the three steps in the process.

The multimedia manager usually retains responsibility for selection, assignment, training, and development of the professional staff. The manager generally delegates to other professional staff members the responsibility of handling paraprofessionals, clerical people, aides, student assistants, and volunteers, remembering, of course, that management can delegate this part of the supervision, but it cannot delegate its final responsibility for the effective and economic fulfillment of objectives by these people. In the personnel management process a supervision and control system must be set up to reserve, for the manager, final judgment and responsibility for overall performance by all employees.

A third step in the personnel management program that the multimedia manager must be concerned with is the development of policies which will serve as guidelines for performance at all levels within the system. Such policies need to be developed by the manager in concert with those other professionals on the staff who will be involved in putting these policies into practice.

It is also necessary for the multimedia manager to include in the preparation of the plan any fiscal concerns or budgetary matters involved in fulfilling the personnel management plan that will bear upon policies and standard operating procedure within the center.

TWO-TRACK PROGRAM

In preparing the personnel management plan, it is well to understand that it will be a two-track program. One track will consist of the personnel management process itself; the actual implementation of the functions of acquisition of personnel, improvement of personnel, and maintenance of personnel. The other track is the management responsibility per se; those activities that are involved in overseeing and directing the total operation. Management has the basic responsibility for preparing the plan, designing the system to carry it out, and then supervising and controlling that system. Delegation of responsibility does not in any way relieve the manager from continued concern with each and every job to be done in the library. It simply clarifies roles and responsibilities up and down the line, and permits the manager to assign tasks and decision making within the staff. Quality and thoroughness of fulfillment of these assignments are still management's final responsibility.

To sum it up: the media manager must establish policies to guide all members of the staff toward the achievement of desired objectives. Policies furnish guidelines for those to whom responsibilities have been delegated, and help them avoid undesirable decisions and misuse of authority. Policies provide standards for action and decision making, standards which are developed on the basis of previous decisions that have been found to be desirable.

The media manager's main concern in preparing the personnel management plan, however, is planning itself. Every good manager is going to have to go through some kind of a creative process involving planning to help determine what should be done in advance of any action. The MBO approach is built upon planning as the first step in management development. The ingredients of good planning are exemplified

by concern for efficient methods, clearly defined responsibility, and careful delegation of authority reflected in, and supported by, thoughtfully developed policy
statements.

RATIONALE FOR THE PROCESS

The first step in any planning procedure for the personnel management plan is
to clearly define its objectives. The total procedure is visually presented in Figure 22.
One of the basic goals of any personnel management plan is to create a staff which
has the skills and motivations to accomplish the stated objectives. As in business,
the multimedia library has a service or product objective. In the case of the
multimedia library it is the creation and distribution of its materials and services for
use by patrons, and, in the newer concept of learning center, to create, as an end
product, learning by its patrons. Not only do the objectives of the specific operational departments or divisions have to be considered, but the personnel objectives
of the staff must be taken into consideration as well. These include such factors as
prestige, recognition, security, and other aspects that affect human and individual
self-concepts.

Certainly the librarian of today is also very much involved in community and
social problems of which the multimedia library, and the people who work and study
there, are a part. Such problems are important factors to consider in determining
personnel policies and in laying out personnel management procedures.

DESIGNING THE PERSONNEL MANAGEMENT STRUCTURE

The next step in the development of a personnel management system, after the
preparation of an overall plan and guiding policies for its implementation, is the
design of a working structure to carry out the plan. In short, the next step is to get
organized so that the duties of each member of the staff having personnel management responsibilities are clearly described, delegated, and understood.

Two components have to be so organized: (1) The overall working functions of
personnel management, and (2) the delegation of responsibility, authority, and
accountability for fulfillment of these functions. The main and most difficult task in
this step is the development of a conceptual plan which can relate each and every
one of these functions so that all of the many jobs performed in the personnel
management scheme contribute to the working efficiency of the total system.

Let us now restate the three functions which are central to the personnel
management process: acquisition of personnel, improvement of personnel, and
maintenance of personnel. Each of these is considered a function because each is a
task that can be simply and easily viewed apart from the others. The basic principles
and premises involved in organizing a personnel management system were covered
in the earlier chapter on Organization (Chapter 2). It is well, however, to review
these steps again, and give some further discussion to certain of them because the
organizing of any activity utilizes basically the same approach, and many of the same
principles.

One basic principle that must always be observed in organizing an activity of
any kind is that principle which could be said to affect the span of control. Especially
is this true in the development of a personnel management plan because the media
manager must delegate personnel management functions within the prescribed
limits of the span of control felt to be most effective for each of the duties provided.

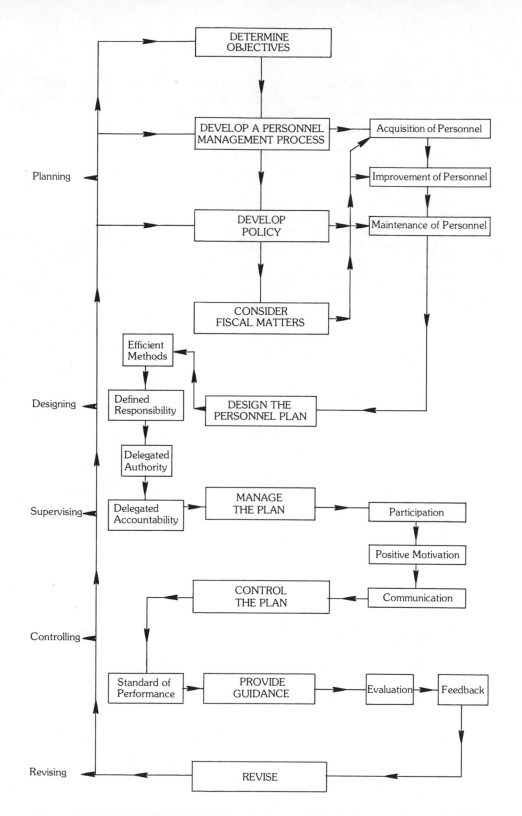

Figure 22. FLOWCHART OF THE PLANNING PROCEDURE FOR A PERSONNEL MANAGEMENT PLAN

Span of control is dependent upon the size of the multimedia library, and the extent of the personnel management function delegated or assigned. Working in a very large system for example, the easiest way to define and delegate span of control is to assign the personnel management function to a separate division or department.

However, developing provisions for a small staff will call for working out a means for delegating personnel functions to individuals within the staff. It is this type of problem looked at here, for in most libraries personnel management is one of the main responsibilities of the multimedia library manager.

Depending upon the size of the library, the media manager may wish to delegate the personnel job to the next lower level of management. Many factors will affect the kind of assignments made when the manager delegates such authority and responsibility. For example, the manager may retain responsibility for handling all personnel matters relating to professionals on the staff, and assign responsibility for all others to some other individual among the professionally trained people. This would be a two-level system.

Or the manager may wish to assign the personnel management functions further down the line. For example, in a three-level organizational structure for personnel management, the media manager would retain responsibility and authority for the management of professional personnel, delegate responsibility to the professionals for the next level of employees, the technicians or paraprofessionals, and, in turn, give the paraprofessionals the responsibility for management of clerical people. A further level in such a system would, or could, give the responsibility for management of student assistants or aides to clerical-level members of the staff.

In a line-type of organization, it is well to remember that in order to create a structure which can be effectively managed by people, it is necessary to create channels by which to provide for the three basic functions of management conduct: responsibility, authority, and accountability. The media manager must clearly delegate at all levels the responsibilities in the personnel management process so that individuals who perform these functions will know their job, have clear authority to do the job, and be accountable in some way for getting the job done.

The principle of authority, especially, is a very important one. It is basic to any effective assignment in management that responsibility to do a job must include the authority to carry the job through. Authority and responsibility go hand in hand.

The media manager still retains final responsibility for all tasks assigned within the organization. Everyone involved must understand the lines of authority and responsibility which have been provided for throughout the whole system, from the lowest to the highest staff member involved.

One final point: each staff member must be accountable to only one superior. Delegation of authority and responsibility should be so structured that every individual reports to a single superior and is accountable solely to that person for the performance of a job. This is what is meant by accountability.

Good accountability is also a two-way process. The media manager is responsible to a superior for the success of the personnel process. The manager is accountable for the performance of all personnel within the organizational unit and for attaining the objectives which have been assigned to the media center.

MANAGEMENT OF THE PLAN

Simply preparing the plan and designing the organizational structure to carry it out, however, do not insure that the plan will work. There remain the important factors of motivation and supervision of the management people themselves to assure that the system will be successful. One approach to accomplishing this has been called *participatory management.*

PARTICIPATORY MANAGEMENT

In all kinds of libraries there is growing pressure from staff for participation in planning and policy decisions as well as other management affairs which particularly affect them. An MBO approach makes such participation especially desirable. Such a management style will improve morale among staff members generally, and encourage their dedication to the overall goals of the organization. Participatory management is based upon the belief that staff members will more readily exercise self-direction and self-control in the service of an action plan containing objectives to which they are personally committed. And where there is a personal commitment to objectives as a result of participation in their development, there will also be a higher degree of motivation toward their achievement.

The principle of participation is very important in creating such motivation. By employing this principle, the media manager creates better personal relationships within the staff. By permitting and stimulating greater participation in decision making and policy formation, the manager creates easier acceptance of policies and supervision because the staff members who are carrying out those policies have contributed to their formation. Cooperation and enthusiasm are encouraged, and a feeling of security and importance is developed. Staff members are encouraged to feel that their input is desirable and important to the system. This leads, in turn, to a greater feeling of responsibility, involvement, and motivation.

POSITIVE MOTIVATION

In utilizing the participatory management style, it is necessary to put positive motivation into action. The manager must approach each staff member as an individual who will respond to different techniques and appeals in a different manner. This means that the manager must take into consideration many separate qualities and attributes of the individual staff member—background, education, sense of values, and beliefs, for example—and then determine what type of relationship will stimulate that individual in a positive way. The principles of personnel management which have been discussed are all guidelines toward creating such positive motivation. However, underlying the use of such principles is the media manager's sincere interest in each of the staff members as individuals.

Interest in individual employees must be a basic working tool of the media manager. Such interest will not dilute the manager's authority or responsibility, but will, in fact, strengthen these qualities. The media manager must be skillful enough in using this approach, however, to maintain a balance between staff discipline and personal initiative and, in any case, to motivate employees to fulfill their job objectives without creating the impression that he can be taken advantage of as a "friend." In utilizing the positive motivation approach, it is important to eliminate the use of fear as a supervisory technique. Fairness, friendliness, and firmness in dealing with subordinates will work more effectively in developing the better staff member each manager seeks to employ.

COMMUNICATION

Providing for good communication within a staff is a very important part of managing the personnel management plan. The media manager must communicate with staff members, and in turn provide for avenues of communication both between and among them, and with management. The effectiveness of the total organization will depend considerably upon its avenues of communication. In the MBO approach, communication tends to take the form more of suggestion than command. Under a democratic management style, it is better to ask, or suggest, rather than command. It is the responsibility of the media manager, however, even while preserving individual dignity and respect for all members of the staff, to make sure that the suggestion or request approach is interpreted correctly, and understood to be a technique employing fairness and respect, not weakness, indecision, or lack of clear purpose. This understanding can be encouraged by explaining to the subordinate the *why* of a directive. When the staff member understands why, it is much easier for the media manager to gain cooperation. Management-by-objectives requires this type of approach. Directions should be given in a friendly way. Flaunting authority creates resistance to direction and interferes with effective supervision.

It is the responsibility of the media manager to insure that communication with the staff be kept as simple as possible. Informative and directive statements must be clear, concise, easily understandable, and reasonable. They should relate to the problems and tasks with which the staff member is familiar. If a directive is unusual or requires an exception or change in policy, it is essential that it be communicated in writing. Where time makes it necessary to give such directives verbally, they should be followed up with a confirmation in writing.

CONTROL OF THE PLAN

The last step in the development of a systematic personnel management plan is controlling the plan. The first three steps have been completed; the plan has been prepared, the structure to carry it out has been designed, and the supervision or management responsibilities for the plan have been delegated. Now it is necessary to design a means for consistent and continuing control of the plan in actual operation. In order to better understand the meaning of controlling the plan, it is valuable to look at the function as three successive steps of management responsibility: guidance, evaluation, and reconstruction. Guidance must be given to personnel at all levels who will work toward the fulfillment of the plan's objectives. Evaluation of the performance of members of the staff who carry out the action plan must be made. And finally, from the feedback obtained in this evaluation process, the manager must make judgments about its effectiveness, and reconstruct the system as needed, or if needed, to strengthen it and make it work. Thus the plan is complete, and is in a dynamic state, responsive to the changing climate of the library community's environment.

STANDARDS OF PERFORMANCE

By setting up performance standards, the manager provides a basis for obtaining the kinds of feedback needed to evaluate the action plan. Standards of performance have been discussed in Chapter 3 as central to the management principle of efficiency.

Standards of performance give management definitive measurements by which to gauge efficiency, evaluate and control current performance estimates, and to plan and reconstruct for the future. It is a principle which must be applied to the personnel management process as a basis for judging the effectiveness of performance, and leads to completion of the cycle of the MBO technique as portrayed in Figure 22.

Standards of performance may be constructed to apply to many variables including factors such as quantity, time, cost, and quality. In the multitude of tasks that are carried on in a multimedia library, all four of these variables are important to management in evaluating both individual performance and the success of the action plan in making objectives obtainable. In technical services, for example, standards of performance can relate to quantity of materials to be cataloged or processed; in circulation, to the number of items circulated; in reference, the number of questions answered per day or hour. Quality criteria can be articulated to provide standards for evaluation of media production, such as videotapes and slide-tape presentations. Time and cost factors are always useful in the evaluation process because they suggest in dollars and cents whether an objective has been worthwhile in the light of what it has taken to achieve it.

Standards of performance are criteria which can be used in evaluating the adequacy of an action plan, and the efficiency of performance of staff in carrying it out. They enable management to produce and maintain an acceptable and realistic level of performance expectations in terms of quantity or quality of staff output. Management, by insisting on adherence to such standards, encourages a working environment in which there are accepted expectations, uniformity of performance, and a reasonable basis upon which to predict successful outcomes. Standards of performance are a useful means of control, and an assurance that fulfillment of objectives can be expected in the well-managed multimedia library.

Performance standards may also be used as a principle in the preparation of guidelines and standard operating procedures. Such guidelines or specifications can be set up both for personnel and equipment. They must include typing speed, for example, or specifications regarding quality and quantity of production to be delivered by equipment. Job specifications and job descriptions may provide standard levels of expectation for implementation within the staff. It is absolutely essential in personnel management to provide standards for performance that are understood and accepted by everyone involved in the business of putting a management plan into action.

GUIDANCE

Let us look now, specifically, at the guidance function in personnel management. It is management's responsibility to give such guidance so that the plan will be carried out successfully and objectives fulfilled. Guidance is accomplished by setting up standards of performance to be expected, standard operating procedures to get performance done, and necessary policy statements to provide guidelines for such performance. Observation and nose-to-nose communication by responsible management people can then be guided by such policy.

As outlined in earlier paragraphs, in management-by-objectives the use of the participatory management technique, supported by standards of performance expectation and guiding policy, helps keep supervision to a minimum. When objectives have been determined, an action plan worked out, and standards of performance established, management simply follows through on a routine basis to see that the standards are being adhered to. Supplemental spot checks as necessary will make management control a relatively painless and effective duty.

EVALUATION

The evaluation function involves two steps: comparison of results with standards of performance, and collection of data in the form of reports and qualitative appraisals which will estimate the success of overall staff performance. This involves comparing results at some point in time with the action plan that was prepared as the first step in the system. If it is found that results do not measure up, it may become necessary to reconstruct the plan and initiate new objectives.

A number of activities or control points can be utilized in obtaining the information needed to make this kind of evaluation. Such activities may be either structured or unstructured. Weekly or monthly reports, for example, either oral or written, are a structured means of accomplishing this. Such reports could be given to management in a seminar or discussion setting where there can be verbal exchange. Another example of a structured method is the written report consisting of narrative or statistical information looked at comparatively. If such reports are included when the objective is written, evaluation actually becomes part of the standard operating procedure. In short, the evaluation procedure is built into the objective. This is demonstrated in Example 5.

EXAMPLE 5
OBJECTIVE EVALUATION

OBJECTIVE

To screen and update the nonprint collection.

PLAN FOR ACHIEVEMENT

Survey the collection to establish correlation to current curricular offerings; review materials as they are damaged or lost and replace with more up-to-date materials if appropriate.

PLAN FOR EVALUATION

All filmstrips, records, 8mm films, and 8mm loop films have been evaluated. Approximately 20 items have been withdrawn as outdated. About 150 other items which were either damaged or outdated have been replaced (or replacements have been ordered) with new copies or newer revised versions.

In addition, a complete survey of the nonbook collection to determine correlation with the curriculum has been completed.

An example of an unstructured evaluation method is simply direct observation by the manager. Use of this technique requires that management be on site long enough to accurately observe performance. It must be emphasized that all of the details and results that are brought together from either structured or unstructured evaluative activities must be organized in such a way that they actually provide effective measurement and lead to judgments which can be used to analyze the effectiveness of the system.

RECONSTRUCTION

The third step in this process is reconstruction. Feedback is no good if it is not applied. New policies or procedures may be needed to make the action plan workable. Reconstruction completes the cycle, permitting the manager to go back and develop or reconstruct aspects of the plan to remedy any faults which may have been revealed in the evaluation. These improvements may require only minor adjustments, or may necessitate major changes in the system. The important thing is that the system be responsive to any change needed to make it work well, and keep it working and improving with time. It is a truism that no system will work if it is rigid or unresponsive to change.

Corrective action in removing problems and trouble sources which can seriously affect standards of performance is a necessity in any working management process. Management must be ready at all times to make decisions which will result in immediate change in both objectives and action plan if such changes are needed to keep the system dynamic, or to plan for improvements that may be made at normal breaking points, such as the end of a fiscal or work period.

In short, the manager must be prepared to establish performance expectations, observe and evaluate them, and then make changes as required to keep the system working well in the accomplishment of desired objectives. This is dynamic application of the MBO technique in multimedia library management.

SUMMARY

Personnel management is an interdependent, decision-making subsystem of the larger, multimedia library organization. It is concerned primarily with increasing the individual effectiveness of the employees of the library. It is a tool of management, a means for controlling library practice, an organized and thoroughgoing, planned system for creating, maintaining, and evaluating people in working relationships within the multimedia library.

This chapter provides a basic view of the philosophy of personnel management in the library environment, stressing the particular importance of motivating staff members, of creating a sense of purpose and satisfaction, and of developing an organizational system within which effective relationships may be obtained.

A key step in developing a personnel program is the preparation of a personnel management plan. There are a number of truths or principles upon which such a plan is based: (1) the *principle of appreciation*, which recognizes that productivity and efficiency are directly related to the sense of self-worth which comes from knowing that efforts are appreciated; (2) the *principle of clarity*, which stresses the importance of making work assignments clear, delegating authority and decision making very carefully, and providing for single accountability in each task assignment; (3) the *principle of fairness*, the creation of a line of trust and understanding which assures that the employee is being dealt with fairly; (4) the *principle of information*, which supports staff rapport and motivation by keeping a positive information flow going; (5) the *principle of initiative*, which encourages staff members to use their own knowledge and experience to take responsibility and exercise judgment within the proper limits of their job assignments; (6) the *principle of consideration*, which reminds the manager of the necessity to give thoughtful consideration to the probable effects on employee attitudes of any rules, directives, or practices put into effect; (7) the *principle of participation*, which stresses the value of staff involvement in the preliminary stages of policy development and decision making; (8) the *principle of praise*, a motivational tool as well as an expression of sincere human awareness of the need to recognize a job well done; (9) the *principle of pride*, an important working principle of human relationships; and (10) the *principle of security*, which assures the employee a certain freedom from threat and uncertainty in the job.

Other principles include: (11) the *principle of selection*, which enjoins the media manager to ascertain, in the hiring process itself, that staff members who are employed be qualified for the jobs they are to do; (12) the *principle of sociability*, which provides for the social aspects of the working environment and sustains necessary interaction opportunity for employees; (13) the *principle of teamwork*, which provides a framework in management philosophy and conduct from which to develop a sense of security and purpose through cooperation and common cause; (14) the *principle of welcome*, which becomes a necessary part of the way in which management relates to the new employee; and (15) the *principle of conditions*, which focuses attention on the important management concerns related to the quality of equipment, physical facilities, and related aspects of the working environment which affect efficiency, productivity, and self-realization on the job. Each of these principles is discussed and illustrated by case study examples.

Finally, this chapter provides specific discussion of the actual development of a personnel management plan. Such a plan begins with determination of objectives, involves a three-step process for accomplishing these objectives (acquisition, improvement, and maintenance of personnel) and the careful implementation of a practicing scheme of management-by-objectives.

This step is, in a very real sense, the final application of the systems approach to multimedia library management, and can be described (in what is admittedly a circular fashion) as a "plan for managing the management plan." Simply working up a good plan isn't enough. The manager must carry it through—in other words, manage it. The functions involved in this process utilize all the principles articulated in this and the previous chapter, including participation by employees themselves, motivation and attention to the working environment, effective communications, control practices in work flow and functioning relationships, standards for performance and guidance in their application, and evaluation and revision as necessary once the plan is put into action. This is in no way a paper plan—it is a dynamic application of the MBO technique in the multimedia library organization.

PART III
THE PROGRAM

CHAPTER 5

BUDGET MANAGEMENT

The important and vital function of planning for the funds needed to support the total program of a multimedia library is looked at in this chapter from the point of view of definitions, planning, and management. It does little good to provide an excellent program and a fine staff without the money needed to support and utilize these resources. We define budget, the purpose of budgeting, goals and objectives for budgeting, and discuss considerations relating to policy, criteria, and selection of objectives. Charts and graphs present much of the essential information of this chapter, and specific discussion is given to selection criteria, the budget procedure, budget calendar, and budget negotiation. Management of the budget and the role of the multimedia manager in the actual directive management of the appropriated or assigned funds for a library unit are given considerable discussion in terms of authority, operations, control, and procedures. Some specific consideration is given to the basic bookkeeping, accounting procedure, and related record-keeping tasks which are required at the operational level to maintain effective management control of budget activity.

One of the most important functions of the manager of a multimedia library is to obtain sufficient financial resources to make it possible to carry out the objectives and goals of the program, the institution, and the patrons served. A budget program, therefore, must be among the manager's primary concerns.

An effective budget program must reflect planning because there are limited financial resources available to multimedia libraries regardless of whether they are public, private, school, or university. Management must, therefore, develop a budget process that will adequately anticipate and communicate the needs of the unit. Other operational programs competing for available financial resources will naturally be making their needs known. The more well planned and justified a budget program is, the better the chances for obtaining adequate funding.

It must be strongly emphasized that the MBO approach advocated in this chapter will effectively implement increasing the multimedia library budget and reduce its problem of insufficient funds.

The basic ingredient that management-by-objectives instills in the budget process is sufficient planning to adequately justify budget requests. The multimedia library program is in competition with other important educational programs for an adequate and fair share of the fiscal pie. In order to obtain a large enough slice, the budget requests must be justified well enough so that the decision makers can readily understand the fiscal need in relationship to the objectives of the organization of which the library is a part.

The budget-planning process should include determination of objectives that relate to implementing the main objectives of the parent organization. If this implementation is communicated well enough to those who make the final budget determinations, the multimedia library will obtain an adequate share of the fiscal pie.

The budget document is the result of a process which develops a formal plan reflecting the financial needs of the library based upon defined objectives for a specified period. These financial needs are projected in terms of specific accounts or categories. The utilization of the MBO approach in such budgeting results in a forecast of action in financial terms. This forecast is the product of research, planning, and actual budget procedures. The basic ingredient of the MBO approach in budgeting is planning and the articulation of specifically defined objectives.

Very often, the multimedia library manager will be provided with, or have the opportunity to develop, a budget plan form of some kind to help both in an analysis of need and the projection of cost. When completed, such a budget plan or document allocates financial resources according to accounts or categories that have been identified by the institution the library serves. Most often, the institution will set up a financial accounting guide indicating the account numbers of designations for categories which the multimedia library must use in determining its financial needs. An example of this is given in Example 6, showing film rentals as Account Number 6120-4523-401.

EXAMPLE 6
FINANCIAL ACCOUNTING GUIDE

6120   Multimedia Library

Professional salaries
1200-401   Supervision
1201-401   Librarians—Full time
1400-401   Hourly librarians and substitutes

Clerical salaries
2100-401   Regular
2140-401   Overtime
2300-401   Student assistants

Operational supplies and expenses
4510-401   Office supplies
4520-401   Audiovisual materials
4521-401   Audiovisual and television supplies
4522-401   Television distribution supplies
4523-401   Film rentals
4524-401   Materials production laboratory
4525-401   Production supplies
4526-401   Equipment maintenance supplies
4540-401   Printing
4590-401   Prior year contracts
4810-401   Replacement of equipment

The budget is a financial or cost forecast in specific detail, the end result of what is described as an action plan based on predetermined objectives, its goal being the highest reasonable expectation of operating efficiency. There are two primary purposes to this process: (1) to limit expenditures to a prescribed amount; and (2) to assure wisely planned spending in any case.

The word budget for most people implies that there is a limitation on expenditures, and that a budget is, therefore, a restriction on expenditures. Certainly, such limitation and restriction of spending are two of the primary purposes of budgeting. Limitation of spending to a prescribed amount should be the outcome of such a program of fiscal planning.

Another way of talking about budgeting is to emphasize its importance as a *forecast* of an action plan in financial terms. A forecast implies that consideration is being given to the future, that a plan based upon estimates is being developed. The budget is the result of such estimates.

These estimates can be blind guesses or guesses justified by planning. The latter, of course, is the more desirable, and in the MBO approach to budgeting, it is essential to emphasize that a primary purpose of the budget process is to insure that spending is done wisely. Thorough planning insures more accuracy, and thus wiser spending.

ESSENTIALS OF BUDGETING

Several factors of importance to the budgeting process need to be stressed at this point, and could be called the four essentials of budgeting. These are *effective organization, support from the chief executive, a good accounting system,* and *research.*

The first of these, effective organization, is a primary requirement. It furnishes the structure that enables library staff to work together toward the fulfillment of those objectives which are to be implemented by financial means. It provides a foundation for the analysis of needs on the basis of task assignments and responsibilities. Such a division of organizational relationships into tasks creates a system for organization of budget, and organization can then be seen in relation to the budget as a device created by management for implementation of both operational and budgetary objectives.

The budgeting structure, then, must be based upon a clearly defined system of responsibility that is carefully planned and understood. Principles of management which will make such an organizational structure work, such as responsibility and authority, have been discussed in the chapter on management and elsewhere in this book.

A second essential to the budgetary process is the support of the chief executive to whom the media manager or the institution itself answers. The media manager must have this support. The manager is usually in a middle-management position and must be able to rely upon the chief executive to delegate, through the organizational structure, sufficient authority and responsibility to permit the carrying through of budget responsibilities.

The third essential of budgeting which needs to be discussed here is means for control or management of the budget, i.e., an adequate accounting system. The media manager must either set up such a system within the multimedia library, or have available from the institution an accounting system that will indicate at prescribed times the amount of expenditures and what balance is available for expenditure.

The amounts of money involved do not really make a great deal of difference in the way a budget operates. A large budget would be expected to be more sophisticated; have more accounts. A small budget might need only a very simple accounting system. An adequate accounting system in either case would only need to give the information necessary to fulfill the purposes of budgetary control.

The final essential of budgeting which needs to be looked at is a program that could be called "research." Such a program of ongoing data collection, analysis, and evaluation is indispensable to the budgeting function.

Detailed information, appropriate statistics, estimates of cost, appraisal of needs, square footage requirements, and so on, can be obtained through such a program. Estimates, which need constantly to be made in any ongoing program, evolve from such research, and are useful in building a budget. But research should not stop there. After the budget for a given fiscal year has been approved, the program of research should be continued and investigation initiated which will provide information about the needs on which objectives should be based for the next fiscal period.

GOALS OF BUDGETING

There are two primary goals of budgeting. The first has already been suggested: to provide for adequate funds to meet the needs of the multimedia library. The second is to make the best use of that money. The first goal is based upon a determination of what the needs are, the second on good management. In the MBO approach objectives are stated, costs determined, and then budget is allocated. Thus, the budget becomes the action plan for the accomplishment of objectives that require funding. With each stated objective, there needs to be a design for achievement which clearly forecasts the cost required to accomplish it, and an operational plan for getting it done. Example 7 indicates how this is done.

EXAMPLE 7
STATED BUDGET OBJECTIVES

SPECIFIC OBJECTIVE

To provide AV equipment necessary to make full use of the AV materials.

Plan for Achieving

A committee composed of the heads of each department and the head librarian determines the following needs in AV hardware based upon the amounts and types of material purchased.

    3 16mm sound projectors
    2 8mm projectors
    6 tape recorders
    3 overhead projectors
    3 microfilm readers
    1 opaque projector
    4 filmstrip viewers

Plan for Measuring

Keep records of how much both AV software and hardware is used. Obtain feedback from patrons on whether they are able to use AV software when it is available or whether they have to wait because hardware is unavailable. Same committee as above will reevaluate its recommendations at the end of the year.

Cost Estimate

16mm sound projectors cost $800 each, and 8mm projectors cost $200. Tape recorders are $150 each, overhead projectors $175 each, microfilm readers $350 each, filmstrip viewers $150 each, and opaque projectors $180 each.

    3 × $800 = $2400   cost of 16mm projectors
    2 × $200 = $ 400   cost of 8mm projectors
    6 × $150 = $ 900   cost of tape recorders
    3 × $175 = $ 525   cost of overhead projectors
    3 × $350 = $1050   cost of microfilm readers
    1 × $180 = $ 180   cost of opaque projector
    4 × $150 = $ 600   cost of filmstrip viewers
              ‾‾‾‾‾
               $6055   Total cost of AV hardware

EXAMPLE 7 (Cont.)

SPECIFIC OBJECTIVE

To improve and extend the periodicals collection and to rebuild back issues in microfilm.

Plan for Achieving

Place subscription orders for an additional 100 titles. Each department will be asked to order its professional journal. The library will subscribe to *Education Index* for the teachers to use in conjunction with these professional journals. In addition the library will purchase 3 racks to display and store the periodicals. Also microfilm copies of 3 years of back issues of the ten most used periodicals will be purchased. The library already has a file cabinet to store this microfilm. Present subscriptions will be continued.

Plan for Measuring

Keep statistical records of reference inquiries relating to periodicals. Ask students and teachers to complete monthly questionnaire regarding periodical usage in library.

Cost Estimate

Magazines cost $6 per subscription (including cost of cataloging). *Education Index* costs $40 per year. Racks cost $114 a piece. Microfilm copy of one year of back issues costs $20. It will therefore cost $60 (3 × $20) to purchase 3 back years of any one periodical title, and $600 (10 × $60) to purchase 3 years of back issues for 10 individual titles.

$$
\begin{array}{rll}
100 \times \$\ \ 6 = \$\ 600 & \text{cost of new magazine subscriptions} \\
86 \times \$\ \ 6 = \$\ 516 & \text{cost of continuing magazine subscriptions} \\
1 \times \$\ 40 = \$\ \ \ 40 & \text{cost of subscription to } Education\ Index \\
3 \times \$114 = \$\ 342 & \text{cost of magazine display racks} \\
10 \times \$\ 60 = \$\ 600 & \text{cost of microfilm back issues} \\
\hline
\$2098 & \text{Total cost of periodical materials}
\end{array}
$$

With this basis to go on, the manager may reasonably expect that operating efficiency will be increased, and that both cost and waste will be reduced. Budget management must always strive to achieve operational procedures which are based upon an expectation of highest efficiency. It is through very thorough planning that this can be achieved. This is why the MBO approach is so valuable in budget management.

OBJECTIVES FOR BUDGETING

RESEARCH

The media manager is concerned with estimating needs and allocating resources to reach stated objectives. Allocating is a difficult task, requiring an analytical approach. Management must determine the costs involved in attaining objectives. This means research: observation, study, analysis, and cost of all functions performed in the multimedia library. It means pulling together all the factors that are related to the fiscal aspects of the library's objectives, analyzing all of the relationships within and among these factors, and coming up with a plan for achievement. It is a task requiring thoroughness. Management must be sure to consider all aspects of each job to be done which might have significant impact upon the cost of the job itself and the total cost of operating the facility.

In the research, the budget developer needs to consider not only the short-term requirements of a given fiscal period, but also any long-term needs that may relate to both current budgetary concerns and future budgeting periods. This means that after the objectives have been determined with costs estimated and budgeted for, a long-range view has to be taken of the whole plan in relation to present and long-term objectives. Thus, priorities become a part of the budget planner's concerns, and time periods for the accomplishment of objectives become of supreme importance. Obviously, a budget is related directly to a specific fiscal period. However, its relation to an ongoing, long-range fiscal plan is equally important. Measurement of progress and achievement in the operational program, which is provided for by the budget, is a final step in fiscal management. Certainly priorities and time factors are paramount in this phase of budget management.

To simply state the point: research as a function of budgeting means gathering the facts and information pertinent to the budget so that these facts may be analyzed in terms of budget provision, plans, and priorities. The simplest way to do this is to set up a file and record the nitty-gritty day-to-day management experiences that pertain to budget and have implications for the library's fiscal policy.

In setting up a future budget file, a very simple approach can be used, or a more complicated multifile system can be developed. The simple approach would be to prepare, for example, a file folder labeled Future Budgets or Budget—1977–78. As day-to-day needs arise that must be funded in the next budget year, a handwritten or typed notation may be made and placed in the folder. These day-to-day experiences could be such things as these: The catalog clerk's typewriter is just not operating well and should be considered for replacement; oversize bookends are needed in the stacks for art books; longer running cassette tapes, such as 90 minute, should be obtained; and the like.

A more structured file system would consist of a file folder for each account: audiovisual materials, film rentals, library supplies, and so on, or main account headings such as Operational Supplies and Expenses. As the day-to-day experiences occur, the notations are prepared and placed in the account files that will be affected. When it is time to start to work on the actual budget itself, the needs shown by these records can be listed and evaluated in terms of priorities. Where more information is needed, research can be started to provide a more adequate basis for considering given problems in the next fiscal period. These alternatives are shown in Figure 23.

For each of the multimedia library's objectives, it may become a routine matter of listing all of the information, facts, and evidence. If a given objective or need is going to require reevaluation or a new process or technique for its attainment, then it is well to set up a flowchart to indicate the necessary steps to accomplish this. Flowcharts and similar devices make it easier to estimate costs and labor involved in the various steps which lead to the fulfillment of objectives.

Input for use in this process can also be obtained from direct observations and interviews with staff members. Sampling is often useful when specific tests need to be made to discover needs and uncover problems. For example, a quantitative objective (such as adding 5,000 titles to the multimedia library collection) may require a sampling process to find out what equipment and human resources are going to be needed and utilized, and how many items can be acquired, processed, cataloged, and put on the shelves in a given amount of time.

FISCAL POLICY DETERMINATION

Policies are established and put into language by top management to guide and control middle management. The media manager must understand and be familiar with all policies that affect the research. The manager must also know where there is a need for policies, or where existing policy may require evaluation and change. Policies are guides to courses of action that have been anticipated by top management to guide the organization. When undertaking research, it is necessary for the middle-management level of administration to clearly understand and follow those policies that have been set down to guide middle management toward the fulfillment of objectives and the making of cost estimates. Example 8 demonstrates the format of a fiscal policy statement.

EXAMPLE 8
FISCAL POLICIES

Requests for audiovisual equipment and supplies (projectors, films, filmstrips, slides, transparencies, etc.) are to be submitted to the media manager for inclusion in the overall budget of that activity cost center. Funds for the above items are *not* to be included in individual budget requests.

PROGRAM SUPPLIES

Program supplies for *all areas* are defined as supplies to be used and consumed by the program during the fiscal year. It is to be noted that this category no longer

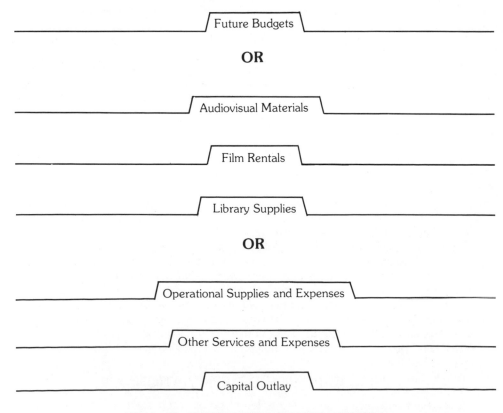

Figure 23. FUTURE BUDGETS FILE SYSTEM

EXAMPLE 8 (Cont.)

includes related expenses such as rentals, conference, travel, consultants, etc., instead the latter group is to be reported under the 5000 account series.

REPLACEMENT OF EQUIPMENT

Funds requested for replacement of equipment must be accompanied by a clear and concise statement of justification. This budget category includes not only replacement of equipment to be traded in but also replacement of equipment which has been lost or stolen, is obsolete or in a condition making it impossible to repair. Items to be replaced must be listed in priority order and with sufficient description to identify the need for replacement.

The media manager must be particularly aware of the need for policies, or changes in policy, which will affect the plan for achieving the fiscal objectives of the multimedia library. Very important in such a body of policy are those statements which prescribe the authority and responsibility of the media manager within the total financial structure of the library. Once a budget has been approved for a given fiscal period, the media manager must have clear authority and responsibility to determine budget needs and to control fiscal activity.

CRITERIA FOR DEVELOPING OBJECTIVES

In developing criteria, or guidelines for the statement of budget objectives, the media manager is concerned about funds needed by the multimedia library to support resources in four categories: labor (human effort), materials, equipment, and facilities.

Labor, today, is the most costly of these, and in most multimedia libraries becomes a fixed cost that does not allow the media manager much room for adjustment, except perhaps in the addition or reduction of staff members. And even in this case, the manager must justify either, and in particular any addition to the staff. Cost of adding an employee is predetermined by personnel management factors, such as established salary schedules or job classifications.

Materials are another important part of fiscal need which must be included in the development of a budget for the multimedia library. Both print and nonprint collections must be expanded yearly, and thus require sufficient funding to keep them up to date. The constant introduction of new materials in multimedia formats makes this a key requirement of fiscal planning.

Facilities planning for the budget means planning for buildings and equipment. In budget terms, such expenditures are considered capital outlay. Facilities items are of a lasting or permanent nature and must be considered as capital expenditures. Equipment of all kinds is a most important ingredient in the multimedia library, with new equipment considered as capital outlay and replacement of equipment considered as a maintenance budget item.

In identifying criteria that can be used for developing budget objectives, it is essential to emphasize that such criteria be tailored to fit the local situation. Thus most criteria will reflect the research which has provided information and knowledge about specific needs to be implemented with fiscal resources. However, there are several standard criteria that may also be considered in working toward budget objectives. These include number of patrons, use of materials, need in general, previous expenditures, previous budgets, advances in technology, problems, opportunities, known constraints, and feedback.

The first of these criteria is *number of patrons*. The number of patrons served by the multimedia library is an important indicator for budgeting and is included in all national and state standards for public, school, university, and community college libraries. Number of patrons served is the basis for determining several important needs, including number of volumes per patron, amount of square feet per patron, number of periodicals per patron, and number of filmstrips per patron, for example.

A second general criterion for determination of budget objectives is need, as reflected in statistical analysis of *materials use* requirements. These requirements can be seen in circulation statistics. If circulation of certain materials decreases, for example, a 40 percent drop in the use of phonograph records for the year, this indicates a need to research this area to see if these materials need to be strengthened with fiscal resources. Even an apparently adequate collection may be underutilized if it is weak or incomplete in some way. Underuse does not always mean absence of need. It may instead mean that a collection needs to be expanded, or weeded and renewed. It is essential in every type of library to carry on continual evaluations of the collection. The results of such evaluations can be utilized to suggest budget objectives that will provide funds to adequately respond to the demonstrated character of materials demand in the multimedia library.

A third standardized criterion for budgeting is simply the term *need*. As a result of ongoing use research, certain needs will be identified. These needs may be in any of the four areas—personnel, equipment, materials, or facilities. Such needs will become visible, and will be useful in making provisions in the budget for specific requirements which will have to be supported with fiscal resources.

There are two standardized criteria that must be approached from what may be called a negative rather than a positive point of view. These are *previous expenditures* and *previous budgets*. The examination of previous expenditures and previous budgets will indicate where funds have not been spent and where funds have not been budgeted. This information is very important in relation to the previous criteria indicated: need, use of materials, and number of patrons. A review of previous expenditures and budgets can demonstrate the adequacy or inadequacy of budgets or expenditures in specific areas. It can reveal where money has been allocated unnecessarily, or where, for example, insufficient fiscal support has been given to needs of the library. For example: bindery funds have not been provided for, resulting in the poor condition of many books. This information will assist the media manager a great deal in planning for the current fiscal period as well as in long-range planning.

The next criterion for multimedia library budgeting is somewhat unique in that it is concerned with technology. This is very important because it reflects the need to be aware of and responsive to *advances in technology*, equipment, and materials. The multimedia library manager needs to ask, for example: What advances have been made in microforms? What advances in television? What advances in computers? These advances in technology become budget concerns because they may mean that technology has solved a problem, or met a need, or created new fiscal requirements that must be reflected in the budget.

Keeping a day-to-day budget file is another valuable practice in the development of criteria for multimedia library budget planning. As the media manager works from day to day, *problems* (or successes) that have fiscal implications are recorded and placed in the budget file. When the manager starts to prepare a new budget, this file is examined for problems that have arisen during the past fiscal period. The file provides guidelines from experience that are useful in the preparation of a realistic and adequate budget for the new year. Such guidelines may be in the area of personnel needs or management, materials, equipment, or facilities. The problem of book loss is a good case in point. It is essential to emphasize that problems having fiscal implications which come to the attention of the media manager must be systematically recorded and used in developing objectives and fiscal requirements provided for in the budget.

On the positive side is the criterion we have labeled *opportunities*. Opportunities will present themselves to the media manager, and in order to take advantage of them, the manager will have to make certain fiscal provisions. These can be in the area of matching federal funds or matching grant funds, for example, or opportunity may simply present itself to implement a multimedia approach in learning or curriculum development. Funds will certainly be required to respond to such an opportunity. The budget objectives and fiscal provisions will need to have sufficient resources and latitude to make such response possible.

Another standard criterion which must be discussed here is *constraints*. What constraints must be considered in the budget process? What will be their impact? Facility constraints, for example, can limit collection growth. These constraints can be policy determinations that restrict the availability of funds or the approach to budgeting; they may be constraints on the techniques and procedures utilized in budgeting, such as being able to budget books into capital outlay but not AV materials. Whatever they may be, the media manager must be aware of such constraints and work within them.

A last important factor in budgeting that may be considered as a standard concern from which criteria may be drawn is *feedback*. In the MBO approach, observation, evaluation, and analysis of the ongoing process of multimedia operations and management are important indicators of what is needed in any budget proposal. Feedback obtained from these activities will provide information on the results of both budget and management objectives. It can be utilized in all of the several criteria discussed here in determining changes needed in existing objectives and determining objectives that must be initiated in new budget development. Feedback is the unique factor in the MBO approach, and essential to the varying, changing, and revitalizing of objectives.

SELECTION OF OBJECTIVES

The result of applying the criteria so far discussed should be a list of objectives that realistically need fiscal implementation. The problem then becomes one of having more objectives than can actually be implemented with the fiscal resources at hand; a question of whether all objectives should be included in a budget request, or only the more important of them. Usually, this latter alternative is the course taken. It is best to set up a selective process according to priority. These priorities may be related to, and assigned according to, the importance of each item in supporting the philosophy and goals of the institution the multimedia library serves. First priority would be assigned to those objectives which the media manager considers most essential to those goals, and to the very survival of the multimedia library itself. Demands and needs of patrons served by the multimedia library are also of primary concern in assigning the level of priority. The assignment of first priority to an objective in any case must be based to a large extent on the best judgment of the media manager, because the manager knows from experience both the needs of the library and the expectations of the administration.

Second priority objectives are those which are important for improvement of the multimedia organization. They are second priority in that they are very important to the improvement of the multimedia library, but not so essential that the library will not function if they are not supported.

Third priority objectives would be those considered desirable but not crucial if eliminated or postponed.

An approach to the task of selecting objectives to be included in a budget proposal is to list each of them by priorities, and then examine them in relation to each other, and in the context of total library need. This is essential especially because the media manager may find duplication or conflict between objectives in the different priorities, or other patterns among them which will suggest changes in final priority assignment. Some objectives may need to be modified, or moved from one level of priority to another.

It is also well to note here that in the budget procedure there is one very important additional step that has not yet been discussed that will affect priorities, and that is the assignment of cost estimates. It is later in the budget development process that a cost estimate is assigned to each objective. But cost may affect the placement of an objective by priority. Using the above approach to the determination of priorities before cost estimates, however, is recommended, because cost estimates inserted too soon into the process may seriously cloud the determination of priority. Objectives should be evaluated first on the basis of what they will achieve in relation to the philosophy and objectives of the multimedia library and the institution itself, rather than on how much they will cost. The realities of money eventually will have to become an important deciding factor, of course. But it is unwise to begin by asking, What can we afford? The first question should be: What must we do, to do the best job we can for the institution? When this optimum service has been realistically reflected in budget objectives, the capability in terms of available fiscal support may then be reassessed.

PLANNING THE BUDGET

Adequate financial support of the multimedia library is mandatory because of the diversity in personnel, equipment, materials, and facilities needed to make all types of media available to the patron. In order to obtain this support, it is necessary to have a budget process that provides for planned expenditures and assures spending within budgetary limits. Planned expenditures are projected on the basis of stated objectives, themselves designed to implement the total library program. A year-round, day-by-day budget process is essential and a budget file that is systematically documented throughout the year will reflect information and experience for inclusion in planning for the next fiscal year's budget.

The budget process is really not too difficult in the MBO approach because management, in developing an action plan for a given fiscal period, will have developed a number of objectives that have been articulated in the action plan for the library. Most of these will have fiscal support requirements, and thus become the basis for cost projections in the budget. Cost estimates will then reflect both priority and importance of given objectives. It is in this step of budget development that the day-by-day file becomes useful.

The budget development process thus becomes a management activity. It is made up of six steps which culminate in a statement of dollars and cents cost for implementation of the action plan of the multimedia library. These six steps will be discussed in the next section.

BUDGET PREPARATION PROCEDURE

The six steps in the budget preparation procedure, portrayed in the Budget Process Flowchart shown as Figure 24, are as follows: (1) determination of objectives; (2) determination of a course of action; (3) design of a program to achieve the objectives; (4) development of fiscal estimates based on the program; (5) review

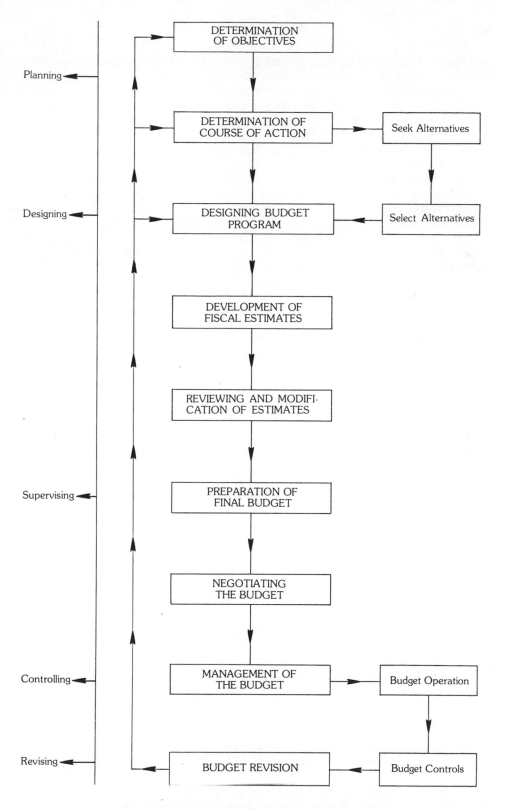

Figure 24. BUDGET PROCESS FLOWCHART

and modification of fiscal estimates; and (6) integration of all steps and preparation of a budget statement.

Management, in carrying out the first three of these steps, is of course involved in a much larger task than just budgeting. As pointed out in previous sections, management must *determine objectives* for the next fiscal period, then develop an overall course of action and a plan for achieving those objectives. Fiscal estimates, the next step, then follow, with review and integration representing the final polishing of the document.

The development and selection of objectives were thoroughly covered in the preceding section so it is not necessary to go into further detail here. It must be reemphasized, however, that the objectives which require fiscal support become the objectives included in the budget and, therefore, budget objectives.

The second step, *determination of a course of action*, is in effect an overview statement which generally points the way toward achieving all of the budget objectives and provides for efforts toward the fulfillment of each.

The third step, *design of a program* to achieve these objectives, is again a culmination of the plan for achieving stated budget objectives, but is much more specific. When the first three steps have been completed, management has a list of objectives that need fiscal support with an indicated course of action and a program to carry out those objectives. It is then possible to move on to step four.

The *development of fiscal estimates* is based upon estimates of cost, and known costs for such requirements as new equipment, replacement of equipment, personnel, materials and supplies, and other needs. Sufficient research needs to have been done to pull together all of the cost factors necessary to make realistic estimates.

In obtaining cost factors for materials, for example, past expenditures can be averaged out; average costs for the book publishing industry are available in many standard publications; jobbers, producers, or manufacturers of equipment will often provide cost estimates when requested to do so.

Time is another important factor. In large expenditures such as those for television equipment, it may be necessary to have budget objectives worked out 30 to 60 days prior to deadline so that accurate cost estimates can be obtained. One of the best resources for cost estimates is past experience of management. Another is the purchasing office of the institution the library serves. Purchasing people often have good contacts with industry, publishing houses, and other sources of supply, and cost information which can be of invaluable service to the multimedia library manager undertaking the difficult job of getting a budget into perspective.

The fifth step in budget procedure is *review and modification of fiscal estimates*. Total estimates have been tallied at this point, and the manager now has a final figure representing the total amount of estimates for all the objectives. It now becomes necessary to decide on the best course of action in relation to the fiscal resources the manager has, or will require. If the requirements are not within the limits set out by higher management, the media manager must make two decisions: hold to all objectives and go with the original estimates, or reexamine each estimate and see if there are alternatives which would lower anticipated cost.

The latter alternative is the one the manager will most likely have to consider. It may be possible to modify an estimate by substituting equipment or other materials that cost less than those originally considered. Careful review of all objectives, with their cost estimates, will permit the media manager to decide whether to modify, reduce, or change any of the items before drawing up the final budget document. Such a review will also strengthen the justifications developed to support both estimates of cost and the procedures used in arriving at these estimates—important information which may be used later when negotiating the budget with top management.

The final phase, or step six, is comprised of the above five phases and the *preparation of the actual budget* in final form. Priorities will have been assigned, a course of action prepared, and all estimates finalized. Along with objectives, a plan for achieving them, and a plan for evaluating, it is now possible to pull all this together and prepare the final budget.

The budget document itself, of course, is simply the summary of this total procedure.

The actual budget summary consists of four columns, as shown in Example 9. The first column shows account titles, such as books, supplies, capital outlay, nonbook materials. The second shows projected cost. The third indicates cost for the previous budget period, and the fourth shows the difference in terms of increase or decrease.

This budget document will also include supporting data, the budget program itself, a statement of specific budget objectives, the plan for their achievement, and the plan for evaluating each objective. Each of the objectives described will also include cost figures which, when totaled, will make up the amounts that are shown in the budget summary.

A justification summary in the form of a narrative statement must also be included. Top management is always concerned with any change from status quo. They are interested in both how and why the budget request for a given new fiscal

EXAMPLE 9
BUDGET SUMMARY

Budget Account No.	Budget Account Title	Next Year's Budget	Present Budget	Increase or Decrease
214.2	*Substitute Librarians*	$ 500	$ 1,000	$ −500
220.302	*Classified Overtime*	1,150	900	+250
220.303	*Student Assistants*	45,257	29,955	+15,302
240.201	*Library Books* (Regular book budget in capital outlay)			
	Replacement	14,834	16,833	−1,999
	Other Expenses General Instructional Supplies			
290.231	Supplies and Expense	16,000	9,000	+7,000
290.233	Audiovisual Materials	11,000 ⎫		
290.233	Audiovisual Supplies	3,500 ⎬ 17,950	17,950	+3,050
290.233	Rental of Motion Pictures Films	6,500 ⎭		
290.234	Materials Production Lab	12,000	10,500	+1,500
290.232	Periodicals and Microfilm	12,000	11,500	+500
290.234.1	Special Printing Service	1,300	400	+900
290.235	Rental of Equipment	2,450	2,350	+100
290.237	Conferences	805	400	+405
290.238	Travel	300	200	+100
	Maintenance of Plant			
730.6	Replacement of Equipment	2,770	1,150	+1,620
790.311	Repair of Equipment	6,025	4,000	+2,025

period is increased or decreased from the budget requirements of the present year. A need for thorough justification arises when there are significant differences in these amounts, particularly when these requirements are estimated upward. In writing this justification, it is essential that the media manager utilize all the information which has become available in the budget development process.

BUDGET CALENDAR

The timing of the budget development process is structured by a budget calendar which sets dates or deadlines for the completion of each step in the procedure. The media manager is concerned with meeting the deadlines of the institution, of which the library is a subsystem, and any deadlines or dates that are prescribed by either institutional policy or by law. Accordingly, the budget calendar includes two sets of dates, one showing deadlines set by the library structure, and another showing deadlines set by the institution or the law. In a small multimedia library it may be necessary for the media specialist to set the deadlines.

In all cases, however, these deadlines will set dates by which each phase is to be completed. For example, in budgeting for a fiscal year that runs from July 1 to June 30, the library must work backward from the date on which its budget is required. The media manager should work back from that date also, so as to have sufficient time to carry out all six steps of the procedure. An example of this may be seen in the budget calendar presented in Example 10. If the library organization is larger, and more involved, it will certainly take more time to do this, and the media manager must include more time when setting up the calendar. If, for example, the completed budget is due on March 1 of a given fiscal year, it may be necessary for the library staff to actually start work on it by December 1.

In a situation where there is a large library staff, the first date on the budget calendar should provide sufficient time to give preliminary instructions to each area within the organization that must contribute to the development of the budget. The second date should provide for a budget conference with each responsible person. That person would then, in turn, complete the six steps in the budget procedure for a given area, setting deadlines for each step according to the final deadline

EXAMPLE 10
BUDGET CALENDAR

On or Before	Action
January 12	Budget proposal forms to supervisors
February 12	Complete budget conferences
March 1	Budget proposals delivered to supervisors
March 15	Budget proposals submitted by supervisors to business manager
April 9	Review of preliminary budget by chief administrator
May 4	Submission of preliminary budget to library board
May 14	Minimum budgetary allocations to supervisors
June 4	Submission of tentative budget to library board
June 15	Adoption of tentative budget by library board
July 1	Requisitions due for next budget
July 15	Submission of publication budget to library board
July 20	Adoption of publication budget by library board
July 29	Submission of official budget to library board
August 3	Public hearing on official budget
August 3	Adoption of official budget by library board

established by the media manager. The third date on the media manager's calendar should specify return of the completed budget requests by the several area supervisors. The manager then pulls together all of these requests by the deadline set by the institution; for example, March 1. Budget conferences and reviews following submission of a request can be expected to follow, as required by higher management.

NEGOTIATING THE BUDGET

Budget reviews or conferences come under the heading of negotiation. The media manager must communicate with an immediate superior, and expect to justify, explain, and modify the budget as the result of these reviews and conferences. On the budget calendar, this takes place between the time the media manager turns it in to the supervisor and the time the supervisor has to turn it in to the next step up in the organization. This is an important part of budget and procedure. The media manager must give enough information to the reporting senior so that this administrator can justify the budget and negotiate for it successfully with the final authority. Armed with sufficient justification and adequate information, the senior member of the administration team who has to present the final defense of a budget is able to do a much better job of assuring that the multimedia library will receive adequate funds.

SUPERVISING THE BUDGET

Sufficient authority must be assured to supervise and control the budget for which the media manager has been given responsibility. Where there is allocated responsibility for an activity such as budget there must be commensurate delegation of authority. The media manager must have complete control of the spending activities in the library.

It goes without saying, therefore, that the media manager must have authority to set up an accounting system which will provide the details needed to control expenditures. This is not always an easy thing to do because the business office of the larger organization which the library serves often wishes to retain this authority.

EXAMPLE 11
BUDGET MATERIALS FUND ACCOUNT

Date	Vendor	P.O. No.	Encum-brance	Adjust-ment	Balance
7-17	Wise Unit Pubs.	9077	$ 8.68		
7-17	Landing Spur	9079	8.25		
7-22	A & Z	9076	756.14		
7-24	A & Z	9080	756.55		
7-24	Oakwood Museum	9083	8.47		$33,037.54
7-24	Product Education	9084	143.92		
7-24	Landing Spur	9085	32.38		
7-29	A & Z	9058	968.43		
7-29	Thesbian Play Service	9082	32.27		
7-29	Wise Unit Pubs.	9091	50.00		$31,810.54
8-1	A & Z	9086	1,075.13		$30,735.41 (Free Balance)

Experience shows, however, a detailed accounting system to control the book account and other material accounts is best served by having individual accounts kept in the acquisitions area or a department of the library. Libraries at all levels have found that having an acquisitions clerk keep all materials fund accounts works better than anything else in controlling the budget. An illustration of how this is done is shown in Example 11. Also, it is strongly suggested that the media manager centralize all record keeping and bookkeeping in general. Centralization allows the media manager to obtain meaningful accounting information quickly and rapidly with a minimum of inconvenience and clerical time. These records and accounts can be summarized once a month, and by keeping close observation of these summaries, the media manager can keep the budget within desired limits. With centralization, the media manager may even exercise daily control over expenditures, further reducing the possibility of excessive expenditure, and providing for adjustments and revisions of the budget as may be required.

DELEGATION

The media manager, having set up the total system, must now delegate by area or function, the authority and responsibility to expend the funds the budget includes for each area. This delegation must be given to the immediate supervisor or employee responsible for that area or function.

While authority and responsibility can be delegated by the media manager, the manager's own accountability for the overall operation of the budget cannot be delegated. Accordingly, a coordinated and cooperative effort between the media manager and immediate subordinates is most necessary. Channels of communication need to be set up so that the media manager is informed at all times and can in fact retain overall budget control. Policies and operating procedures act as guidelines for such a system, and enable both the manager and the subordinates to operate within a reasonable framework of understanding and procedure. So it is to be emphasized that definite, clear-cut policies must be originated and passed down to all levels. The media manager and the responsible staff members must agree on objectives, policies and principles, and spending procedures.

In summary: budget objectives are established, authority is delegated, and necessary policies are provided. The media manager sets up budget controls and supervisory procedures by which to hold each area and function accountable for performance within the specified limits of the operating budget.

CONTROL

Budget control really is concerned with budget accounts (see again, Example 11). In budget operation, the media manager has assigned certain accounts to subordinates. This delegation requires that for budget control the responsible staff member is charged with a monthly review of expenditures to make sure that the budget is indeed under control. Accurate coding is helpful in this process, and supports accurate accounting so that at the end of each month, it becomes possible to arrive at a balance. In the matter of budget control it cannot be overemphasized that the job of media management is to make sure that the course of management practice is always toward fulfillment of budget objectives. Control is aimed at preventing deviation from the provisions of budget and procedure. Remember, management creates the budget and related policies and procedures as control measures. The budget itself is a tool to control expenditures of funds. So it becomes a strong responsibility of management to stay within the provisions of the budget and to hold to the objectives prescribed by the budget. Under the MBO concept the budget is viewed not as an estimate but as an action plan. Management becomes responsible for enforcing and carrying out this plan.

Now to the question of procedures. To enforce control of the budget, management must be concerned with (1) setting up such procedures, so that expenditures will indeed stay within the budget; (2) providing for continuous comparison between estimated and actual operational costs, so that analysis may be made and needed changes instituted; and (3) adjusting the budget to allow for any such changes. There are several means for making such adjustments. It may be possible, for example, to shift funds from one account to another or to let one account go into a deficit while holding sufficient funds in other accounts to offset that deficit.

Two forms utilized in these procedures may be mentioned here: the *requisition* and the *purchase order*. A requisition is simply an order to the business or accounting office to obtain certain materials or items. This requisition can be for materials that must be obtained from sources outside the institution, or from a central stock or warehouse.

If a library requisitions filmstrips or kits, for example, they would normally come from an outside source. If the library is ordering paper or pencils, they are apt to come from a central warehouse within the institution.

The purchase order itself is an official document of the institution and is usually not issued by the multimedia library. The purchase order results from action taken as a result of the request or requisition. When the requisition is received by the purchasing office it is checked as to account title and number, and source of material requested. After the requisition has been approved, the purchase order is prepared and sent out to the actual jobber or producer. This purchase order is initiated by the central business office and used as the basic document for accounting information. When the purchase order is sent out to a supplier, it becomes an official contract between the institution and the supplier.

BUDGETARY RECORDS

Budgetary records within the multimedia library are essential to both control of the budget and to evaluation of its adequacy in providing for continuing needs. Future budget planning also utilizes such information. It is to be expected, of course, that there will be a financial or central business office that will keep accurate accounting records and maintain general procedures for the entire institution. This office will in all probability issue monthly or periodic financial accounting statements which will provide much of the information needed by the library. But it will be necessary for the multimedia library itself to set up its own general accounting or bookkeeping system for internal use. Such a system will enable the media manager to keep abreast of the status of all the accounts.

The difference in use of this information suggests the reason for needing such an internal record keeping system. The central business office, for example, is most often concerned with cash balances in given accounts. The library, on the other hand, wants to know the free balance available at any given time; in other words, the balance remaining for additional purchases after encumbrances have been made. We have suggested that the acquisitions area of the multimedia library is the best location for the production of information on free balances. Acquisitions knows what is being ordered, and is thus the most logical place to have the continuous internal accounting done. Example 11 again suggests the format for a single entry system to show free balance. These figures keep the manager aware of the funds available.

A number of other reasons for recommending the use of an internal record keeping system of some kind can also be mentioned. Many materials may have to be ordered as separate items with no set invoice price available at the time of ordering.

Several deliveries, and thus several invoices, may be received in connection with only one purchase order. Discounts and delivery costs not known at the time of purchase request may develop, and may be shown only on invoices received with the shipments. Central purchasing would eventually have this information all together, of course, and provide it to the multimedia manager. In the meantime, however, the only safe means of knowing how much free money is available to make new purchases at a given time is to know how much has been encumbered (i.e., allocated to pay for something ordered) to date. The internal accounting system will tell the manager that.

It works this way: The manager or supervisor decides to purchase a book costing $10. The acquisitions clerk advises that there is $100 available. The manager sends in a requisition for the book. The clerk *encumbers* (i.e., writes down and subtracts) $10. Now the manager knows there is $90 free balance for other purchases. When the book arrives, the clerk will correct the encumbrance entry and show the exact, delivered, and paid cost of the book.

SETTING UP THE SYSTEM   In setting up a system of budgetary or bookkeeping records, there are three basic steps: (1) to determine what information is needed, (2) to determine how to classify and record it, and (3) to devise a means of presenting the collected information to make it useful. It is important to emphasize that after devising a records and reporting system, the manager may then delegate this activity to the media technician who handles the acquisition of materials or financial records of the multimedia library.

In following through on the first step, it is necessary to keep the record keeping or accounting procedures at a simple level so as not to duplicate the accounting and bookkeeping done in the centralized or business office. Decisions have to be made as to what information is really needed at the media management level. Encumbrances and expenditures as they occur, and information which will show what the free balances are in the different accounts make up this body of records. With this information the media manager may control the budget and know how much money there is for ordering.

The second step is to determine how to classify or title the accounts. Generally, of course, the multimedia library would follow whatever uniform coding system of accounts the institution has already established, although in some cases a system will have to be devised by the manager according to individual needs for information.

Certainly, it would be necessary to have a record of encumbrances and expenditures. The encumbrance record would keep an accounting of committed amounts of money to cover purchase requests and orders, while the record of actual payouts based upon invoices would give the manager an accurate picture of the free balance. Other files that would be of value would include purchase orders and requisitions so the activity of the budget could be verified at any time.

The actual form of an encumbrance or expenditure record will depend upon how the bookkeeping is actually set up. One format has been suggested in Example 11. Notice that there is a column showing date, vendor to which the order was sent, purchase order number, and amount of encumbrance. A column for the free balance is also shown with an additional column which can be used to show adjustments. The adjustment column is used, for example, where there are credits or other changes that give a better picture of the balance available for ordering after the money committed for a purchase has been subtracted from the previous free balance.

The expenditure record is similar. It shows a date, and includes a column in which to note the vendor. This record also has a column for the more specific information now available including invoice number, purchase order number, actual amount as shown on the invoice, adjustment, and balance. Some accounting methods combine encumbrance and expenditure records in one ledger showing the original budgeted figure, the amount of each encumbrance, any adjustments, and a column for posting of invoices. A final column shows the free balance. Unless it is a very large budget, however, and there is a need for weekly or daily free balance figures, it is much easier to handle encumbrances and expenditures as two separate accounts. Monthly or weekly comparison will keep control of the budget.

This method is most conveniently referred to as encumbrance accounting. It is a single entry system that is easily utilized by the library clerk without any special training in bookkeeping or record keeping. It is, in fact, very much like writing a check against a balance in the bank. The budgeted amount, or balance, is entered as the income (like the deposit). Then, with each order sent out, a certain portion of that balance is encumbered (i.e., reserved or set aside), although the amount is not actually spent until the purchase order has been completed and the invoice cleared and paid. Like subtracting the amount of a check from the balance in a checkbook, however, the encumbered amount is already committed when the check is written, even though it may not clear the bank for a few days.

It is essential to reemphasize here that these budgetary records are not just book work, but are specific aids to management. They are useful in preparation and control of the budget, evaluating internal efficiency, future planning, reporting, and comparison of budget activities with other multimedia libraries.

BUDGET REVISION

It is essential that the budget be flexible enough to adapt to changes and emergencies. This explains why the media manager who has the responsibility for initially preparing the budget must also have the authority to revise it to meet changing needs and conditions. The basis for revision of a budget must be developed out of the analysis of changes which have occurred. Justification for abandonment of previous budget figures and rationale need to be carefully worked out. Obviously, when performance of objectives is no longer possible, and when previous budget estimates no longer represent a realistic basis for accomplishing the objectives of the library, revision is needed.

Such changes, of course, are to be expected in a vital and changing economy. Budget estimates may have been developed as much as six months to a year previous to actual expenditure of the money. In that time there may have been changes in prices, transportation, the tax structure, and so on, and therefore a need for revision arises despite the fact that increases in cost have been anticipated.

Renewing a budget in this way may not always mean pumping new money into the total figure however. Budget revision may take the form of transfer of money from one account to another. When a budgeted need does not materialize, for example, because of such factors as change in state or local law, change in personnel, change in facilities, or enrollment drop, funds that are not going to be utilized as planned for can be transferred to another account. Authority to transfer funds under circumstances such as this must involve the media manager.

SUMMARY

Budgeting is the activity involved in estimating and providing for the fiscal requirements of a multimedia library. More than just forecasting anticipated costs on the basis of some kind of intuited insights, however, or by some general review of what it cost last year, the manager who is utilizing the MBO approach needs to look at budget from the point of view of purpose, goals and objectives, procedures, and so on. The manager needs to consider a wide variety of factors affecting budget, and to provide for each of the needs anticipated in terms of dollar support. It does little good to provide an excellent program and fine staff without the money needed to support and utilize these resources. It is strongly emphasized in this chapter that the MBO approach will effectively implement increasing the multimedia library budget and reduce its problem of insufficient funds.

Planning is the essential ingredient of the multimedia library budgeting process. Planning insures accuracy in forecasting needs, and thus, wiser spending. It assures the attainment of the two primary purposes of budgeting: limitations as needed upon spending, and best utilization of available funds in any case.

The four essentials of good budgeting are these: (1) effective organization, (2) administrative support, (3) effective accounting, and (4) research. Good organization provides the structure within which to plan and carry out fiscal programs. Administrative support by the executive to whom the media manager reports provides a realistic environment within which to plan. Effective accounting procedures keep the manager apprised of the fiscal position, and research, used in this context to mean records, data collection, analysis, and evaluation of the program, assures an overview from which budgeting can be done realistically and in keeping with known factors in the library's ongoing program.

In discussing these four essentials, it is pointed out that the objectives for budgeting include a number of practical, day-to-day tasks in their implementation. A budget file is recommended, in which records can be entered daily or as needed to provide a basis for estimating needs. Policies, articulated by executive administration, often provide useful guidelines on the kinds of information needed in such files to provide the insights required for realistic projections. Program supplies, for example, or the replacement of equipment versus capital outlay requirements, are defined and identified in policy statements.

A number of criteria for fiscal objectives are suggested as they relate to record keeping and the facts needed to guide the budget process. These include number of patrons, for example, materials use statistics, needs of the program as related to growth, new curriculum and the like; previous costs, advances in technology which have cost implications, problems which, though unresolved, promise to have impact upon budget requirements; opportunities and constraints which loom upon the anticipated budget period, and the like. From these, objectives directly related to realistic budgeting can be anticipated.

Selecting appropriate objectives from among the many which present themselves, however, is another important step in the budget process, and one involving determination of priorities. The following order for priorities is suggested. First, those items in the budget which are most essential to the primary goals of the multimedia library itself, and without which the very survival of the library is at stake. Second, those objectives which relate most directly to the improvement of the library, but which, if not implemented, will not endanger the continuance of service and activity on a status quo basis. Third priority would be those objectives which are considered desirable but not crucial to the program if eliminated or postponed. Among these the media manager must expect to find duplication or conflict. Objectives in different priority groups may need to be changed or adjusted before any final determinations are made.

It is unwise to begin by asking, "What can we afford?" It is best to begin by asking what must be done and what can be done to best serve the institution.

The actual planning procedure, the budget process, begins after objectives (the first step) have been finalized. It includes setting a course of action, designing a budget program, developing fiscal estimates, reviewing and modifying estimates, and preparing the final budget—the document in which the actual statement of dollar needs is articulated. This process is complex enough to require a budget calendar in which various steps in the process are given a timeline perspective to let those working on it know when various parts of the budget must be ready, and when it will be reviewed for preparation in final form. This is referred to as budget negotiation. The media manager should expect, at this point in the process, to have to deal nose-to-nose with an administrator who will expect careful justification for every item in the proposed budget request.

The final portion of this chapter discusses management of the budget, the manager's role in supervision and control of the budget once it is finalized, in terms of in-house accounting, record keeping, and related procedures. The importance of these functions, which are aids to management and an important task of the multimedia management job, is stressed.

CHAPTER 6

MANAGING MULTIMEDIA RESOURCES: SELECTION

Selection, acquisitions, cataloging, physical processing, and shelving or storage are the central processes and functions which comprise the management of multimedia resources. The goals and procedures of management as related to resource development and the practical applications of these factors in managing the resources are central to any consideration of library management, as it is the resources which represent the basic collection of human knowledge managed for the public by the institution.

The task of management is to organize the various processes so they operate together with maximum effectiveness and efficiency, and minimum cost. Without management each process tends to become an isolated unit in itself that does not recognize its relationships with other processes in the system. By identifying not only the objectives of the overall process of resources preparation but also the objectives of each separate process which is a component in the overall process, management-by-objectives can design a plan that will synthesize the accomplishment of all objectives so that coordination is achieved. This interaction is demonstrated in Figure 25.

Of course, a collection of resources does not assure communication of knowledge to the public. The multimedia library must ascertain that the resources of knowledge can be easily utilized. To prepare resources for use requires several processes performed in such an ordered sequence that the output of the first contributes to that of the second, and so on down the line until the entire preparation process is completed. The process begins with selection, continues through acquisitions, cataloging, and physical processing, and terminates with storage. In addition to the sequential relationship there are other to and fro relationships wherein the work performed in one process may be of benefit to all processes or to one which does not follow in the prescribed order. For example, the data recorded in the selection process is necessary not only in acquisitions but also in cataloging. At the same time, to ascertain what resources the library already has and to determine what subject areas need additions, selection uses the records produced by the cataloging process.

The selection process, as the first in a sequence of steps, is given considerable in-depth study. Discussion of management of selection in this chapter should be considered a prototype for application of the MBO process to resource management. Diagrammatic graphics provide visual access to the relationships in the process. Detailed coverage is given to the procedures involved in recording information about materials for selection, supervision of the process, and control factors. Goals and objectives, personnel factors, tools of the trade, and actual handling procedures and policies are discussed.

APPLICATION OF BASIC PROCEDURES

The design of any process requires the practical application of the methodology of management-by-objectives. The major steps in this methodology—planning, designing, supervising, controlling, and revising—have already been discussed in Chapter 3. In practice, each of these major steps is subdivided in logical segments that can be more easily manipulated. Thus certain procedures can be determined which remain the same no matter what the process under consideration. These procedures constitute a basic procedural plan that acts as a guide to the manager who uses it when designing each process, supplying the information and routines pertinent to that particular process.

IDENTIFY THE GOAL OF THE PROCESS

Fulfillment of the goal of the entire process establishes the purpose for all procedures within the process. Too often procedures are continued because they have always been in existence. Past performance can be a useful guide in working out procedures, but cannot be considered a criterion of effectiveness because the conditions for which the procedure was originally designed will have undergone many changes. The only true test of the validity of a procedure is its contribution to the goal of the process. Each procedure must be judged on the basis of how successful its output is in accomplishing that part of the goal of the whole process for

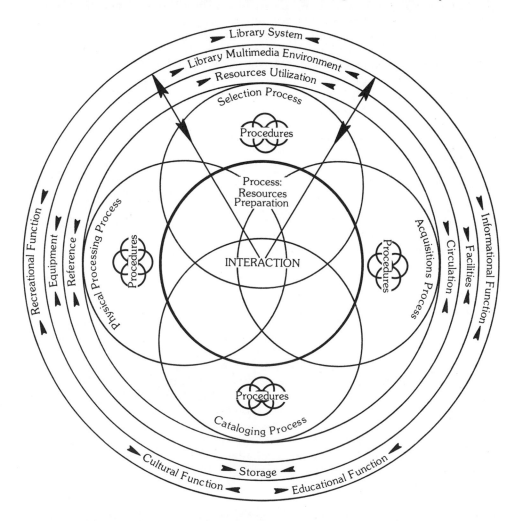

Figure 25. INTERACTION OF PROCESSES IN THE MULTIMEDIA LIBRARY SYSTEM

which it is responsible. In essence, the goal of the process is the basic evaluation instrument for each procedure. Therefore, before any work on procedures can begin it is essential that the goal of the process be identified and stated in understandable terms.

IDENTIFY THE GOAL OF MANAGEMENT

Once the goal of the process has been established management can proceed to clarify its own goal. The distinction between managing a process and performing the tasks involved in carrying out the process is one that the manager must understand and clearly delineate. In many instances it may seem that the easiest course to follow is for the manager to actually do the work. The manager may thus become so overburdened with routine and detail work that the goal of accomplishing a specific task becomes a substitute for the real goal. The manager must know how the various routines will proceed and fully understand their significance while remaining free to achieve the true goal of producing, with maximum effectiveness and efficiency, the results demanded by the goal of the process.

To fulfill the goal the manager creates a structure of procedures designed according to the basic principles of management using the methodology of management-by-objectives to ascertain that these procedures operate successfully. Since staff participation is basic in management-by-objectives, it is essential that the manager be in constant communication with both executives and subordinates while proceeding through the successive steps in the methodology. The manager begins each major step by stating its desired outcome in terms of major objectives, then refines and restates these objectives as dictated by the specificity of the procedures involved.

PLANNING AND PLANNING OBJECTIVES

Planning is one of the most important of the manager's tasks. Efficient planning demands a broad and in-depth knowledge of the conditions that exist in the library and in the library community, of the work that has to be done, and of the various factors that may affect it. Prior to any planning the manager must acquire this knowledge by means of input data. To gather information about needs, opportunities, problems, organizational and financial constraints, and the human and materials resources it may be necessary to use one or several methods. The manager may conduct surveys, utilize formal and informal reports, hold interviews, and/or devise other practical means for obtaining the facts required. At the same time the manager furthers knowledge through personal observations. Input data is an essential prerequisite to planning, but its acquisition has certain built-in dangers which the manager must recognize. It may easily become an end in itself instead of a means for implementing the objectives of planning. The collecting of input data may grow insidiously to the point where it becomes a deterrent. The amassing of unnecessary details and the overconsumption of time can prevent the manager from beginning the planning phase of the work. The manager, therefore, must ascertain that the data-collecting instrument is so designed that there can be no misunderstanding concerning the kind and amount of information required and the time allotted for completing the data.

Efficient planning requires not only knowledge but also analytical skill and clear thinking. The manager must be able to assess the relative importance of facts in the input data in order to determine priorities (i.e., the sequence in which problems, opportunities, procedures, and so on need attention). The manager must also be able to project the probable effects of determined priorities on the total system and visualize feasible procedures for attaining the objectives of these priorities.

Efficient planning should provide the answers to these six basic questions:

1. Why is the work performed?
2. On what materials is the work performed?
3. By whom is the work performed?
4. With what tools is the work performed?
5. What are the interrelationships of the work performed?
6. How is the work performed?

To avoid confusion and to ensure maximum coverage in the design of the process, the manager states these basic questions in terms of major objectives. It should be emphasized that each of these objectives can be fulfilled only within the parameters of the total system of which the process is a part. In fulfilling each objective, therefore, the manager must work within the organizational structure of the system and determine that the plan is not in conflict with established policies, regulations, and criteria. In essence, the assessment of the effect of existing conditions is one of the standard operating procedures that the manager repeats in each step of process design.

There are six major objectives of planning intended as a basic guide and checklist for the manager. In the designing of each process specific pertinent objectives would also apply. Objective 1 is *to analyze the goal* of the process to determine why the work is necessary, the essential components of the process, and the parameters imposed by the total system. Objective 2 is *to provide the materials* component required to fulfill the goal of the process. Objective 3 is *to provide the personnel* who have the knowledge and expertise needed to fulfill the goal of the process and to establish responsibility and authority of personnel in line with the organizational structure of the system. Objective 4 is *to provide the tools* needed to carry out the process, whether these are informational tools, equipment, or facilities. Objective 5 is *to establish relationships with other processes*, which will probably take the form of services to other processes and services from other processes. Finally, objective 6 is *to create the plan* of the process. To do this the manager would survey all possible procedures that can accomplish the work, select procedures that will work best, including possible alternatives, chart the organizational structure of the overall process, and chart the workflow of the overall process. The six planning objectives are discussed more fully later in this chapter.

DESIGNING AND DESIGNING OBJECTIVES

In translating the process plan into an action plan, the manager works out in detail the various procedures selected in planning. There is, of course, a great deal of overlap in planning and designing, and it is often difficult to separate the two. For example, in selecting procedures in the planning stage the manager must envisage the workflow and accomplishment of each procedure before deciding which will work the best. Consequently, much of the work of designing has already been done in planning, and it should be understood that their listing in this outline as individual consecutive steps is for guidance purposes and does not negate their intermingling.

In designing, the manager provides specific answers to these basic questions: How is the work done? Who does the work? When is the work done? As in planning, the manager states these basic questions in terms of major objectives.

These objectives are: (1) *to design the action plan* that will operate to produce the results required to fulfill the goal of the process; (2) *to delineate the organiza-*

tional structure of each procedure, including personnel for each task in the procedure and responsibility of personnel for each task in the procedure; (3) *to identify the objectives* of each procedure and the objectives of each task within the procedure; (4) *to apply work simplification techniques* such as standard operating procedures for repetitive tasks and standard forms for data recording; (5) *to chart the workflow* of each procedure and of each task within the procedure.

SUPERVISING AND SUPERVISING OBJECTIVES

The action plan has been prepared and it is now put into operation. Supervising is a continuous activity in which the manager engages and is one that cannot be practiced on a hit-or-miss basis. Success in management depends upon a well-planned program of supervision that covers every aspect of all the work performed and puts into practice all the principles of personnel management.

In supervising, the manager's major objectives are: (1) *to direct the operation* of the action plan; (2) *to ascertain that personnel understand the action plan*, and to assure that understanding by explaining the coordination of objectives of procedures, and explaining the coordination of functions of personnel; (3) *to manage personnel*, which would include training and advising key personnel, and to motivate and communicate with personnel on all levels.

CONTROLLING AND CONTROLLING OBJECTIVES

In this phase of management procedures, the manager observes and evaluates the action plan as it operates. In controlling, the manager's major objectives furnish answers to these basic questions: How successful is the operation? What modifications are needed? The objectives are: (1) *to evaluate the action plan*; (2) *to ascertain necessary redesign* of the action plan; (3) *to provide standards* as instruments of measurement for evaluation, both qualitative and quantitative standards of performance for each task; (4) *to evaluate*, on the basis of objectives, the overall process and each task in the process which is specific for a given fiscal period; (5) *to evaluate time requirements* for each task, and output for a specific period of time, such as the fiscal year; (6) *to evaluate cost* of the overall process, of each task in the process, long-range budget, and short-range budget for a given fiscal period.

REVISING AND REVISING OBJECTIVES

To improve the action plan, the manager must have, in addition to the data gathered through personal observation and evaluation, information on what has been done from other sources. The manager receives such feedback both through the lines of communication established in the formal organizational structure and through the various means of communication used by informal groups.

In revising, the manager is concerned with two basic problems: the modification of objectives and the modification of the action plan. Consequently, the major objectives in revising are: (1) *to assess the validity of the objectives of the action plan* to determine if no changes are needed, if minor changes are needed that can be made immediately so that revisions of the action plan can proceed, or to determine if major changes are needed that necessitate the identification of new objectives and the designing of a new action plan; and (2) *to modify the action plan* to ensure that its operation will produce the required output.

Figure 26 charts the flow of basic procedures utilized in designing and managing the processes through which the resources of knowledge are prepared for the

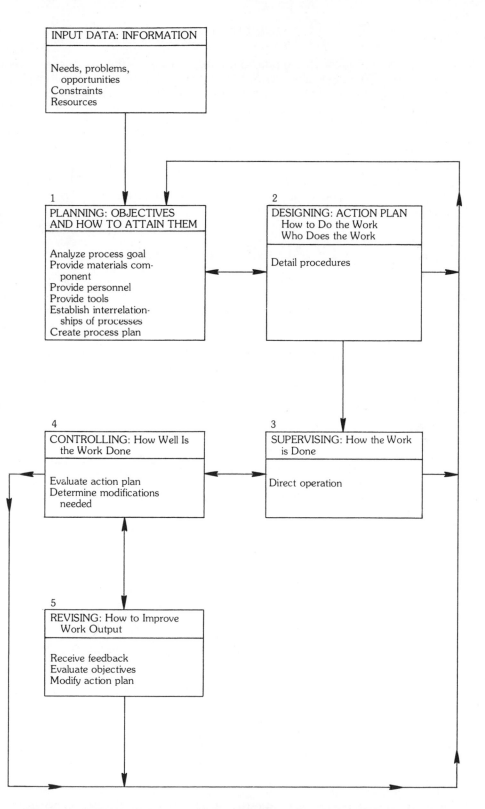

Figure 26. FLOWCHART OF BASIC PROCEDURES IN PROCESS DESIGN

patron's use. Visualization of the procedural workflow gives the manager an overall view of duties and responsibilities, and provides a basic guide even though the specifics of each process may require variations in procedures. The discussion of the management of each process indicates these variations and demonstrates the practical application of managerial procedures.

Process specifics and procedural application are analyzed in detail in this chapter for the selection process. Discussion of theory and procedures that are basic to all processes and that, with pertinent specifics substituted, logically apply to acquisition, cataloging, and physical processing, is not repeated in Chapter 7. The selection process is intended as a sample that should be referred to in designing the other processes.

GOAL OF SELECTION

The ultimate goal of selection is to choose from among the many available resources of knowledge those that best serve the needs of the library's community. It is evident that as long as the library exists the practice of selection must continue and that, to fulfill its goal, selection must cope with change both in materials and in patrons' needs.

Too often, unfortunately, materials are acquired that prove to be inadequate. This problem occurs where there is no structure of responsibility for selection and no guidance in identification of needs and evaluation of materials. The basic goal of management of selection is to provide that process which will function continuously and within any given time and budget limitation to ensure the fulfillment of the goal of selection.

PLANNING THE SELECTION PROCESS

The six planned objectives described earlier may now be examined with specific application to selection.

ANALYZE THE GOAL

Why is a selection process needed? An organized process is essential for the successful performance of the informational, educational, cultural, and recreational functions that constitute the goals of every multimedia library. The acquisition of all the resources of knowledge that are currently available in so many different formats would be self-destructive, not only because it would be financially impossible, but also because it would generate so many additional complications in informational and physical accessibility. Consequently, each library is faced with the problem of deciding which materials it should add to its collection.

Many factors will influence this decision: the goals of the institution of which the library is a part, the changing needs and demands of the library's clientele, the availability and quality of materials, and the limitations imposed by budget, staff, equipment, facilities, and time. All these, as well as other interrelated factors, must be considered in selecting materials. Without an organized procedure there can be no assurance that all these aspects will be covered completely enough to result in good selection.

The essential components of the goal of selection are the needs of the library's community and the resources of knowledge. The process of selection brings these two components together. The accomplishment of this union depends upon professional expertise that combines good judgment, objectivity, and imagination with a thorough knowledge of the library's populace and both a comprehensive familiarity with those resources already in the library's collection and those available in great variety through purchase, local production, or other means of procurement.

PARAMETERS IMPOSED ON SELECTION   There are parameters imposed on selection by the goals of the total system. The materials selected should contribute to the fulfillment of the goals of the library as a whole and of the larger system in which the library is a subsystem. For example, the resources chosen by a school media center, while furthering the educational aims of the school and the district of which the center is a part, must also relate to the specific needs of the students and teachers of that particular school; those chosen by a special library must reflect the subject and research interests of the institution which it serves. In designing the selection process, therefore, the manager must ascertain that its focus remains on the goals of the total system.

The organizational structure of the total system also imposes parameters on selection. The organizational structure of the selection process must be compatible with that of the whole library. Currently, evaluation of materials may be accomplished through a variety of different approaches that range from tightly controlled individual professionalism to wide participation, both voluntary and mandatory. Selection may depend upon the recommendations of appointed committees, subject specialists, library patrons, or periodically issued lists. Each library must determine whether one or a combination of several of these methods is the most feasible in its own local situation, and each library must emphasize to top administration that its support of the selection process is essential. Unfortunately, top administration, assuming that selection is something that just gets done along with other duties, often disregards selection as an entity in itself and neglects to provide the moral and financial support that is needed for good selection. Whatever the methods chosen, the mechanics of selection should be set up so that authority, responsibility, and lines of communication are clearly delineated and conform to the organizational pattern of the total system.

A materials selection policy that is clearly stated and officially adopted is essential in the selection process. It establishes the basic principles and limits of selection, and provides policies, procedures, and criteria that are used as a guide in selection.

The materials selection policy covers all types of resources and, depending upon the local situation, may consist of general statements or very specific details. It may include general criteria for the evaluation of all kinds of materials; specific criteria for each type of material and for particular subject areas that may be of a controversial nature, such as sex, and political doctrines; policies for handling special questions such as gift acceptance, attempted censorship, and discriminatory pressures; and clarification of the goals on which selection should focus. All the aforementioned subjects may be treated in the materials selection policy, or each may be set out as a separate policy. Whether general or specific, it is extremely important that there be a stated policy that has total administrative support. In planning the selection process, the manager must analyze policies, regulations, and criteria very carefully to ascertain that they permit enough flexibility to adapt to change, promote continuous growth, and encourage creative thinking. Such a critical analysis may reveal that existing policy constitutes a detriment to selection, in which case the manager may have to exert pressure to bring about policy changes that are more conducive to good selections. If, on the other hand, as is too frequently the case, no policy exists, the manager may have to initiate action that will result in the establishment of the needed policy.

The availability of funds can become a major problem since it can set very definite limits to selection. In planning the selection process, the manager must consider the budget of the current year, the budget that can be projected for several years ahead, and possibilities of additional income from various other sources. The obvious limitations imposed by the budget may often be extended considerably by the manager who takes the time to preplan short- and long-range programs and employs imagination and business acumen in using the funds that can be obtained to the best advantage.

PROVIDE THE MATERIALS REQUIRED
TO FULFILL SELECTION GOALS

It seems axiomatic to state that in order to select resources of knowledge for the multimedia library a variety of resources from which to make selections must be provided. However, the supposition that materials for evaluative examination are always easily available too often results in a collection that is lacking in quality, quantity, and in proportion to needs. The building of a collection that will fulfill the goals of the multimedia library depends upon selections being made from a broad spectrum of materials which, at any given time, may pertain to all subjects in general, or may focus on a specific subject. Such comprehensive coverage necessitates an organized program that ensures continuous access to available materials and/or information about them.

An actual hands-on scrutiny of all the materials that are currently produced is an impossible task. Practicality demands that limits be set to the number of materials provided for evaluation. Thus, in determining which materials should be reviewed, the process of selection is already in operation, and the manager must design a procedural plan that effectively coordinates all those factors that can influence these first decisions. Therefore, to accomplish the second major objective in selection process planning, the manager sets up guidelines that pertain to general criteria. The philosophy and goals of the particular multimedia library constitute the primary criteria that determine which materials should be considered for evaluation. While certain basic reference resources for general knowledge information are widely appropriate, the specific subjects and educational level of materials selected must in some way further the purpose of the library. For example, an electrical engineering company library need not be concerned with curriculum materials specifically produced for the primary school media center. Although the differences in the purposes of the two libraries in the foregoing example are obvious, these differences are seldom as evident in a comparison of libraries of similar type and level.

It is essential for the selection process, therefore, that the purposes of each library be formulated in terms of general criteria that cover subject content, scholastic level, and type of media. It is equally important that these general criteria be flexible enough to permit priority variations in content, level, and type, as dictated by changes in needs and conditions.

A long-range program which indicates what percentage of materials on various subjects should be acquired each year is a quick reference base for eliminating evaluation materials that deal with unwanted subjects. The program should cover at least a five-year period and the subject percentages should be based on an assessment of needs, future programs, and gaps in the collection.

The subjects and percentages specified in such a plan should be used only as a guide, however, not as a rigid instrument of measurement. Strict adherence to the plan disregards the need to cope with changes that inevitably occur over a period of time and consequently negates the purpose of selection. In each fiscal year a refocusing of subject content as dictated by prevailing needs should take place, and the materials procured for evaluation should reflect revised subject emphases.

At any time, in addition to the major subjects specified in each year, current interest may create an unforeseen demand for resources on particular topics that necessitates immediacy in evaluation. The mechanics of procurement must be designed so that materials on these subjects, or information about them, can be supplied rapidly enough to allow for a fair evaluation. If this is not done, the pressure of instant demand often results in the purchase of materials that have not gone through the selection process and are found to be entirely unsuitable.

The manager must also set up selection guidelines that pertain to quantity. Recommended national and state standards for various types of libraries suggest the number of different types of materials that would be adequate to carry out the services in which the library is engaged. (*See* Bibliography for Chapters 6 and 7 which includes listing of standards.) These quantities should be regarded as goals to be reached and can be used for guidance in determining the number of materials of various types that should be reviewed. If, for example, the number of books and filmstrips in the collection of the multimedia library has already reached the quantity denoted in the standards, and there is a notable deficiency in items in other media, such as tape recordings, 8mm films, and slides, the majority of the materials supplied for evaluation should be of the type that is lacking in the collection, and the number of each kind should be roughly proportioned to the quantity needed to meet the standard and keep the collection current.

The cost of different types of materials, the expense of procurement, the budget, and the time involved in reviewing, are additional factors that impose realistic limits on the number of materials that should be provided for evaluation. An even balance must be established between the temptation to practice overly assiduous selection that insists on reviewing everything available and the limitations dictated by economic conditions. By computing a feasible and flexible ratio of the number of items procured for review to the number that can actually be purchased, the manager provides a procedural guide that speeds up the selection process and minimizes its costs.

The simplicity of the logistics of book reviewing as compared to the complexity of those of nonprint previewing that entail special time periods, facilities, and equipment, is not a valid reason for supplying print materials in such an amount that resources in other formats are largely excluded. The use of standards as a quantity guide for all types of materials has already been discussed. Of prime importance, however, is the need to determine what type of material can best reach the library's patrons. A work may be available in several different media: as a book, a sound recording, a filmstrip, a motion picture, or a set of slides. Which of these formats, or combination of formats, will be most appropriate for the present and potential users is the principal factor that determines what type of material is procured for evaluation.

Policies that pertain to the procedures of the selection process should be clearly stated and understood, and should not be confused with materials selection policies. Procedural policies are primarily concerned with the methodology of the process, which is usually not detailed in materials selection policies. Procedural policies should be established only after discussion by both professional and clerical staff has resulted in a consensus.

POLICY FOR SELECTION THROUGH REVIEWS   The proliferation of materials currently being produced makes it imperative that a policy be established which ensures that, in the time available, selection be made from evaluations of the greatest possible number of materials. To accomplish such wide coverage necessitates dependence upon reviewing that is not performed in-house. Critical evaluations by authoritative and widely recommended reviewers can be accepted as a suitable substitute for local evaluations made from an actual perusal of the material. If an item on a desired subject has been recommended by several reliable review sources, it can be designated for purchase without further evaluation. The time that would have been spent in evaluating this material can thus be devoted to appraising those materials that cannot be found in reviewing sources, as well as those from less well-known producers and publishers. Although such resources may be relatively unknown because they are not nationally advertised, many of them are of excellent quality and may have merit, especially for the local situation.

In selecting materials by the review method there is always the temptation to acquire materials that have majority recommendations. Caution must be exercised to avoid using reviewers' consensus, instead of suitability, however, as the principal criterion of selection. It is extremely important, therefore, that before a decision is made the entire review be read to ascertain that the material in question does indeed meet the criterion of suitability.

The policy for selection through reviews should state the evaluating sources that are acceptable and be kept up-to-date by addition or deletion of sources as warranted by changing conditions. It should also indicate the basic number of favorable reviews needed for final selection, and outline a procedure to be followed when reviewers disagree in their assessment of the worth of the material. The following policy statement, shown as Example 12, applies to an elementary school media center. By particularizing the details, a similar one may be formulated for any multimedia library.

EXAMPLE 12
SELECTION THROUGH REVIEWS POLICY

GENERAL POLICY

Materials may be considered for purchase on the basis of qualified review sources, evaluator's recommendations, requests, and other means. The following sections describe the sources which may be used as a basis for selections, and the terms and conditions under which evaluators' or reviewers' statements may be utilized as a basis for selection.

1. Materials recommended by the following review sources may be considered for purchase without further evaluation. (Note: To update, always include the latest edition and/or supplements, unless the source has been deleted.)

Date (Additions Deletions)	Source	Type of Material
1971	*AAAS Science Book List for Children.* American Association for the Advancement of Science	Books
	The Booklist. American Library Association. Semimonthly	Multimedia Books
	Books for Elementary School Libraries: An Initial Collection, compiled by Elizabeth Hodges. American Library Association	Books
	Bulletin of the Center for Children's Books. University of Chicago Press. Monthly	Books

EXAMPLE 12 (Cont.)

Date (Additions Deletions)	Source	Type of Material
	Children's Catalog. H. W. Wilson. Quinquennial, 4 annual supplements	Books
	The Elementary School Library Collection, edited by Mary V. Gaver. Bro-Dart Foundation. Annual, 1 supplement	Multimedia
	Horn Book Magazine. The Horn Book, Inc. Monthly	Books
	New Educational Materials, a Classified Guide. Citation Press. Annual	Multimedia
	Periodicals for School Libraries: A Guide to Magazines, Newspapers, and Periodical Indexes, compiled by Marian H. Scott. American Library Association	Periodicals
	Recommended Paperback Books for Elementary Schools, edited by David Cohen. Book Mail Service, Inc.	Books
	Resources for Learning: A Core Media Collection for Elementary Schools, edited by Roderick McDaniel. R. R. Bowker	Nonprint media
	School Library Journal. R. R. Bowker, Monthly	Books
1972	*A Multi-Media Approach to Children's Literature.* American Library Association	Multimedia
	Previews: News and Reviews of Nonprint Media. R. R. Bowker. Monthly	Nonprint media
1973	*The Best in Children's Books.* University of Chicago Press	Books
	Picture Books for Children. American Library Association	Books

2. The number of evaluator's recommendations needed before an item may be considered for purchase without further evaluation are: for print materials—4; for nonprint materials—3. (The state of the art of nonprint materials reviewing and the number of evaluating sources available are not as advanced as are those for books.)

3. If reviewers disagree in their assessment of the value of the material, a simple majority of favorable opinions may constitute a valid basis for considering an item for selection. However, before the final decision is reached, any predispositions or biases of the reviewing sources should be explored to determine the validity of their recommendations or rejections. By familiarizing one's self with the peculiarities of individual reviewers, the selector is better able to put disparate opinions in a more objective perspective.

If there is wide divergence of opinion in an evaluation, the material should be procured and evaluated directly in the library's selection process.

The list of review sources in the example policy is not intended to be comprehensive, of course. Its purpose is to show, by a sufficient number of examples, the kind of information that would be included in a selection through reviews policy and the manner in which it could be presented.

POLICY FOR SELECTION THROUGH REQUESTS   The selection of materials that are specifically requested is a matter that calls for diplomacy and good public relations. To strike an even balance between selection that is based on accepted principles and selection that is made because of pressure requires a great deal of finesse. A policy that publicizes the procedure adopted concerning the selection of requests is therefore essential to minimize the difficulties involved. A written policy that points out the necessity for requested items to be evaluated in the same way as other materials assists the staff in handling requests in a satisfactory manner, and the requestor in understanding why the material wanted is not immediately made available. Of prime importance in this policy statement is the emphasis on the positive attitude that the staff must maintain vis a vis the requestor. Indispensable to this effort is communication, either verbal or written, with the requestor. Common courtesy demands that the requestor be informed about a desired item. This report, then, is of the highest priority.

Communication may begin when the requestor submits the request. A standard form, such as the one shown in Figure 27, is easy to fill out, and, in addition to the

P.O. Number	Class No.	Cost Price	Cancelled OP OS	Date Rec'd

For Science #110	Author (Last Name First)
	Title; No. & Type of AV Material
Dealer Demco	Sand dune succession: 2 filmstrips, 2 cassettes

No. of Copies

1

Publisher/Producer   Educational Dev. Corp.   Date 1975   Edition/Binding/Cat. No. #231340400

List Price 28.95

Requested by: Henderson
Recommended: B 11/15/75:487

Date Ordered 4/1/76

LC Card No. 75-735800
Catalog Card   LIBRARY
Yes   No   Address

✓ BOOK
   AV
   ORDER

Figure 27. AUDIOVISUAL MATERIAL REQUESTED ON MULTIPLE-COPY ORDER FORM

required bibliographic information, asks for the reason for the request. This helps the staff to determine the relative importance of acquiring the material. In a college situation, for example, the works that a professor designates as essential for the course being taught are more likely candidates for first consideration than are those of a recreational nature that are submitted from the general public.

The communication which goes back from the staff to the requestor should report action taken. If the material is to be purchased, a tentative date of availability should be indicated. If the material is not to be purchased, the reasons for rejection should be briefly and clearly stated. In such cases, the importance of suggesting alternate titles and/or media formats should be stressed.

PROVIDE THE PERSONNEL

To build a collection of resources that enables the multimedia library to perform its informational, educational, cultural, and recreational functions successfully requires participation in selection that goes beyond the personnel of the library. Good selection is a many-faceted operation that necessitates contributions from those who have knowledge of the whole community, of individuals in the community, of the goals of the institution, of media materials, and of subject content. Such a breadth of knowledge and specialized expertise calls for the involvement of persons who are not directly connected with the library. The manager, therefore, plans the machinery of selection so that these personnel become part of the selection team. One extremely important part of the plan which is often neglected is the provision, where needed, of a training program in selection principles, criteria, and methods.

Responsibility and authority for selection may be formally structured so that all those who are involved in the evaluation of materials are assigned to various committees or groups that have well-defined functions. One group may be primarily concerned with materials for a specified grade or age range, another with books only, another with nonprint resources only, another with materials on all subjects. Conversely, an informal grouping of personnel may prevail wherein evaluations are made by individuals or by groups that have formed temporarily to accomplish a particular project or satisfy an immediate demand.

The flexibility and response to community needs that are essential for good selection can be obtained through a combination of formal and informal groupings. One type or the other may predominate at any time, but the basic pattern of these combined groupings must be compatible with the structure of responsibility and authority of the whole system. In planning the selection process, the manager first determines the responsibility that should be delegated, and the authority needed to carry it out, and then clearly designates the personnel to whom this responsibility is assigned.

In the Hicks High School, for example, the manager has been successful in forming an evaluation committee in which each of the subject departments, the student body, and the library are represented. The committee holds monthly meetings to review and discuss the evaluations completed by the members during the month and to recommend for purchase the resources deemed the most suitable. The manager delegates the responsibility for these meetings on a semester basis to one of the members of the team and also gives authority to take the steps that are needed to produce the required results. The person to whom this responsibility is delegated then delegates parts of the task to other members. The representative of the science department becomes responsible for the procurement of all types of materials on science, ecology, energy conservation, and science fiction, and for their distribution for review. The business education department representative assumes the task of seeing that evaluations are completed on time and that necessary clerical work is performed. In the same way, and usually on the basis of subject-matter expertise, other members are assigned responsibilities. Even though the manager is considered responsible for final selection, this delegation of responsibility makes possible a broader spectrum of materials reviewing and permits the manager to focus on problem areas instead of on routine matters.

PROVIDE THE TOOLS

To operate effectively the selection process depends, in addition to materials for evaluation and personnel, on the availability of what may be called the tools of the trade. These include informational tools, equipment, or facilities.

In using *informational tools*, selection criteria for all types of material, for specific types of material, and for equipment, are the basic guides for evaluation. They may appear on a standard form as abbreviated statements that are to be checked on a rating scale. However, to make a valid judgment, the evaluator needs to clearly understand the meaning of each criterion and the various factors that have to be considered in its application. This understanding can be accomplished by providing all evaluators with a document which explains succinctly and summarizes in key words each criterion.

In addition to the selection aids already discussed in Policy for Selection through Reviews other sources of information about materials should be made readily available. These would include evaluative reviews and selective compilations that do not appear on the library's official list, descriptive reviews, and catalogs from producers and publishers. Which of these tools are acquired will vary with the current conditions in each library. Provision should be made, however, for furnishing a basic collection of this type of selection tool. Publishers' and producers' exhibits are an invaluable aid in gaining familiarity with materials. Arranging for exhibits to be brought to the library and funding attendance at local, state, and national conferences provide opportunities for personnel to examine the various resources that are on display.

The use of standard bibliographic reference works in the selection process eliminates duplication of evaluations and of work in other processes. Identification of materials and verification of authors, titles, formats, editions, publishers, producers, distributors, prices, and availability are not only factors that influence selection, but are also a means of determining if the material has not already been evaluated under a different title or series, or as part of a package of multimedia materials. The information acquired in the bibliographic search in the selection process is passed on to the acquisitions and cataloging processes. This procedure minimizes the time and work needed for bibliographic search in acquisitions and cataloging, thereby speeding up the flow of materials to the library user.

The availability of *equipment* and *facilities* can often be the factor that determines what audiovisual materials will be evaluated. Equipment needed to preview all types of media should be furnished and kept in good repair. To give the evaluator greater latitude in time and place for previewing, circulation of equipment that can be easily transported is advisable. A previewing room that has adequate outlets, lighting, and darkening facilities is needed for viewing and listening. Space is also required for selection meetings where reviews and discussion can take place without interruption.

ESTABLISH RELATIONSHIPS WITH OTHER PROCESSES

The procedural plan of the selection process indicates in what way and to what extent its product can be used to provide services to other processes in the system. Bibliographic information is one of its main contributions which is of benefit to both acquisitions and cataloging. Reviews and materials often supply cataloging information such as classification numbers, subject headings, and Library of Congress numbers which if recorded at the time of selection will reduce the time needed for cataloging. Annotations, descriptions, and reviews assist staff members in their reader guidance services and library users in their search and choice of resources for their own particular purposes. The most important aspect of this part of selection process planning is to identify the services that can be beneficial to other processes, to specify which processes can use these services, and to establish communication between all processes involved. When the flow of information is presented graphically, the concept of a within-the-system information network takes shape. In this way, each process knows what services are its responsibility, where they should be directed, and how and when they should be delivered.

The selection process can also expect to receive services from other processes. Information from cataloging and acquisitions prevents needless evaluation of works already in the collection or on order. Acquisitions renders service by procuring the reference tools and preview materials required in selection. Cataloging renders service by organizing reference works for easy accessibility. It also furnishes a subject analysis of the works in the collection which assists selectors in determining subject priorities in new materials. These and other services from various processes facilitate the work of the selection process and their relationship to selection should be clearly delineated. Figure 28 graphically describes the interrelationships of selection and other processes.

CREATE THE PLAN

The first five major objectives in planning the selection process are concerned with the work that has to be accomplished to fulfill the purpose of selection. The task now is to plan how the work can be most efficiently performed. The manager gathers data to *survey all pertinent procedures*, including those that already exist in the library and those that are used in other libraries. The manager assesses their feasibility in relation to the organization and conditions within which they must operate and their capability in relation to the projected plan. The methodology of evaluation, for example, can generate many problems when its structure conflicts with the philosophy and organization of the institution. The techniques employed in one library to secure wide personnel involvement in evaluation may not be successful in another library because they are at variance with traditional established concepts and administrative support.

In many instances, evaluation breaks down because there is no overall design that coordinates the machinery of evaluation in such a way that it not only functions on a continuous basis but also swings into action to meet an immediate demand. This machinery will not function efficiently unless the procedures used in its operation detail the number, competencies, and organization of personnel, the frequency of task assignments, the workflow, and the expected outcome.

From among the possible procedures studied the manager *selects procedures* that will produce the best results, as well as possible alternatives which may be substituted should unforeseen complications appear in the actual procedure performance. The procedures chosen may be some that are already in practice in the library, some borrowed from other libraries, and some devised by combining the best elements from several procedures.

The manager will chart the organizational structure of the selection process. Figure 29, the organizational chart of the selection process in a school district, exemplifies such a chart. It shows relationship of components, lines of authority, and delegation of responsibility.

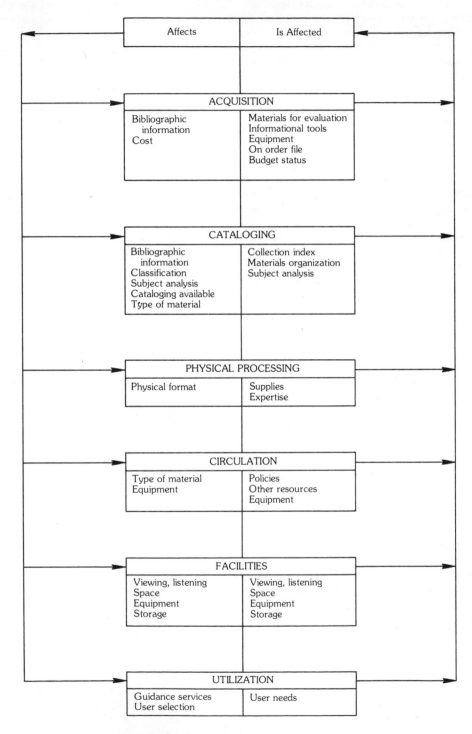

Figure 28. SOME INTERRELATIONSHIPS OF SELECTION AND OTHER PROCESSES

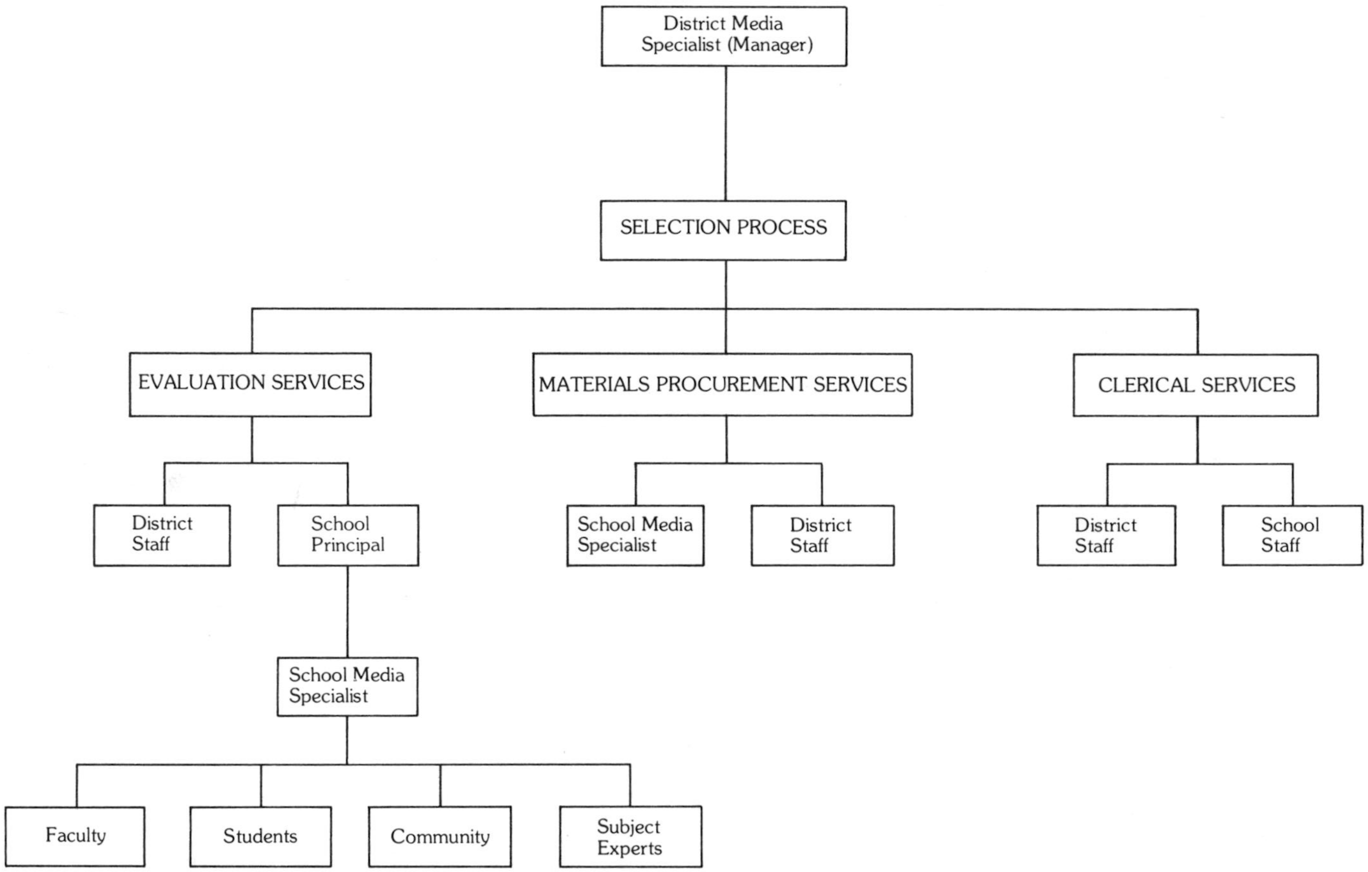

Figure 29. ORGANIZATIONAL CHART OF THE SELECTION PROCESS IN A SCHOOL DISTRICT

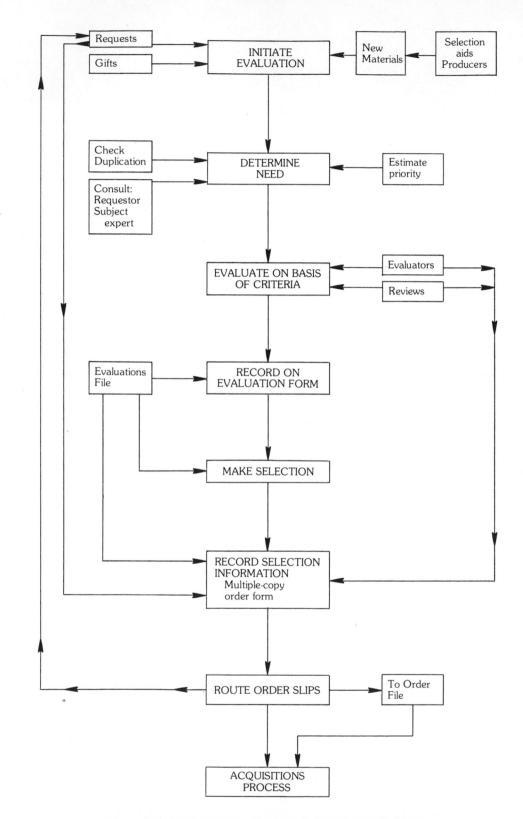

Figure 30. FLOWCHART OF THE SELECTION PROCESS

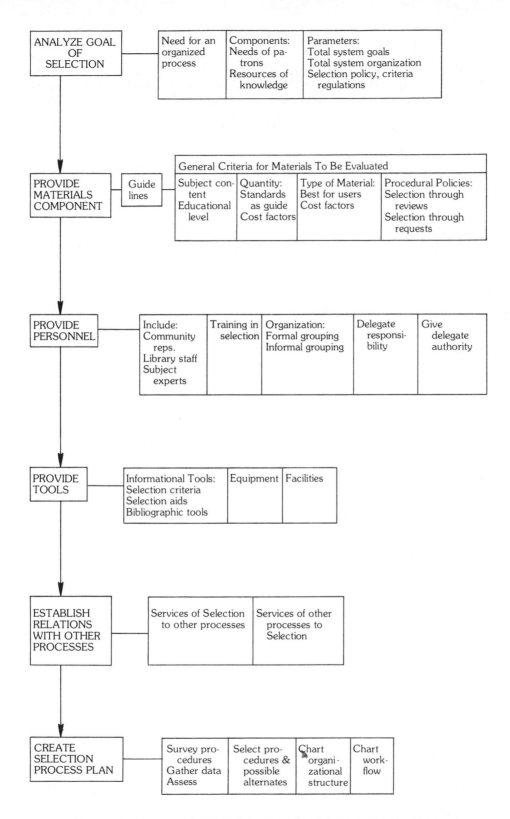

Figure 31. MODEL OF PLANNING THE SELECTION PROCESS

The manager then will chart the workflow of the selection process. An example of such a chart is shown in Figure 30. In this chart the major steps in the work performed in selection are presented in a coordinated sequence. This type of chart establishes the relationships of tasks to each other and to the total work accomplished, and is instrumental in increasing motivation and decreasing task insularity. The details of each procedure do not appear in this chart. These may be worked out in consultation with personnel and presented in various charts in the designing phase of the process. The entire planning phase of selection is shown in Figure 31.

DESIGNING THE
SELECTION PROCESS

The objective of designing the action plan is to lay out the details of all the procedures that are needed to accomplish the work of the selection process. Designing the action plan requires the cooperation of all professional and clerical personnel involved in selection. Each person should contribute to the plan by providing an analysis of the tasks performed, including a statement of objectives, a step-by-step breakdown of the procedures followed, and recommendations for change if needed. The manager should not assume the task of working out all these details personally. The task in designing the action plan is to organize the procurement of procedural information, to evaluate the existing procedures, and together with staff, finalize the design of the action plan.

Four other major objectives of process designing that have been identified in the basic management procedure are concerned with the organizational structure, objectives, standardized routines, and workflow of each procedure and of each task within the procedure. How these objectives are handled in the selection process is demonstrated in the following treatment of one procedure—the recording of information about material that is being considered for selection. Other procedures in selection and in the other processes can be patterned after this example.

EXAMPLE 13
PROCEDURE FOR RECORDING INFORMATION
ABOUT MATERIALS FOR SELECTION

THE OBJECTIVE

To provide the information that identifies the material and also contributes to the data needed in other processes.

THE PERSONNEL

Requestors, evaluators, and library staff record the information. The staff that is responsible for carrying out the procedure is required to have skills in typing, filing, and bibliographic searching. Responsibility for the completion of the work is assigned to one person who has the authority to organize and supervise the work of staff members, and who also ascertains that other personnel are provided with the instructions and means that will assist them in recording the necessary information. The responsible staff member reports through established channels of communications to the person who is in charge of the selection process. The number of workers needed to carry out this procedure is based upon the anticipated volume of materials that will go through the selection process.

EXAMPLE 13 (Cont.)

THE INFORMATION

There are two main categories of information required for each item. Essential information needed to identify the work: author, title, type of material, number of parts and other types of material included in the work, and publisher/producer. The source of recommendation or request and reason for request should also be noted.

Additional information, if available and applicable, that gives assistance in evaluation, acquisition, and cataloging: date, edition, producer's catalog number, price, binding, classification number, subject headings, catalog card numbers (Library of Congress, Wilson), availability of cataloging kits, intended audience, and the number of copies requested if more than one.

WORK SIMPLIFICATION TECHNIQUES

Basic routines are used for repetitive tasks in finding and recording information. Sources of information are specified and numbered in the sequence in which they are to be searched. The standardized terminology, abbreviations, form of entry, and so on that are used in all processes are followed in recording information. Information is recorded on preprinted evaluation, request, or multiple-copy order forms. To facilitate the transcription of information from one form to another the same sequence of information appears on all forms. Final recording of information is on the multiple-copy order form. Whenever possible, to minimize typing time, the information is recorded initially on the multiple-copy order form rather than on one of the other forms.

SUPERVISING THE SELECTION PROCESS

The manager's overall objective in supervising is to ascertain that, in directing actual operation of the action plan, all procedures are functioning as they have been blueprinted in the plan, so that the goals of the selection process are fulfilled. The two other major objectives of supervising are comprehension of the plan and management of personnel. These are basic in accomplishing the primary objective and are an integral part of the manager's supervisory procedure.

To supervise the selection process the manager plans a program that will provide a continuous overview of the accomplishment of the various procedures. Such a program enables the manager to assess the amount and kind of supervision that may be required in each procedure at different times. To facilitate the supervisory task the manager may draw up a checklist that will assist in identifying the procedures that are in need of additional supervision. In the selection process, some of the major areas on which the manager will focus supervision are objectives, work assignments, and coordination.

Further explanation may be needed to clarify the objectives of the selection process and of each of its procedures so that personnel understand why the work is being done. For example, in the procedure for recording information about materials for selection, those who perform the tasks should know why the data they provide is necessary not only for selection, but also for acquisition and cataloging. This knowledge will assist them in determining what data is essential and reduce the amount of time that is spent in researching and recording information that may be either inconsequential or more efficiently provided in one of the other processes.

In reviewing work assignments, the manager may find that an individual is not making the best use of personal capabilities because the task performed is not related to that individual's training and skill. For example, the checking of reviews for suitable materials is the responsibility of the professional who has knowledge of community needs, materials, and evaluation techniques that are needed in selection. If the professional also does the work of recording choices, time is spent on the routine tasks of typing and filing that can be efficiently handled by a nonprofessional. In situations of this type, the manager exercises supervision by discussing the task requirements with the person involved, suggesting alternate ways of doing the work so that the professional can devote time to the completion of the work which only that staff member can perform.

In supervising coordination, the manager ascertains that the product for which each procedure is responsible is available at the time that it is needed. If a bottleneck occurs, the manager identifies the procedure that is not accomplishing the work as scheduled, determines the cause of the delay, and supervises corrective measures. In some instances the problem may be easily solved by recommending a simple rearrangement of the sequence in which the tasks in the procedure are performed. In other cases, the solution may become more complicated. If the procedure depends upon services from another process, for example, the manager has to assess the effects of the proposed remedy on the other process as well and arrive at a conclusion that will be beneficial to both processes. If regularly scheduled evaluation sessions are part of the selection machinery, materials for evaluation must be provided for these meetings. If they are not available as anticipated, and it is the responsibility of the acquisitions process to obtain them, the manager must supervise the acquisitions procedure that is used to obtain preview materials. The manager may suggest modifications in the procedure, but not to such an extent that the acquisitions process will be disrupted. Rescheduling in selection may also be required to achieve the desired coordination.

CONTROLLING THE SELECTION PROCESS

While supervising, the manager also evaluates. Supervision is primarily concerned with the operation of the process, which is observed continuously. Control focuses on the product of the process with the objective of evaluation at periodic intervals. The process should be in operation long enough to provide a sufficient amount of data to make the evaluation valid. Such formal evaluations are usually conducted over a yearly period that coincides with the fiscal year. At that time, information on the production from other processes is also available. By bringing all this data together a comparative analysis can be made that indicates what factors from other processes influence the production of the selection process and must be considered in evaluation.

For a true measure of output, data must be interpreted from several different points of view. Both quality and quantity should be measured. In addition, the process should be evaluated in terms of fulfillment of objectives, of time requirements, and of cost. In evaluating the selection process, the manager uses the data on hand to answer questions such as: Is the number of items selected sufficient to meet the demand of the library's patrons? Does the number indicate that satisfactory progress is being made toward achieving the quantities recommended in established standards?

Typically, the manager asks many other questions. Does the quality of the materials selected show evaluation according to established criteria; a broad involvement of knowledgeable personnel; a thorough understanding of the needs of the people that the library serves; a comprehensive coverage of all types of materials and of all subjects? Does the process function at a pace that keeps up with the production of materials and the demands on the library's service? Is too much time being spent on unnecessary procurement and previewing of materials? Will additional reviewing sources, simplified and standardized evaluation and work forms, reassignment of tasks, and changes in task sequence result in a more productive use of time? What is the cost of the selection process? Has it exceeded its allotted budget? Is there an imbalance in the amount of money expended for professional and clerical staff, for procurement of materials, for reviewing aids, for previewing facilities? To what extent have emergencies depleted available funds? Does the production of the process fulfill the ultimate goal of selection? Does each procedure in the process achieve its formulated objective? What contribution do procedure objectives make toward achieving the overall objective of selection? Does misinterpretation of objectives exist? Do the objectives ensure the continuous practice of selection? Do they permit the flexibility that is needed to take care of change?

While supervising, the manager becomes aware of the areas in which changes may be needed. An evaluation indicates more precisely where modifications are needed and in what order of priority they should be made. If, for example, the evaluative data shows that a large percentage of requests for resources remains unfilled, the manager focuses on redesigning that part of the action plan through which knowledge of the people's needs is communicated.

REVISING THE SELECTION PROCESS

Since the functioning of the process is based on the accomplishment of stated objectives, the first step in revising the action plan is to review and assess the validity of these objectives. In addition to information from supervision and evaluation, the manager must have feedback from those who are actually working in selection. Are objectives stated in terms that are understandable and specific? Is further clarification of objectives needed? Are the objectives attainable? Is the amount of work they demand unrealistic and overwhelming? How does a particular objective assist in accomplishing the major objectives of the selection process? Is the cost of carrying out an objective in proportion to the contribution it makes?

To set up a center for the examination of materials, for example, is theoretically a sound objective. However, in certain situations it may prove to be invalid. It may be too expensive; it may not be extensively used; it may require so much time and work that other aspects of selection will not progress satisfactorily; or the provision of materials for evaluation which is the purpose of the objective may be more efficiently accomplished through the coordination of other means of procurement.

The last step in the manager's procedure is to redesign the plan in those areas that are weak in production. Decisions and corrective measures are based on an analysis of all the data that the manager has accumulated through supervision, evaluation, and feedback. To ensure that the changes are beneficial the procedural cycle of planning, designing, supervising, controlling, and revising is repeated. Figure 32 displays a model for managing the entire selection process.

SUMMARY

Selection is the first in a series of activities which concern the library resources. Managing the selection process has been analyzed in detail both because it is central to the functioning of any library, and to serve as an example or prototype by which

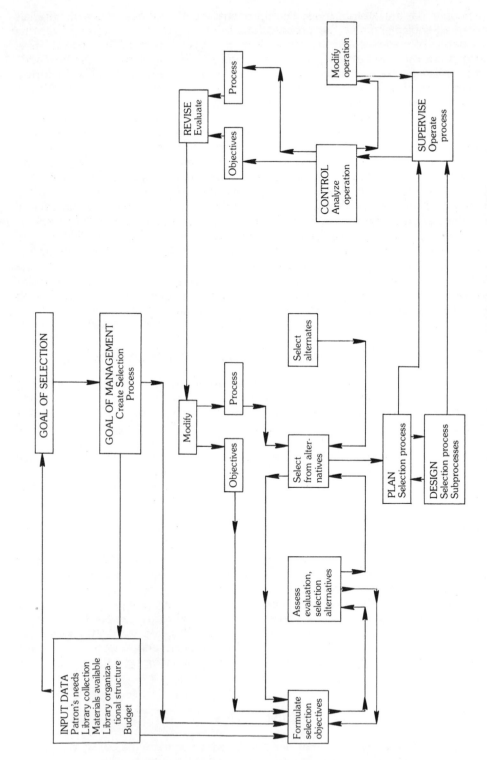

Figure 32. MODEL OF MANAGING THE SELECTION PROCESS

to analyze similarly the other resource management processes of acquisitions, cataloging, and physical processing.

The chapter applies the principles and sequential steps in management-by-objectives to the areas of operational activity under discussion. It reviews the basic procedures in process design, identifying the goals of management in the context of the process, and execution of the management function in planning, designing, supervising, controlling, and revising the process.

Planning is discussed in terms of six criteria in question form: (1) Why is the work performed? (2) On what materials is the work performed? (3) By whom is the work performed? (4) What tools are needed to do the work? (5) What interrelationships can be seen between and among the several task assignments? (6) How is the work performed? These questions provide a planning base for the design of an action plan to get the operational job done.

The main body of the chapter is given to comprehensive discussion and application of these questions and factors relating to selection.

CHAPTER 7

MANAGING MULTIMEDIA RESOURCES: ACQUISITIONS, CATALOGING, AND PHYSICAL PROCESSING

An important part of a learning resources center is the technical support services provided to maintain all audiovisual and television production equipment. (Courtesy of Learning Resources Center, Solano Community College.)

Acquisitions, cataloging, and physical processing follow selection as key activities in the management of the multimedia library. Acquisitions has to do with a variety of tasks which get the resources into the collection in the first place; cataloging provides a means for locating and retrieving these resources, and physical processing prepares the materials themselves for actual use by the patron. It is important for the multimedia manager to conceptualize the goals, planning, and parameters which apply to each of these activities, the policies and procedures needed to implement them, and the relationships of each of these as a function to the other processes of management.

This chapter looks at the four major procedures of acquisitions: searching, ordering, accounting, and receiving; the specialized knowledge, tools, and procedures which apply to cataloging, including description, analysis, classification, and catalog production; and the careful and important tasks of physical processing which permit owner identification, location identification, borrower identification, and resources protection. These are the actual operational staff functions of the multimedia library, and a central responsibility for the manager.

ACQUISITIONS

GOAL OF ACQUISITIONS

The major goal of acquisitions is to procure the resources that are needed to achieve the library's objectives. The meaning of the term *acquisition*, as used in library literature, may vary considerably. It may be used comprehensively to cover all the factors that influence collection building in addition to selection, such as budget, personnel, accounting, business practices, and so on. Acquisition may imply selection in the sense of acquiring the most suitable resources, in which case the words "acquisition" and "selection" may appear as synonyms. In many instances acquisition focuses primarily on the procedures required to actually procure the resources designated through selection. It is in this later sense that acquisition is treated in this discussion. Referring generally to this total process, the term is most often used as a plural-appearing singular: *acquisitions*.

The goal of management of acquisitions is to organize the acquisitions process so that the money expended procures the largest possible number of the selected resources within the period of time that they are required. Management's concern is to get resources to the user as quickly as possible and to do this as economically as possible.

To achieve this goal the manager follows the basic procedure that has already been outlined and exemplified in the selection process. The discussion of the acquisitions process, therefore, will not repeat the details of each step but will focus on identifying some of the factors that are peculiar to acquisitions and some of the major objectives of acquisitions procedures.

PLANNING THE ACQUISITIONS PROCESS

Efficient planning in acquisitions requires not only the general knowledge, analytical skill, and clear thinking previously discussed under planning in Chapter 6, but also specifically requires an understanding of accounting, proficiency in budget analysis, and a knowledge of book publishing and media production.

The manager should be informed about the book and audiovisual trade and be alert to the latest developments in the trade which could affect the operation of the acquisitions process, such as company mergers or new management of a company which may result in changes in service, discounts, and the type of resources offered; new jobbers; new contractual, consignment, approval, and purchase plans, and so on. If, for example, the manager is not aware that materials which were always obtained through a jobber become available only through direct purchase from the producer, the cost of these items may be increased. Reordering is expensive, not only in terms of the money expended for duplication of work but also in time delay in service to the patron. Input concerning conditions in the trade may be acquired through direct communication with publishers and producers, membership in their associations, and perusal of trade periodicals, reports, and other literature.

Acquisitions is essentially a business operation and therefore is subject to business principles. Consequently, in planning the acquisitions process, the manager must understand the principles of good business in designing the various procedures that must work together in the process.

The product of acquisitions can be evaluated better by quantitative measurement than can those of other library processes. Although it must also be evaluated qualitatively, its service deals basically with tangible items and specific monetary amounts which can be manipulated to produce a greater output. Haphazard procedures and inadequate records will not achieve this increased production. Procurement procedures lend themselves particularly to a structured organization. The detail in the final design of each procedure will vary in complexity in accordance with the size and kind of library and its established policies and business practices, the type of materials to be acquired, and the different agencies with whom business is conducted. However, they have many characteristics in common which are basic to their operation and which, once determined, are repetitive in nature.

Every order sent to a vendor must bear purchase authorization, for example. This may be a purchase order number, a contract, a brief letter, a signed standardized form, and so on. The work involved in the procedures for obtaining authorization, ascertaining that the vendor has it, and noting it in the appropriate acquisitions record can be performed in sequential steps. This sequence of task performance becomes the basis of a repetitive routine which remains unaffected by the format of purchase authorization, the method of purchase, or the type of material ordered. Operational procedures, therefore, can be systematically organized and charted so that time is used to advantage, motion is not wasted, and coordination of needs, budget, and procedures is achieved. Work simplification methods can be adapted and work duplication can be minimized by the use of standard forms. Through an organized acquisitions process the procurement of needed materials will be accomplished at a reduced cost and with increased efficiency.

PARAMETERS IMPOSED ON ACQUISITIONS As in other processes, the procedures of the acquisitions process are subject to the parameters imposed by the goals, organizational structure, and policies of the total system. In acquisitions especially, there are certain identifiable constraints which, in effect, actually determine the objectives of a procedure and dictate its basic workflow pattern. Business practices and accounting techniques for the entire library system are usually well established, and provide a predetermined mold into which acquisitions routines must be fitted. Some of the procedures in this category are those which are involved in requisitioning, authorizing purchase, invoicing, confirming orders, encumbering, paying, closing orders, and recording expenditures. A prescribed method of purchase may constitute an additional constraint depending upon how restrictive or permissive it is and how specifically its application is demanded.

The stipulation that all materials must be procured through the process of bidding, for example, may be adhered to so rigidly that the successful achievement of the goal of acquisitions becomes impossible. In such cases, the manager's principal task is to communicate with those who are responsible for setting the policy in question so that changes will be made that will permit the flexibility required for acquisitions to function with maximum effectiveness and efficiency. In the same way, the manager will have to work for changes in budgetary policies which result in narrowing even more the definite limits set by the budget. Funds that are divided into narrow categories and are not transferable and time schedules for ordering, for fund expenditure by percentage, and for closure of orders impose often unrealistic limitations on how funds can be spent. The advantages that could be gained by grasping opportunities and employing business acumen are lost.

POLICY OBJECTIVES IN ACQUISITIONS   Acquisitions and selection policies are interrelated, for the decisions concerning what materials should have priority of purchase must be based on the same criteria that are used in selection. Since the budget imposes realistic limits on the number and kind of materials that can be acquired, the decisions made in acquisitions are, in essence, completing the selection process.

Policies should be established concerning when and to what extent materials should be procured by means other than purchase, such as through rental, free loan, exchange, or gift. For example, the purchase of an expensive 16mm film may deplete the budget to such an extent that other needed resources cannot be bought. It may be advisable to obtain the film through rental if it will be used only a few times. Acquisitions policies furnish guidelines for making judgments of this type.

Policies may also treat such matters as the extent and type of service required from vendors, the extent and type of bibliographic and other information provided for vendors, the extent and type of necessary records, and the extent and type of claims on vendors that should be pursued. Policies of this kind should be sufficiently general in statement to permit application on a broad scale. Using the policy as a guide, the various specific details required to perform the work can be explicitly stated in the workflow designed for the particular procedure.

PROVIDE THE PERSONNEL   The type of work required in the acquisitions process can be very adequately performed, for the most part, by paraprofessional and clerical personnel. A paraprofessional who has been trained in the functioning of the various procedures can be assigned the responsibility of day-to-day supervision. When repetitive routines are established and understood, members of the clerical staff can assume responsibility for the satisfactory completion of their assigned tasks and be motivated to work independently. By delegating responsibility in this way and by maintaining open lines of communication, the staff is encouraged to participate in identifying problems and suggesting possible solutions. Thus the manager need not be concerned with the actual details of each procedure unless they constitute a problem, and can fully utilize personal expertise to solve problems, extend work simplification, improve workflow, and perfect coordination.

ESTABLISH RELATIONSHIPS WITH OTHER PROCESSES   Services rendered to and received from the selection process were shown in Figure 28. In the same manner relationships with other processes should be identified and charted. Duplication of work is minimized when the results of work already performed in acquisitions are made available to other processes. For example, bibliographic search need not be repeated in cataloging if acquisitions records the information accurately and passes it on to cataloging. Acquisitions' records, reports, and statistics provide essential information for budget analysis, preparation, and projection. They are also important for long-range planning since they indicate trends in the cost and availability of resources, and the needs of the library users.

CREATE THE PLAN   In creating the plan of the acquisitions process the manager must first determine the type of process that will yield maximum returns for a particular multimedia library. The process may be manual or automated; cooperative, centralized, or individualized. To make a valid assessment of these alternatives the manager must become thoroughly familiar with what is involved in the total operation of each type of process, and relate this knowledge to the existing conditions and future expectations of the library. Decisions will be influenced by such factors as the size, type, and goals of the library; current and projected budget; long-range plans and expected growth; and the kind and amount of information required from the process.

At first glance, for example, a manual process appeared to be the best type for the Perez Public Library because of its present size, finances, geographical area served, and needs of its clientele. Further analysis revealed, however, that better service could be obtained from an automated process at a comparable cost if certain routines in some of the procedures were revised. In addition, changes in local conditions indicated that the library would have to extend its service over a broader geographical area and that the needs of a larger, heterogeneous clientele would require a larger collection of resources in many different media. On the basis of this analysis the manager decided to plan an automated process.

BASIC PROCEDURES IN THE ACQUISITIONS PROCESS AND THEIR OBJECTIVES

Irrespective of the type of process, the work of acquisitions can be grouped into four major procedures or subprocesses: *searching, ordering, accounting,* and *receiving.* Different ways of grouping tasks should be studied in designing the routines within each procedure.

Routines may be set up according to the type of material to be procured, for example. Separate routines may be established for ordering books, periodicals, pamphlets, duplicates, out-of-print items, and resources in audiovisual media; or one routine may handle all print materials and another one may be used with nonprint materials; or one routine may be responsible for ordering all types of resources.

Similarly, routines may be structured on the basis of the method of procurement, such as by purchase, free on request, gift, rental, free loan, lease, exchange, or local production; or on the basis of method or source of purchase, such as by bid, approval plan, blanket ordering subscription, direct ordering, or ordering from a jobber. The alternatives selected for the basis of routines must be those which conform best to the conditions which exist in the particular library and which achieve most efficiently the objectives of the major procedure of which they are a part. A brief discussion of some of the objectives of each of these procedures will facilitate an understanding of the acquisitions flowchart which appears as Figure 33.

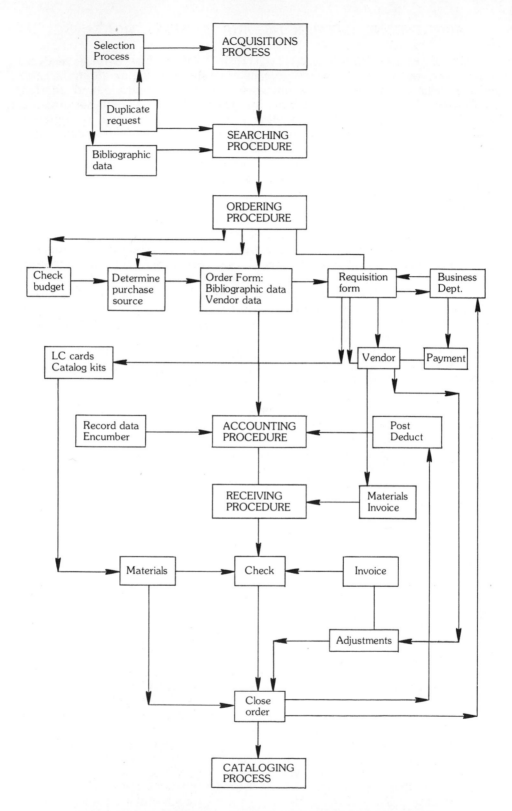

Figure 33. FLOWCHART OF THE ACQUISITIONS PROCESS

Objectives of the *searching* procedure are to minimize duplication of orders and work, and to provide required bibliographic data. The request forwarded from the selection process may duplicate an item already on order, or already received but still in process. Appropriate files should be checked to avoid unnecessary expenditures for unwanted duplicates and needless work repetition. If it is found to be a duplicate, this fact should be noted on the request, and the request form returned to the requestor.

The bibliographic information required includes those basic elements that are essential for identifying the title to be ordered. If this data has not been completed in the selection process, a search for the missing elements will have to be conducted in various bibliographic and reference sources. Personnel should be provided with a checklist of these essential elements even though the library uses a preprinted order form on which they are indicated. (Note: The reader may wish to refer back to Figure 27 for a sample of an order form.) In ordering nonprint materials it is extremely important to designate the medium and the number of items in the package since resources with very similar titles are often produced in different media.

The *ordering* procedure objective is to place orders as rapidly as possible. Accurate information about the materials and the number of items ordered should be given and orders should be submitted in the form prescribed by the business office and by the dealer. Ordering routines should be kept simple and the number of record-keeping files minimal. Complexity in files and procedures increases the cost of materials and personnel time.

Typing time for example will be saved by using a preprinted multiple-copy order form designed so that both materials and catalog cards may be ordered by typing the information only once. If certain kinds of order information are demanded only occasionally, maintaining separate files to provide such information is not warranted. Each file and routine should be carefully evaluated to ascertain that it really accomplishes enough to contribute to the efficiency of the ordering procedure and the acquisitions process. Orders should be placed at regular intervals to maintain a steady flow of resources into the library and an even distribution of work load in acquisitions, cataloging, and physical processing.

Also in ordering, one objective is to determine the vendors of all types of materials who will give both the largest discount and the best service. Written agreements should be made with vendors specifying what the library requires from the vendor and what the vendor requires from the library. Purchasing through a jobber who can provide the largest number of materials rather than from individual publishers and producers is the least expensive. The work required to prepare requisitions will be reduced to a minimum, and volume buying will obtain better discounts.

Discounts, however, must be in balance with good service. If a vendor cannot fill a large percentage of an order, a high discount is of little value. Even though the discount may be less, it is advisable to choose the vendor who can supply the largest number of materials possible and deliver them without undue delay.

Although service and discount must be considered, the resource selected is the principal factor which determines the source of purchase. In some instances procurement must be from a vendor whose prices are high and shipping and billing services inferior because the particular material is not available elsewhere. This situation occurs most frequently with nonprint materials which are often produced by small companies that are not geared to efficient business methods. Since a substitute of comparable quality and relevancy may not exist, the vendor in question should not be boycotted, however, even though his terms are not the best. In such cases direct communication between the manager and the vendor often results in more beneficial arrangements, especially in the area of service.

Agreements with chosen dealers concerning discounts, services, procedures, order submittal, returns, adjustments, payment, and so on, should be clearly understood. Communications with vendors should be kept open so that needs and problems can be discussed and mutually satisfactory arrangements can be made with a minimum of delay and expense.

Accounting procedure objectives are two: to maintain accurate and current balances for all budgeted funds, and to keep authorized personnel informed of the status of funds. Accounting routines should be kept up-to-date on the posting of encumbrances, authorized payments and credits, and the calculation of fund balances. This information is essential when orders are placed to ensure that accounts are not overdrawn. It is also needed to determine how funds may be transferred from one category to another to satisfy a pressing current need.

Finally, the objectives of *receiving* procedures are to determine that the materials received are as ordered, to route materials as quickly as possible to the cataloging process, and to close orders. Checking materials against invoices and matching materials with order slips from the on-order file are the principal routines in the receiving procedure. Checking materials for imperfections and damage should also be done if it can be accomplished rapidly. Checking nonprint materials, however, may be expensive and impractical since special handling, equipment, and facilities are required. Imperfect and damaged audiovisuals should be returned to acquisitions when they are first used.

Orders should be closed so that payment can be authorized and the exact amount of the order can be deducted from the appropriate budget account. Routines for making satisfactory adjustments with vendors for wrong titles, imperfect materials, and the like are involved in the closing of orders. Correspondence concerning adjustments need not be lengthy or time consuming if a preprinted form is used that requires only checking to indicate the complaint. Orders should be closed as soon as all claims are settled.

A model for managing the entire acquisitions process is portrayed graphically in Figure 34.

CATALOGING

GOAL OF CATALOGING

The comprehensive goal of cataloging is to assist library users and staff in the determination and the location of available resources which will best suit their specific needs and best satisfy their particular purpose.

The goal of management in cataloging is to ensure that the instrument for accomplishing the total goal of cataloging, i.e., the catalog, has the greatest possible capability and the most continuous currency, and that it be provided as economically as possible. Management, therefore, focuses on organizing the cataloging process so that it produces a catalog with the required entries, makes the resources which the catalog describes rapidly available, and operates as inexpensively as possible.

As demonstrated in the selection and acquisitions processes, the manager organizes the cataloging process using the basic procedural plan for process design as a guide. Some of the major decisions and objectives that pertain specifically to cataloging procedures are analyzed in the following paragraphs.

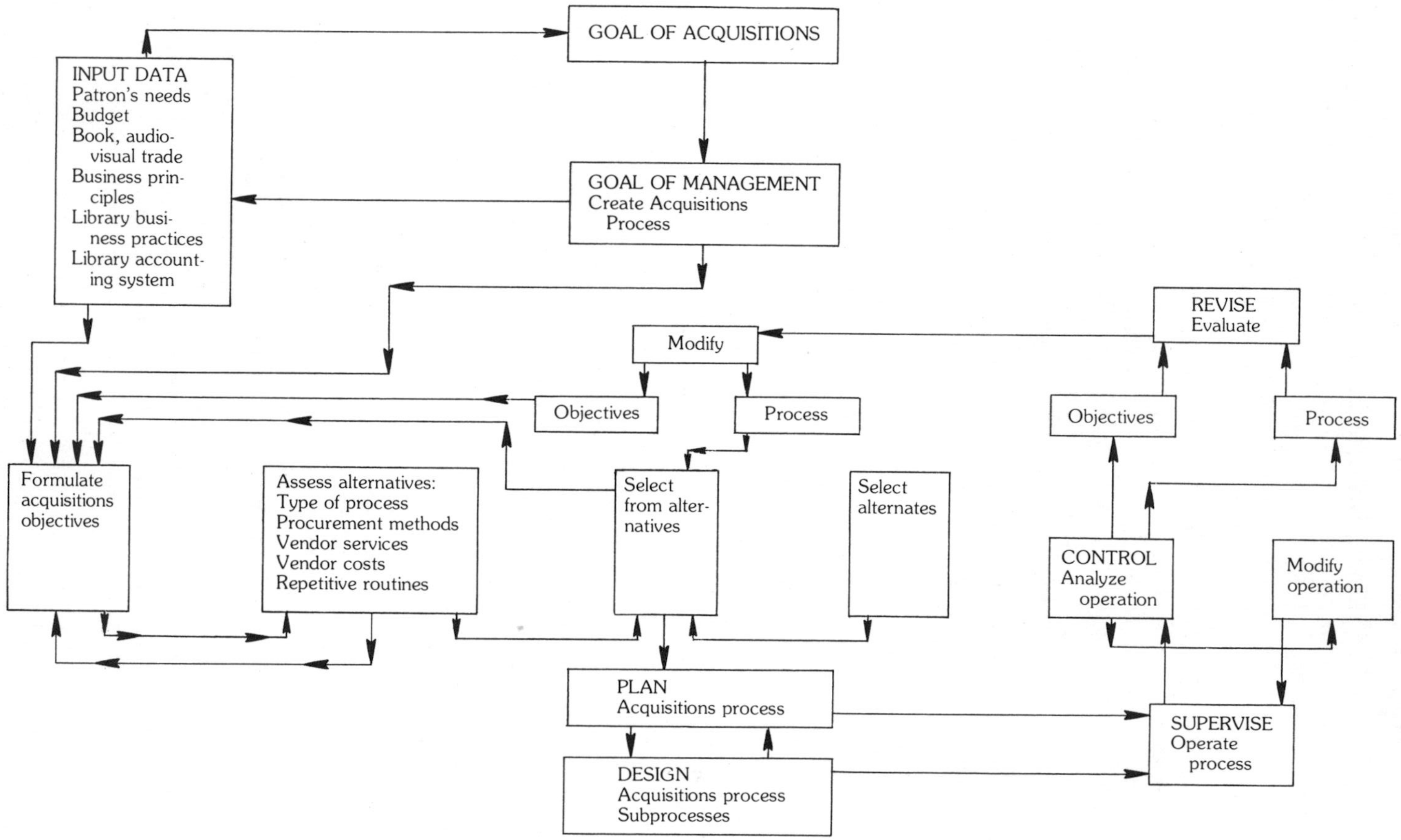

Figure 34. MODEL OF MANAGING THE ACQUISITIONS PROCESS

PLANNING THE CATALOGING PROCESS

In addition to the general knowledge, analytical skill, and clear thinking needed to plan a process efficiently, planning the cataloging process also requires a body of specialized knowledge. Knowing the details of the rules for cataloging is not necessary (unless, of course, the manager is also the cataloger) but a familiarity with the rules is essential. The manager should keep abreast of the latest developments in the establishment of national and international standards for the bibliographic control of all types of materials and should have an understanding of the basic elements of various systems of information storage and retrieval. The manager should be informed about the availability of commercial cataloging services and, with staff participation, be sufficiently proficient to assess the worth of such services for the cataloging process.

If, for example, the library's books are cataloged by a commercial company which is forced to discontinue its service, the manager must provide a substitute source of cataloging, either by adding professional personnel to the staff, which budget limitations may prevent, or by procuring service from another cataloging firm. In such a situation decision and action must be rapid in order to prevent a breakdown in the coordination of work in the cataloging process. If the manager is uninformed concerning the availability and quality of other cataloging services, and their compatibility with the library's cataloging, an appropriate research will have to be conducted which may take a considerable amount of time. During this period a backlog in cataloging can build up very quickly, resulting in the withholding of materials from the user for an excessively long period of time. The manager must also be aware of technological advances which may improve both the efficiency of the cataloging process and its effectiveness, such as better methods of reproducing catalog cards and book catalogs, equipment for enlarging or reducing catalog cards, computer assisted catalog searching, indexing and index locating by mechanical means, and the like. Cognizance of standard and new bibliographic, cataloging, and reference works which are aids to cataloging that will increase the rate of production is also necessary in planning the cataloging process.

The effectiveness of the output of the cataloging process depends primarily on the major decisions which are, in essence, subject to the judgment of the professional librarian. Knowledge of user needs and capabilities and knowledge of cataloging are both required to assess the amount and kind of information that must be provided and the means by which it is conveyed.

Specialization of labor is essential for efficiency in the cataloging process. The basic work performed in the process requires the knowledge and skills of professional personnel who have been trained in all aspects of cataloging. However, there is also a necessity for many tasks with a repetitive pattern which can be accomplished adequately by trained paraprofessionals and clerical staff. Unfortunately, there is a tendency for the professional to expend time and energy on tasks which demand only the skills of the nonprofessional, probably because the work is of such a nature that its various parts seem to merge and flow together.

In many instances, for example, it may seem simpler and faster for the cataloger to type the complete card while cataloging a work. If the cataloger does not happen to be a good typist, the typing of basic information that is easily ascertained and recorded in a set pattern (e.g., author, title, imprint) and the correction of typing errors can consume valuable time which should be devoted to cataloging and staff supervision. In the overall process, it would be more advantageous for the professional to take the time to train paraprofessional and clerical personnel in the handling of these essential but routine elements and the card format required in cataloging. Doing this permits the cataloger to limit the data personally recorded to particularized information for the work in hand, and to use an established abbreviated notation that is understood by the staff. How efficiently the cataloging process operates may depend, therefore, on the manager's competency in analyzing the work required, dividing it into precisely defined segments in which the work to be done is definitely specified, and assigning these tasks to members of the staff who have the appropriate training and skills. How successfully the process operates will then be affected by the manager's proficiency in coordinating these tasks to achieve an unobstructed sequential flow of work.

ORGANIZATION   An analysis of the goal of cataloging emphasizes the fact that organization is the essential requirement for goal achievement. The user must know what resources are available, if they are what is wanted, and, if so, where and how to find them. In addition, this information must be provided as a service which minimizes bother to the user. The service must be easy to use and must supply satisfactory answers as quickly as possible. Materials, therefore, must be furnished with instruments that are sufficiently standardized and consistent so that knowledge of their use can be successfully applied in the majority of libraries. Consequently, not only must the materials themselves be organized, but the pertinent facts about them must also be systematically organized. An effective scheme of organization provides an inventory of the resources available within the particular multimedia library and an index to them, and if required, supplies similar information about resources in other libraries.

To assist in augmenting the functions of the multimedia library the catalog must be instructional as well as informational. The reader may wish to refer back to Example 1 in regard to this. The essential bibliographic and descriptive elements and the analysis of a work presented in the catalog should alert the searcher to the broad spectrum of related subjects and resources that will enhance learning.

Further analysis of the goal of cataloging reveals that the characteristics of the catalog must relate directly to the four principal functions of the multimedia library. The catalog is often considered only an informational tool. This is a valid point of view if the focus is only on the needs of the searcher, and are interpreted as primarily informational. However, if the focus is also on the specific purpose which motivates the user to look for information, the catalog must also be regarded as a means for educational, cultural, and recreational satisfaction.

From the foregoing analysis, it becomes apparent that cataloging is responsible for a versatile output. To channel the different facets of this output into one effective instrument and to ensure that their coverage is comprehensive and complete requires a high degree of coordination requiring a systematically organized process.

PARAMETERS IMPOSED ON CATALOGING   As shown in the selection and acquisitions processes, the design of the cataloging process must also conform to the constraints of the goals, organizational structure, and policies of the entire system, and it must operate without imposing unacceptable limitations on any other element within the total system. Effective cataloging reflects the type of institution which it serves, and the peculiarities of background, degree of sophistication, and educational level of its clientele.

For example, the various descriptive and analytical elements that are emphasized in cataloging in a special library in an automobile manufacturing plant will differ from those that are highlighted in cataloging in a special library in an agricultural firm. In an elementary school library, the amount and kind of information in the catalog entry and the degree of vocabulary simplicity will mirror the capabilities of the elementary school student and will differ from what is included in a secondary school or community college catalog, which should reflect the intellectual and educational capabilities of their respective clientele.

Parameters are imposed on the cataloging process not only by the total system of which it is a part, viz., the multimedia library, but also by the suprasystem in which the library is a subsystem. Cataloging is especially subject to continuously developing constraints which are established in response to social and technological conditions in modern society. The ability for rapid communication has advanced to such a degree that the entire world must now be regarded as a suprasystem which demands an instantaneous exchange of ever increasing information. The recording, storage and retrieval of information can no longer be planned with only an isolated area in mind but must be designed to integrate into a worldwide system. Consequently, rules for national and international bibliographic control of information in all formats, designed to accommodate mechanical and electronic implementation, must be accepted as the basis for cataloging. Traditionally, these cataloging rules are considered authoritative and many catalogers who adhere strictly to them are reluctant to depart from them in any respect. However, the limitations imposed by these rules can be flexible if the rules are interpreted as guidelines, permitting certain adaptations pertinent to local conditions.

POLICY OBJECTIVES IN CATALOGING   Policy objectives provide guidance in determining the best methods for handling different types of resources and for the most advantageous expenditure of time in achieving the goal of cataloging. Cataloging provides one part of the bridge between information and the user. Therefore, policies should be established that assist staff in deciding the methods of handling different types of resources that will meet the specifications for building that part of the bridge for which cataloging is responsible. The pattern for conveying sufficient information will differ for books, pamphlets, periodicals, vertical file materials, pictures, audio recordings, and the like. The various patterns and the conditions under which they are applied should be indicated in a policy statement so that staff will be alerted to the different ways of treating materials and will have a basis for judging the adequacy of description in the pattern suggested for the type of material of a particular work in question. Such a policy statement also assists in orienting the user to the different kinds of resources that are available and what information the user can expect to find about them in the catalog.

Policies should also treat such matters as the amount and kind of descriptive detail to be included in the catalog entry; the necessity for original cataloging; acceptance of commercial cataloging and criteria for assessing quality and compatibility with existing cataloging; revision of accepted commercial cataloging; and other methods of handling incompatibilities resulting from commercial cataloging.

Cataloging is often considered a bottleneck in the total process of preparing resources for use. To avoid a buildup of uncataloged works that obstructs the steady sequential flow of materials from one process to another, policies are needed which indicate the acceptance and use of cataloging aids (e.g., purchased catalog cards), the expenditure of time on essentials and nonessentials (e.g., extensive revision of commercial cataloging), and the basis for priority in the order of processing (e.g., subject, type of material, acquisition).

Many specific details are involved in the work of cataloging. No attempt should be made to identify these details in policy statements. They are numerous, and many constitute exceptions to the established pattern. Consequently, it is better to delineate them specifically in the particular routine to which they pertain. Policies should be formulated in general terms that are yet specific enough to alert the staff to the existence and importance of these details and to provide the guidance that is required for the worker to make decisions and to act upon them.

PROVIDE THE PERSONNEL   In the section on planning the cataloging process it was pointed out that specialization of labor is a prime requisite for the efficient performance of the work involved in cataloging. The staff must include a professional librarian who is also a cataloger and whose duties include not only cataloging, but also staff training and supervision. Sufficient paraprofessional and clerical personnel should be assigned to the cataloging process to take care of the output of the cataloger and the processing of those resources which do not require the cataloger's attention. If the work load is such that another cataloger should be added to the staff, it is poor economy to attempt to reduce the work load by hiring a paraprofessional or clerical person instead. In many instances the result of this kind of personnel policy is to increase the work load of the cataloger and decrease the amount and perhaps the quality of cataloging output. The addition of personnel who do not have the necessary knowledge and skills actually creates an extra drain on the cataloger's time. Too many unskilled workers on the staff exert a deleterious pressure on the cataloger who is faced with the problem of keeping these workers gainfully occupied, and who may thus be forced to attempt to create output beyond realistic capabilities.

Many professionals tend to specialize in cataloging only one type of material such as books, serials, or government documents, and are reluctant to assume the responsibility of cataloging other types of resources which may necessitate adaptations or changes in the work to which they are accustomed. The problem of specialization of labor on the part of the professional is particularly acute in the multimedia library since book catalogers often resist becoming involved in cataloging nonprint materials. In the multimedia library the cataloging of resources in audiovisual media ranks in importance with the cataloging of books. Consequently, the manager must provide leadership and motivation to overcome the cataloger's resistance to change, and through additional training and in-service workshops assist the cataloger in acquiring the special knowledge and skills needed for cataloging nonprint materials.

PROVIDE CATALOGING TOOLS   Using the analysis of the tools of the trade in the selection process as a guide, the tools required to attain and maintain efficiency in the cataloging process can be determined. In addition to the tools that are used in common in all processes, there are certain tools that pertain especially to cataloging, such as the National Union Catalog. Many of these tools, which are essentially cataloging aids, may be very expensive. The manager, in consultation with the cataloging staff, should assess where their use and contribution is sufficient to warrant the large expenditure of funds. In arriving at a decision on the advisability of procuring these aids, the manager must, of course, make an assessment within the framework of the total system, taking into consideration such factors as the number of acquisitions, the amount and kind of information needed for the clientele, budget allotment, plans for future growth, catalog maintenance, types of resources, and so on. For cataloging nonprint media materials, for example, several different aids are essential since standardization in the bibliographic control of resources produced in audiovisual formats is still in a developmental state.

ESTABLISH RELATIONSHIPS WITH OTHER PROCESSES   Relationships of the cataloging process with other processes should be charted as was shown for selection in Figure 28. A visual analysis of how the cataloging process can be affected by the procedures and output of other processes and how it can also affect the operation of other processes helps to focus attention on those procedures that can be streamlined or eliminated when the services of other processes are advantageously used (e.g., subject analysis from selection). In addition, the charting of process relationships often opens up new lines of communication between processes (e.g., between cataloging and reference) which results in more efficient and effective total library service.

CREATE THE PLAN　The first step in creating the plan of the cataloging process is to determine the best type of process. The discussion in acquisitions of some of the different types of processes—manual, automated, cooperative, centralized, and individualized—also applies to cataloging. Because acquisition and cataloging are very closely related in many respects, there is usually less disruption of workflow, greater economy in time and money, and more efficiency when both acquisitions and cataloging use the same type of process.

BASIC PROCEDURES IN THE CATALOGING PROCESS AND THEIR OBJECTIVES

To fulfill its overall goal, the cataloging process must supply the library user with data which describes, analyzes, and classifies available resources. Therefore, four major procedures or subprocesses may be set up to perform the work of *description, analysis, classification*, and *catalog production*. In designing the routines within each of these procedures, various ways of grouping tasks should be considered. Work may be divided according to the type of material since specialized skills are required to catalog materials in different formats and media. The size of the work load and the amount of description required may necessitate a narrower specialization with consequent refinement in task grouping. For example, the handling of print and nonprint materials may be the basis for dividing the work into two separate routines. The tasks in the nonprint routine may be further subdivided on the basis of specific type of material. One routine may be responsible only for 16mm motion pictures, another for filmstrips, audio recordings, slides, and the like.

While the design of the cataloging process must conform to the conditions which exist in the particular multimedia library, the nature of cataloging work itself is an important factor in structuring the process. Most of the work involved in the description, analysis, and classification procedures requires the knowledge and skills of a professional and is so interrelated that, in practice, it may be more efficient to combine the professional work of these steps into one major procedure. Similarly, nonprofessional tasks might also be combined into another major procedure. In this way, also, work that is the same that must be repeated in each procedural step, such as checking original cataloging, or revising commercial cataloging, need be done only once. Whatever the procedural structure deemed to be the most efficient, the basic criterion for its selection from among the various alternatives is always the attainment of the objectives of the four major procedures. To emphasize the importance of always directing the work toward these objectives, the division of work and the sequence of its performance as shown in Figure 35 are structured on the basis of the four major procedures. Clarification of some of the objectives in each of these procedures will be helpful in adapting to the local situation the procedural structure suggested in the chart.

Objectives of *description* are to provide information to identify and describe a work sufficiently to satisfy the needs of the library clientele, and to determine main entry for a work to assist the user in finding it. In order to identify a work and distinguish it from any other work, certain basic elements of information are essential, such as author, title, medium designator (for audiovisuals), and imprint. These elements are recorded in an established sequential pattern. Descriptive information includes elements which describe the physical characteristics of a work, its bibliographic history, and the nature and scope of its content. The extent of the

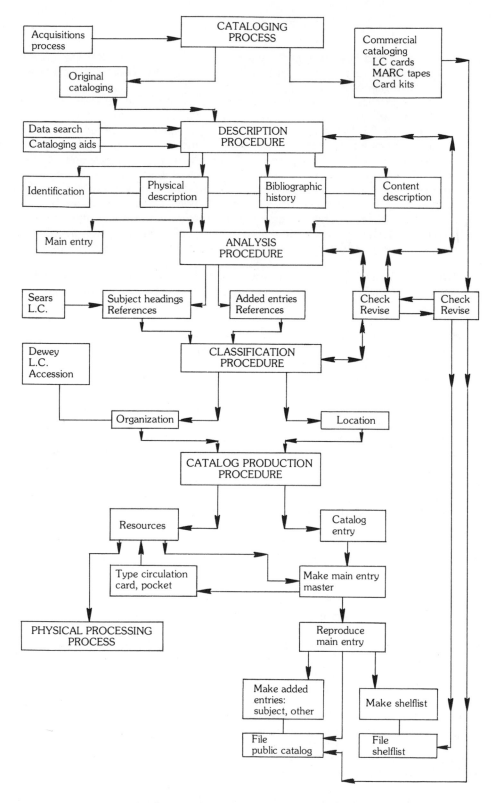

Figure 35. FLOWCHART OF THE CATALOGING PROCESS

information provided in excess of the essential elements required for identification and description will vary in accordance with the goals and needs of the clientele of the particular multimedia library.

For some works, the data required may not be available or easily accessible from the work itself and must be obtained by searching in the appropriate cataloging tools. The need for a data search may occur very frequently in cataloging nonprint media materials since it is often too inconvenient and time consuming to examine a work in its entirety, and discrepancies in identification data are common (e.g., variations in title, series, etc.). Using cataloging aids will also reduce the amount of time needed to determine and record identification data and main entry. Consulting such aids as the Library of Congress catalogs, *Booklist*, and *Previews* can be a very effective means of increasing the quantity of nonprint resources output from the description procedure. The content and bibliographic information given in the description procedure assists the analysis procedure in assigning subject and other added entries.

The procedure of *analysis* is performed with the objective of providing an index to a work which enables the user to find it by subject and by other names by which it may be identified. The analysis procedure is responsible for analyzing the content of a work and determining the descriptors which best convey to the searcher the subjects which it treats. Descriptors should be taken from an accepted standardized list of subject headings such as the Sears or Library of Congress compilations, and the same list should be used for materials in all media formats. Subject analysis assists the classification procedure in placing a work in the most appropriate place in the classification scheme used.

In the analysis procedure, in addition to subject analysis, a work is analyzed to determine other possible names the searcher might look under to find the work, such as title or joint author, and added entries for them are indicated. Both subject and added entry analysis include the provision of those references which will assist the user by bringing the description of related works together in the catalog. They also prevent the catalog from growing at an excessively rapid rate.

The purpose of *classification* is to organize resources for easy retrieval, and to indicate location of resources. Grouping like materials together in a prescribed order helps the user find what is wanted more easily and quickly, and also points to other available resources which may be useful for a particular purpose. In the classification procedure, therefore, using an accepted standardized classification scheme and information from the analysis procedure, the class which is most appropriate for a work is noted on the catalog entry. A classification scheme which systematically organizes knowledge by subject, such as the Dewey Decimal or Library of Congress classification system, is preferred for both print and nonprint resources. An accession number system and a system of grouping by type of material are often used to organize resources in audiovisual media. The decision as to which classification system will be the most efficient and effective will be influenced by such factors in the particular library as storage facilities, size of the collection of various types of materials, policy on public access to resources, and so on. For example, in a library which has a large collection of 16mm reel films which is not open to the user, it may be more efficient to organize the films by accession number and size of reel.

When different types of resources are stored in separate collections and the classification notation does not serve also as a location device, the location should be indicated in the catalog entry. This may be done by coding or some other means which will assist the user in finding the desired material.

The *catalog production* procedure is responsible for the actual production of the catalog which should be in a form easy and convenient to use, and should provide information as economically as possible. The form of the catalog and how it

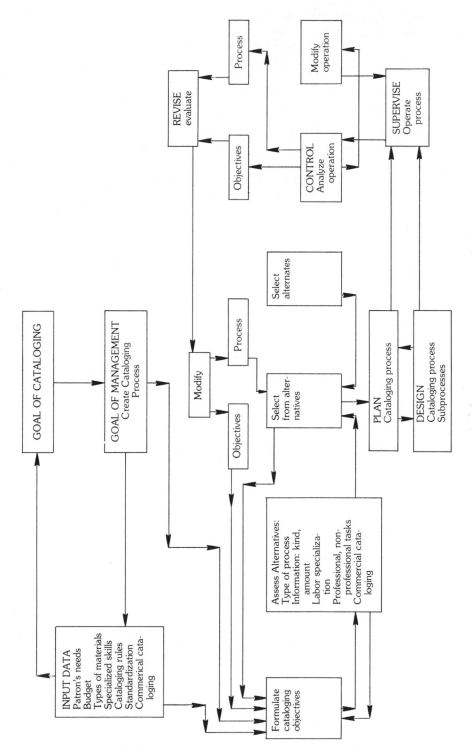

Figure 36. MODEL OF MANAGING THE CATALOGING PROCESS

is produced are directly related to the type of process used for the cataloging process. In an automated process the catalog may be in card or book form; in a manual process the catalog is in card form. In an individualized process where only one set of cards is needed for a work, all the cards may be typed; in a centralized process where several sets of cards are needed for the same work, cards may be reproduced by mechanical means such as xerography and offset printing. In the multimedia library a union catalog which informs the user about all the resources available in various media should be maintained even though many materials may be housed in areas removed from the library. For these resources provision should be made for an additional catalog in the area in which they are stored.

Recording acquisitions information on the shelflist card and filing in the shelflist and public catalog are part of producing the catalog and should be kept up to date. Time and motion will be saved by producing the circulation card and pocket together with the catalog cards rather than in the physical processing process.

Management of the entire cataloging process is portrayed by the model in Figure 36.

PHYSICAL PROCESSING

GOAL OF PHYSICAL PROCESSING

The goal of physical processing is to prepare sources so they can be obtained easily and quickly.

The goal of management in physical processing is to ascertain that resources are so equipped that they may be loaned and returned for continued use without delay.

In the circulation of resources there are established routines through which the resources must pass. Delay in completing these routines is frustrating to the user. Management's job, therefore, is to plan a physical processing process that will operate as efficiently and economically as possible in preparing resources adequately enough so that delay in the mechanics of loan and return is avoided.

PLANNING THE PHYSICAL PROCESSING PROCESS

Besides the general knowledge, analytical skill, and clear thinking that are requisites for efficient planning, physical processing planning requires some additional qualities and special knowledge. Familiarity with the physical characteristics of all types of materials is essential. The shapes and sizes of books are standardized and there are relatively few departures from the standard. For audiovisual materials, however, standardization of shapes and sizes has been slow to develop, and even when a standard has been established, continuous technological research and experimentation produces new materials which do not conform to the standard (e.g., video recording cassettes and cartridges). The manager must be aware of technological advancements which affect the size and shape of new productions and which promote the development of more usable and less expensive containers and storage equipment.

Incompatibility in the sizes and shapes of materials, containers, and storage facilities can add considerably to the cost of resources. For example, full value is not received for funds expended on a separate cabinet for housing filmstrips if the cabinet cannot be used to accommodate filmstrips in cartridges or those of a nonstandard width which require containers of a larger diameter and height.

Familiarity with the physical characteristics of resources coupled with up-to-date information on available processing supplies and equipment can result in further economies. For example, a comparative analysis of sizes and shapes of materials and labels may reveal that instead of using labels of several different sizes and shapes which must be purchased in minimum quantities that exceed the number that the library can use, labels of two sizes only can adequately take care of the majority of the labeling required. Reduction in the variety of labels acquired permits the library to take advantage of discounts for quantity buying since a larger number of the two multipurpose labels will have to be provided. This same kind of analysis for other supplies needed for specific sizes, such as plastic jackets for books, can result in additional monetary savings.

The manager should also be informed about the availability and operation of mechanical processing equipment such as pasting machines, label protectors, laminators, and so on, so that it is possible to realistically judge whether the quality and efficiency of physical processing are increased sufficiently to warrant the cost of such devices. An understanding of assembly line techniques and work simplification methods and how to apply them will result in a smoother coordination of tasks and a greater degree of efficiency and produce an increase in physical processing, another factor which may influence the planning of the process and about which the manager should keep informed so as to make a valid judgment as to its quality, cost, availability, and completeness of coverage of all types of materials.

Efficient planning of the physical processing process calls for imagination and ingenuity, especially in the multimedia library where the inherent nature of materials in various media generates problems in circulation and storage which relate directly to their physical preparation. The manager must be able to visualize how the materials will be placed in the storage facilities, anticipate the kind and extent of damage possible from handling, and the physical deterioration from continued use which may be expected. The manager must exercise ingenuity and aggressiveness in designing and using inexpensive means for solving problems in the housing and protecting of resources. In addition, the manager should always be conscious of the necessity of promoting the use of the library's resources and services, and strive to enhance the multimedia environment by making its resources physically attractive.

In planning the physical processing process the manager proceeds through the steps of the basic procedural plan seen in Figure 26, using information and selecting alternatives pertinent to physical processing in the same manner and in the same detail exemplified in planning the selection process. The manager will study the parameters imposed by the library system and by its clientele, and formulate policies to provide guidance in such matters as the extent and placement of owner identification and labels, the degree of resource protection required, the care and handling of resources, and so on.

Since physical processing tasks can be very adequately performed by nonprofessionals, the manager should provide for sufficient clerical personnel who rate high in manual dexterity, and for training of these personnel in handling processing equipment and in performing specific physical preparation tasks such as pasting in pockets, applying book jackets, protecting labels, and the like. The manager should delegate to one member of the staff the responsibility for supervising the day-to-day operation of this process; selecting equipment, tools, and supplies such as pasting machines, tape dispensers, and preprinted labels that will promote work simplification; charting the interrelationships of physical processing with other processes such as cataloging, circulation, and facility planning; and planning the process so that identified services to and from other processes are used to full advantage.

CREATE THE PLAN   The nature of the work performed in the physical processing process lends itself to a structure that is similar to that used in assembly line

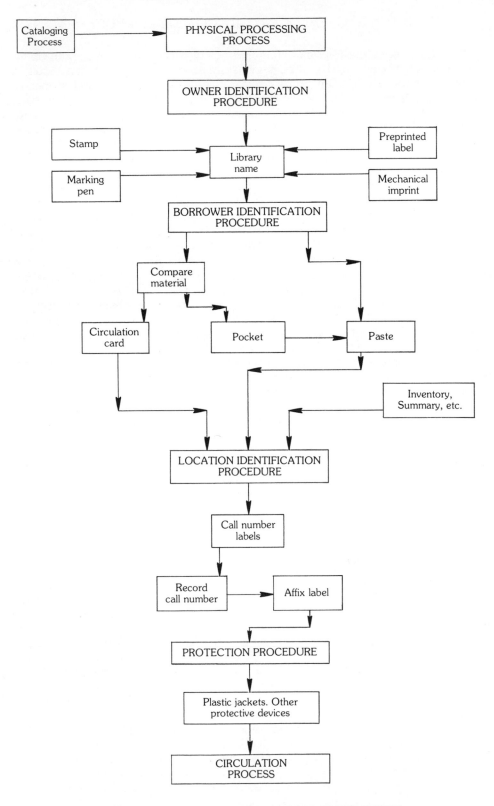

Figure 37. PHYSICAL PROCESSING FLOWCHART

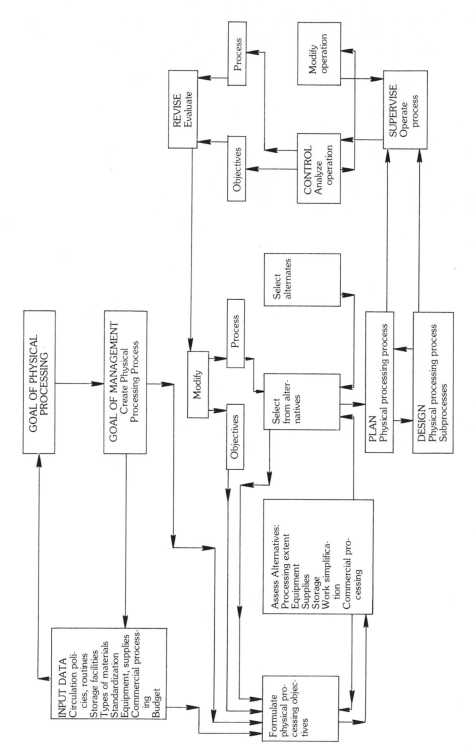

Figure 38. MODEL OF MANAGING THE PHYSICAL PROCESSING PROCESS

production. The overall goal of the process can be translated into four major objectives: to provide *owner identification, location identification, borrower identification*, and *resources protection*. Therefore, the design of the process is based on these four major procedures. Tasks are grouped together and performance routines are established within each procedure. Some of the tasks in each procedure are indicated in the physical processing process flowchart which appears as Figure 37.

The work performed in each procedure is very specific. Its accomplishment requires specific tools and supplies, and there is an uncomplicated, straightforward flow of work from one procedure to another. The procedures may be delineated as work stations structured in an assembly line pattern, and designated by the predominant type of work performed at each station. Thus the owner identification procedure may be called the stamping station; the borrower identification procedure becomes the pasting station; the location identification procedure translates as the labeling station; and the protection procedure is known as the applying station.

Although delineation of this kind is helpful in familiarizing staff with the type of work involved in physical processing, it does not promote objective orientation since it does not indicate why the work is being done. While the workflow pattern is the same, the importance of objectives in work accomplishment and the steady progression toward the attainment of the overall goal of the process should be emphasized by identifying the major procedures by their objectives. The procedure for managing the physical processing process is depicted in Figure 38.

SUMMARY

Acquisitions, cataloging, physical processing, shelving, and storage of the resources of the multimedia library are important areas of management concern which support the circulation and reference services the public sees as the library. These primary supporting activities, along with selection, are the actual operational staff functions of the multimedia library and the central responsibility of the media manager.

Chapter 7 describes procedures in each area of activity at the heart of the whole process, and the need to set them up in terms of their value in making the total process work. Discussion is given to each of the process areas in light of management concerns relating to goals and objectives, scope and limitations, interrelationships, procedures, and related management considerations.

CHAPTER 8

MANAGING PUBLIC SERVICES: CIRCULATION AND REFERENCE

Student viewing educational TV programs. This college has nine RF modulated channels for the main floor of the learning center. (Courtesy of Cuesta College.)

Reference and circulation services in the multimedia library are defined and discussed; their need for management, goals, and objectives defined and described, and procedures overviewed in light of patron needs and expectations and the specific characteristics of the given library. We look at a variety of topics relating to policy, objectives, and procedures in various functional areas of reference and circulation. Discussion is given to the charging system, discharging activities, statistical and record-keeping functions, collection control, security systems, and sensitive processes such as fines and overdues. Weeding and inventory procedures and policies are discussed, together with criteria of importance in planning and carrying out these functions. Implications of contemporary technology for reference and information area management are discussed. Considerable stress is placed upon the philosophical emphasis in reference today, which is seen as one of essentially informational resources management as contrasted with the traditional search and location functions of reference per se. We differentiate between the ivory-tower reference posture of the past and the enterprising position of the present, the difference being one largely of taking a positive, outreach posture toward the patron, and of seeking out needs, rather than simply responding to requests.

This chapter is concerned with the management of the process, or procedures, by which the resources of the multimedia center are made available to the patron, as contrasted with the previous chapter which dealt with preparation of material resources for patron use. More specifically, we are talking about the management of the reference and circulation services of the multimedia library, both print and nonprint.

Reference service is that function of the multimedia library which provides direct aid to patrons in their search for information and knowledge through the material resources available, and the management of those materials.

Circulation pertains to lending material to the patron and assuring the return of such material. The procedures and processes by which these functions are carried out are the primary concern of this chapter. All formats of materials are included in multimedia, of course, and so for purposes of this chapter, all materials will be deemed as integrated in both circulation and reference areas. It is understood, of course, that in the practical instance, integrated shelving of books, tapes, cassettes, and kits, for example, with standardized classification of all formats and standardized circulation procedures for all media, both print and nonprint, may not always be practicable. However, the ideal is to have all such materials together, and in this chapter we will be treating the ideal.

To create effective circulation and reference services, management is needed particularly in the area of cooperative human effort. Management in this context can be considered, in fact, as the process by which the diverse interactions of people involved in helping patrons find and use information are given direction and guidance and controlled in such a way as to provide for the fulfillment of recognized objectives. Good management leads to effective effort on the job and to effective patron service in the areas of reference and circulation.

It is important to stress that the management process in the context of these activities is largely concerned with cooperative human effort. In both circulation and reference, it is the collective human effort of technical and professional employees alike that meets the needs and wants of the multimedia patron. Management integrates the work of these several individuals, and puts it together in the larger context of the multimedia library.

In Chapter 6, considerable discussion was given to management functions and basic procedures in process design. The basic procedures in process management and process design shown in Figure 26, including planning, designing, supervising, controlling, and revising, are directly applicable to the areas of reference and circulation just as they are essential to other areas of the multimedia library.

CIRCULATION

GOAL OF CIRCULATION

Circulation is a primary task of the multimedia library. Its goal is to maximize the availability of all materials to the patron and to actually implement the use of such materials. Unlike the strictly book environment, the challenge of circulation in the multimedia library is to handle a variety of additional formats that depend upon newer technologies, and involve, in addition to just lending materials, the distribution of information and knowledge by electronic and other methods.

Audio and video materials, for example, are often distributed or delivered for use, but not physically lent to the patron. A centralized listening system, providing access to audiotapes or recordings, is a case in point. In other instances, the circulation person has to distribute and demonstrate equipment needed to permit the patron to use materials. The cassette player, for example, the filmstrip viewer, and the slide viewer are some of the portable equipment pieces that are handled by the circulation staff in the multimedia environment.

These differences in format, nonstandardization of physical size, and equipment technologies are all factors which create problems as well as opportunities for the circulation person and for those concerned with the management of the circulation process.

Efficiency and economy are the primary goals of circulation in the perspective of active and creative use of the collection. This means creating effective charging systems and procedures for all types of media and equipment. It means policies which will serve to make materials optimally available to the patron while assuring effective control of those materials. It means procedures which make the handling of books, filmstrips, or large art prints simple, yet comprehensive and workable. It means equipment, from 16mm motion picture projectors to audiocassette players, which must be made available as needed.

Management, in achieving these goals in the circulation area, follows the basic procedures of management-by-objectives as detailed in earlier chapters of this book and as shown in Figure 39.

PLANNING THE CIRCULATION PROCESS

One of the most important aspects of any library service to patrons is the circulation process, and planning is essential in this area to insure quick, efficient, error-free procedures. To many patrons, in fact, the contact made at the circulation desk is their only one, and, thus, the circulation process becomes a strong public relations factor for the library itself. The manager must be concerned with the ease

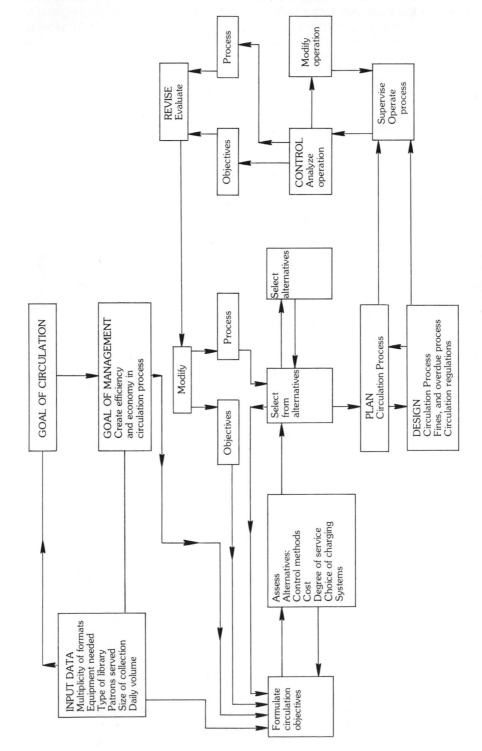

Figure 39. MODEL OF MANAGING THE CIRCULATION PROCESS

and simplicity involved in circulation for both the patron and the staff in using and operating the process. The simpler the process, the easier it is for both the patron and the staff.

In planning the circulation process, there are many factors that management must consider. Some of these are discussed in the following paragraphs.

In handling many types of media, it is necessary to provide for a *multiplicity of formats*. Models, cassettes, filmstrips, art prints, and 8mm loops, for example, may be circulated, as well as conventional book and periodical materials. The circulation of cassettes and 8mm loops also necessitates circulation of the equipment needed to utilize these materials. The process utilized to do this must be planned to handle the size of the collection, the daily volume expected, and the types of materials circulating. The larger the collection and volume of circulation, the larger and more involved will be the circulation process.

A public library and a school library will often have different circulation processes, reflecting the *different patrons served*. The public library, for example, serves an entire population with a range of patrons from child to adult, while a school library would have a captive population with a much narrower range of interests and needs. The school library would also probably have more control and access to patrons, and the circulation process could be much simpler.

Degree of service given is an additional factor to be given careful consideration when planning. Are all multimedia materials to be circulated? Is equipment to be made available to the patron for home use? These kinds of questions must be answered by management to help decide the kinds of patron services to be offered. It is well to be reminded that in answering these questions, the goals of the institution and the specific objectives of the multimedia library must be considered as the basis for any decisions reached.

The last factor, but certainly not the least to be considered in planning, is *cost*. The major items involved are personnel, equipment, supplies, and the maintenance of any automated or mechanical equipment used for the circulation of materials. Planning must include the necessary research to assure that the circulation process is an efficient and economical one.

The patron needs the flexibility of using materials when and where they are wanted, to the extent that this is reasonable and possible. There is a *need for a workable circulation process* which is efficient, simple, and economical. When materials are lent out many other needs are created, such as registering patrons, collecting statistics to measure efficiency, and setting up controls to assure security, housing, and storage. Processes involving inventory and weeding of the collection must also be developed.

A final need in the circulation process is the cancellation of the patron's responsibility for materials after their return. This process, in turn, creates overdue and fine work plus the return of materials to storage so they can be readily used by the next patron.

Parameters imposed on circulation arise from several factors: type of library, basic philosophy, and goals and policies of the public the library serves. The public library, for example, is set up to circulate materials. A special library for a business may not circulate material, but simply act as a reference source.

In the case of the multimedia library, the need for parameters is amplified by the number of different materials that do not readily lend themselves to circulation. Materials such as videotapes, fragile models, specimens, and the like, may not be suitable for circulation. If 16mm films are circulated, a decision must be made as to whether the projector is circulated also.

Circulation regulations usually describe the parameters which apply to circulation. Many libraries have limits on the number of items that a patron may check out.

A school library, for instance, might have a limit of six books at any one time. Other considerations include the length of time the material may be kept (two weeks, one month); whether or not the material may be renewed and if so, whether renewals may be made by telephone. Is there a varying circulation period according to the material (two weeks for books, 24 hours for filmstrips)? Are fines to be charged on overdues, and if so, what is the amount per day? These concerns determine the parameters of the circulation system.

The circulation system itself becomes a parameter. A sophisticated system that is difficult for the patron to understand and use will effectively limit use patterns. Ease of use is an important determinant in the success of a library loan program.

Provision of personnel is another factor for management consideration. The circulation process can be operated quite adequately by paraprofessionals, clerical personnel, and student aides. Professional involvement generally would be restricted to determination of basic policies and procedures, and general supervision. When the basic process has been established, including policies on handling overdues and fines, a lead paraprofessional or clerk can handle the day-to-day supervision.

The manager will have to operate on the basis of exception. Needs may occur which are not covered by policy or process. In these cases, the manager will be called on to make a decision or take some other appropriate action.

OBJECTIVES IN CIRCULATION

POLICY   Policy objectives in the circulation area of the multimedia library relate to, and are determined to a greater or lesser extent by, the type of library, the character of the patron population, the nature and variety of the collection and its supporting equipment, and other factors. Public, school, special, university, and college libraries, for example, each have different needs based upon these many factors, and thus have differing policies to support objectives related to these needs. Special problems related to these several factors also have an impact upon the nature and type of policy developed, and accordingly, upon policy objectives in general.

Policies that set up a framework for control of the use, abuse, and theft of library materials, for example, relate directly to these factors, as do policies relating to charge-out periods, fines for overdues, and the like. Where management is concerned with security aspects of its collection, it must decide what kind of a security system is needed, a decision, in turn, which will depend on the type and size of the library plus the interests and objectives of the institution or community the library serves. More and more the necessity of protecting materials so that all patrons have equal access to them, plus consideration relating to the cost of replacement, makes some kind of security system mandatory. These factors, combined with the cost of such a system itself, are prime concerns in decisions in this area. Policy supporting any decision to provide security for the collection must of necessity reflect cost as a factor in any implementation in design.

Management must make basic decisions of a policy nature relating to what materials will be protected and how. Carrying this a step further, it is also plain that such decisions can affect other policies relating to the integration of materials in general as related to storage and shelving.

Certainly a basic circulation policy that must be of concern to the multimedia library manager is what materials and equipment are to be circulated in the first place. Limited circulation of some items, for example, is almost always feasible and necessary for a variety of reasons. Length of period for which materials may be charged out, and to whom, is another concern. In school libraries, for example, it is not uncommon to find policies which provide for checking out of nonprint materials, such as slides, to faculty only. It is not unusual to find varying check-out periods according to format in many libraries. A seven minute, 8mm loop, for example, might have a 24-hour circulation period, while an art print might have 30 days.

The age-old problem of overdues and fines is another area in which the need for policy objectives and policy statements is a recognized management imperative. The professional literature is full of pros and cons relating to this problem. And of course there are other areas in which clear policy objectives toward which statements of policy and procedures for implementation can be articulated. It should suffice here to note these few examples, and to stress again that management must be prepared to give primary and concerned interest to policy considerations in the areas of circulation generally, security of the collection, fines, overdues, renewals, and the like.

The objectives of circulation have to do with the actual lending of materials to patrons in the most effective and efficient manner. To maximize the availability of materials to all users without excessive delays is a highly important circulation objective.

LIMITED CIRCULATION   In carrying out these objectives in the multimedia library, a concern of primary significance is the need for limited circulation. Nonbook or audiovisual materials, for example, usually require restricted or limited circulation. In theory it would be desirable to treat all media as unlimited in access. However, practical considerations generally force the manager to impose some kind of restrictions or limitations on the circulation of such materials. Formats change, of course, and thus technological and related factors change, and the need for restrictions should be expected to change accordingly. Phono discs, for example, may be considered fragile because they are easily damaged by improper care and faulty use; the uniqueness of large maps, mockups, and models makes their control a matter of importance.

Other technical considerations as well as limitations in the availability of equipment can also affect circulation. Microforms can be used only with proper readers, for example, and so the bulk and cost of the readers necessitate that they be restricted to use only in the library itself where they are housed. Perhaps the portable lap reader will change this, and eventually microforms can be circulated in the regular lending pattern.

Technology will, in time, alleviate other equipment restrictions. The development of the audiocassette in recent years, for example, makes it possible to circulate audiorecordings using inexpensive cassette players. Equipment for 16mm and 8mm films still presents problems, however; the main one being the cost of having sufficient projectors to circulate them. And of course it will be some time before the average person will have a personal home videotape player. Thus, videotapes are apt to be limited to library use for some time to come.

CHARGING SYSTEM   A central and highly visible function of the typical library is the charging system. To the average patron, in fact, it is the library. Some examples of charging system objectives are accuracy, economy, and ease of patron use. To these may be added the need of such a system to provide for rapid return of materials to storage or shelving for further use and flexibility and simplicity for clerical, library aide or student assistant implementation. In short, to be effective a charging system must be accurate in detail, easy to implement, and within budget and personnel constraints and capabilities. The charging and discharging activities of circulation alluded to above are varied, and there are innumerable systems in use and commercially available ranging from the book card Newark System to mechanical and computer based systems. In selecting a system, management must weigh initial staffing, equipment, and continuing supply costs. The manager must select a system that will handle all of the circulating material, including nonprint items. The system must be able to charge out a book or pamphlet as easily as a model or filmstrip.

Simplicity, another factor suggested above, is of great importance, assuring less chance for error and enhancing borrower participation. A rule of thumb the multimedia library manager should always keep in mind is that the less the borrower has to do to check out material, the more willing the patron will be to return as a user. Charge-out cards or slips, for example, should be easy to retrieve and replace in the material. The process should be convenient and visible to both the patron and the staff member, allowing the patron to experience the least pressure while withdrawing an item, and the staff member more time and ease in working directly with the patron.

REGISTRATION   The objective of registration, a key element in the charging system, is to correctly identify all active patrons of the multimedia library. As noted in the previous section, the type of charging system used will significantly influence patron use of the facilities and services of the library. This also holds true for registration.

DISCHARGING MATERIALS   The primary objective in the discharging of materials is to cancel in the most efficient and accurate method possible the borrower's responsibility for the materials. In the time-honored book card system, it is simply a matter of going through the circulation file, retrieving the card from the date due section and returning the card to the pocket or other container on the material. In the process of returning the card, it is necessary to check the material on the pocket or other container to be sure that the correct card has been pulled and is being replaced.

Management must also decide at this point on how far to go in inspecting for wear and damage. A great deal of staff time can be spent, for example, inspecting nonprint materials because they are often not easy to inspect. A book can be examined rather quickly; in most cases, in a very few seconds. It is rarely possible to readily discover damage to an 8mm film loop, however, without running the entire loop.

One of the most important factors in discharging materials is accuracy, both on the part of the staff member and of the process itself. Inaccuracy in a discharging system will create animosity on the part of a borrower for a variety of reasons, the most common being receipt of mistaken overdue and fine notices.

Good public relations is perhaps the term which needs to be stressed here. Many times the impression a patron obtains of a library is directly related to the degree of efficiency that patron experiences in the discharge procedure. Errors in the procedure directly affect relationships with the library and can give the patron a very poor opinion of the library even though all of the other services and activities are of the highest caliber.

As suggested above, an important aftermath of the discharging procedure is overdues and fines and what is done about them. Much has been written on the pros and cons of fines, but the fact remains that overdues are a problem, and management must decide what to do about the borrower who holds materials past the due date. The type of library and patron, of course, determines to some extent the position taken about fines. It is not unusual for an elementary school library, for example, to eliminate fines, while a university or college library will stress the use of fines to keep the materials coming in. In any case, whatever management decides to do, it is important for good public relations that the patron be fully informed about overdues and fine procedures.

Another very real management problem is to decide where to draw the line on abuse of borrowing privileges and what to charge for such abuse when it occurs. The main objective of fines is to encourage the borrower to return materials on time so that others may utilize them. Fines and overdue penalties are intended to be incentives, not punitive measures levied against the borrower.

The problem facing management in this kind of situation is that if they put the fine too low it does not encourage the patron to return the material. If the fine is put too high it discourages the patron from borrowing altogether. Theoretically it would be possible, of course, to set up a fine system that would be so effective, on a punitive basis alone, that there would be no need for fines; there would also, however, probably be no circulation. Somewhere within the extremes possible there needs to be a figure which serves as an incentive to responsible borrower habits.

A word needs to be added here about fine rates as related to different types of loans. It is usual, for example, for a fine on a reserve book which is checked out for 24 hours or less to be considerably higher than the fine on a general collection book that is checked out for two weeks. Again, decisions and recommendations on how much such fines should be need to be based upon a realistic appraisal of the needs of the collection, the character of the library and its users, and the usefulness of the fine procedures in assuring prompt return of materials.

In dealing with overdues, management must decide on how to make the system most useful and capable of implementation. For example, how many notices are sent out to remind the borrower that the material is overdue? The more notices sent out, for example, the more staff time must be spent on this function.

Management must also consider, insofar as staff time is concerned, when to send out the first notice. It has been found, for example, that most overdue material is returned within the first five days after actual due date. Therefore, if the first overdue notice is not sent out until the sixth day, staff time is reduced considerably. In many school libraries, of course, it is extremely important to get materials back without delay, and overdue notices may be sent out the first day. Management in this instance must provide for the considerable staff time required to handle this type of volume.

It is worthy of note here that records relating to overdues and fines can be extensive. Keeping these records up to date can be one of the most time-consuming tasks in circulation, particularly where flagrant violators are concerned. These patrons accumulate huge fines and can create such a problem that the library must have procedures that may even lead to legal action. Confronting the violator with this possibility may be a deterrent against further abuse of privileges. In any event, unpleasant as it may be, management may have to make decisions on how far to pursue the flagrant violator. The point: To deter other patrons from abuse of borrowing privileges, the multimedia manager must have some kind of system by which to impress the violator of the impracticality of abusing library privileges. Again, looking at fines and related procedures as incentives rather than punitive measures it is nevertheless necessary to have the capability of "putting teeth" into the system if needed. In public libraries there have been cases where police or other public enforcement personnel have been sent to the borrower's home. In college and university libraries, laws have been passed allowing the institution to withhold grades or transcripts until fines have been paid or materials returned or replaced.

In the collection of these fines and fees it is important to have an accurate and foolproof accounting method so that there is no problem with theft, misappropriation, or misplacement of the money collected. The fine, for example, should be paid at the time the material is returned so that additional records and files are not needed. A simple calculation process should be used so that it is easy for the staff member to calculate and for the patron to understand.

Finally, fine collection procedures should include provisions by which a written record of a fine payment is provided and where accountability for further disposition of the money received is assured by the staff member. Questions at a later date on the payment of the fine should be a matter of written record. A sample of such a record is included as Example 14.

Other charges that management in the multimedia library must consider are those levied for lost, damaged, or otherwise altered materials. Most often the patron who has lost material is charged the replacement cost plus an amount to cover the expense of implementing that replacement. Replacement charges or fees must be validated, of course, on the basis of actual figures determined by responsible authority in the library. Examples of such charges include repair costs for damaged materials such as 16mm films, filmstrips, maps or globes, and the like, or the cost of rebinding a book.

The circulation area may also have to be concerned with rental fees or charges for such services as photocopying. Different kinds of services have to be kept separate as far as accounting is concerned because fines for overdues and the like, in many cases, are utilized differently than are charges for lost books, rental fees, and photocopy service. It is important for the multimedia manager to set up appropriate record-keeping procedures to take care of the receipt, processing, and forwarding of these various monies according to the policies and directives of the institution with which the library is associated.

EXAMPLE 14
SAMPLE FINE RECORD

HICKS COLLEGE LIBRARY
FINE RECORD

Date _____

Patron's Signature	Title of Material	Fine Amt.	Lost Amt.	Recd. by

STATISTICS   Again, accuracy, efficiency, and comprehensiveness are keynotes in the statistical collection activities of the multimedia library. The objective, of course, is to provide a basis for understanding, planning, and carrying out the circulation job in terms of user demand and use characteristics. Statistics on the volume and types of materials circulated as was shown in Example 4, and the incidence of overdues, fines, lost materials, and patron use, are among the variety of data that is not only helpful, but in fact crucial to management in identifying problems, finding solutions, and making decisions.

Statistics that show a sudden drop in circulation, for example, or an unusual increase, can alert the multimedia manager to a developing problem or need. Statistics can also be used to enhance efficiency by dramatizing comparative figures. Many statistical studies done at individual libraries have led to innovation and improvement in circulation procedures and methods. Even simple surveys have led to improved, patron-oriented circulation systems, increased circulation of materials by type of subject, and other important changes in multimedia library practice. Statistical record keeping is of course enhanced greatly by computer-based circulation systems. Terminals giving the library on-line capability can be used to produce statistical information of all kinds on demand with little or no manual record keeping required beyond that needed to provide the input data required by the program.

COLLECTION CONTROL   The main objective of collection control is to assure that materials are readily available and that adequate space has been provided for their housing and storage. Collateral objectives include security of these materials against theft, abuse, and damage. Inventory and weeding, which are key collection control tasks, serve the objective of keeping the subject matter current and records accurate. Management of the storage area itself must assure that all materials are kept in their proper places for easy patron access. The ideal is to have open stacks or storage areas completely accessible to all patrons, but there are some factors which limit the attainment of this ideal. Some media materials, for example, are fragile, and cannot be made directly available to the patron. Some equipment needs to be utilized in the other functions of the multimedia library, and therefore must be maintained in a controlled access area.

Accordingly, one of the first management decisions that must be dealt with in a multimedia library is that of deciding what materials will be given open patron access. As the collection grows, more important management decisions will need to be made on policies relating to growth or to addition of auxiliary storage areas, and concomitantly, to the question of access to such areas.

A useful example of restricted access is the reserve shelf. Reserve collections are found particularly in college and university libraries. They include materials which are placed there by faculty members or the library staff and specified for a given (restricted) loan period to allow access to a greater number of patrons. These materials are usually kept in a closed access area for control, which requires that a staff member serve the patron in a request for use of the material. The loan period is always different and generally shorter than the regular circulation period, and can be as brief as one hour. Control is obtained by noting on the card catalog or other source that the material is on reserve. Set apart from the regular collection, these materials must be quick and easy to find and to return to their shelving location. A backlog of unshelved materials in the reserve area can create breakdowns in service and bad impressions with patrons. It must be emphasized that materials not so shelved, or misshelved, are not readily available to the patron. Special searches for lost or misplaced materials, particularly in a restricted access collection, require a great deal of valuable staff time, and create problems that damage patron goodwill.

Reshelving of materials in the reserve collection, however, is not the only problem area of concern to multimedia library management as related to the return of materials. Materials in general that are used by the patron in the library and not reshelved are a primary matter of concern—as are those attempts by well-meaning patrons who reshelve themselves, often incorrectly. It is a usual procedure for libraries to indicate to patrons that they should not reshelve materials, but leave them on a carrel or table for reshelving by staff members. Management must then develop a procedure to support this practice which will assure that such materials are then reshelved very quickly by staff.

Most print materials, of course, such as books, are shelved according to a classification system which is basically subject oriented. Other multimedia materials, such as filmstrips or transparencies, many times are shelved according to format or by an accession number system. Staff members must understand the need for such special handling and adapt carefully to this requirement.

A main concern of management in this regard is to motivate the staff doing the shelving to be efficient and accurate. Shelving of material, particularly, can become an unattractive, boring task. Shelf reading, one of the important aspects of this function, is often less than stimulating, and essentially routine. A procedure which provides for adequate staffing and supervision therefore, in shelving and related tasks, is essential to effective management in this area of multimedia library operation.

SECURITY SYSTEMS   A primary objective of management is to protect and control the materials collection so that the availability of all materials to the patron is maximized. A major problem encountered in accomplishing this, however, is the utilization of a system that does in fact provide the needed security, while impairing and restricting the circulation of materials to the least extent possible. Ill will and distrust on the part of the patron are considerations that must be guarded against carefully.

Management, on the other hand, wants the patron to know that there is a security system, because this knowledge tends to discourage the impulsive removal of materials by patrons who would not ordinarily steal, as well as restrict outright, deliberate theft. Many patrons, in point of fact, do not really mean to steal the material, but there are those who simply do not want to take the responsibility for the materials in an official way by signing or otherwise formally having the materials lent to them. In many cases such patrons actually intend to return what they remove. But management must guard against this practice in any event, recognizing of course that security systems requiring a complicated or elaborate method for checking out or charging of material, or which create a serious threat of search to the patron, can reduce circulation and the use of materials in general. The patron's privacy and integrity must be taken into account, on the one hand, while sufficient precautions are being taken to protect the collection for use by all.

Cost is another important factor in management decisions on security systems. Cost will affect the decision on whether or not to have such a system in the first place. If the cost of replacement of lost or missing materials is very low, for example, it may be better to take that loss rather than to incur the expense of installing a security system which has a dollar impact as well as a possible alienation effect on patrons. A study on loss activity and replacement cost is a good basis for approaching such a decision.

In this regard, it is important to stress that the percentage of book loss should not be figured in terms of the entire collection. To say, for example, that book loss is only 1 or 2 percent of the book collection is to use a comparative base which does not provide a valid picture. The more useful relationship to consider is what percent of the yearly acquisitions is being lost. For example, a loss of 2,500 items per year might be a low percentage of the entire collection, but it might be 40 or 50 percent of new acquisitions. And since most surveys of losses show that the materials taken are frequently part of the newer acquisitions, this insight becomes significant as a decision factor. It is very difficult to keep an adequate and contemporary collection of materials if a large percentage of new acquisitions disappears each year.

The actual cost of installing a system will depend upon the individual facility. Factors which will affect the decision will include, for example, how many turnstiles, and what number and type of security system consoles will be necessary to control the exits of a particular library. The multimedia manager will want to obtain estimates of installation costs through representatives of the security systems available. Continuing annual cost must also be a consideration.

Another factor of importance when making a decision on whether or not to install a security system is abuse of sensitive material when circulated, and the extent to which access to the collection must be limited because of this factor. Audiocassettes, for example, films, microforms, and the like, are subject to considerable damage from handling and negligence.

Finally, in the multimedia library there is the management decision on what materials to protect. All security systems do not provide protection to all nonbook materials. Generally most nonbook materials can be protected by the sensors, but depending upon the system used, magnetic tapes may have to be handled by a different procedure than that used on print materials so that magnetic tapes do not go through the desensitizing process.

Perhaps to say more here would be to overstate the case. Suffice it to say that the question of whether or not to install a security system in the multimedia library is one which must be carefully considered by management in light of loss factors, cost, patron needs, and the characteristics of the physical facilities themselves.

WEEDING AND INVENTORYING   The weeding process has as its objective the withdrawal from the collection of materials that are no longer useful. To put this another way, the weeding process is a means for keeping the collection current. And currency, in this context, means usefulness of items in the collection to support the needs of the patrons; in the educational environment, the student and teacher. Weeding is normally best and most conveniently accomplished as a part of the inventory procedure. Criteria that may be used in weeding materials include the following: (1) The physical condition of the material. If a book or nonprint item is badly damaged and must be rebound or extensively repaired, the better alternative is to consider removing it and replacing it with a new edition or model; (2) The age of the material. Has the material been in the collection so long that it has deteriorated and is no longer usable? Microfilm, for example, or books that have deteriorated from age should be weeded and replaced; (3) Is the subject material contained outdated to the point where it should be replaced with newer material? Many times the copyright date is effective in determining the appropriateness of the material; in other cases, the subject matter department or division of the institution may provide a judgment when a copyright date suggests possible obsolescence; (4) Has the material been superseded by better or more up-to-date material, even though it is only a year or two old? Again, a review of the literature and other appropriate evaluative procedures may suggest removal and replacement of an item; Finally, (5) Is the material no longer suitable to the collection? In a school or academic library, for example, where the curriculum has changed to the point where the material is no longer pertinent, there is reason to weed.

In any case, weeding should be considered both as an important function in keeping the collection current and as a part of the selection process as well. Obviously, in weeding out material, the same care and professional skill must be applied as is used in selecting materials for the collection in the first place. Often more people may be involved in weeding than in selection, because, although it is not unusual for one person to select materials, it may take a concensus to justify withdrawals. In academic libraries, for example, a librarian may withdraw a piece of material from the collection for replacement, renewal, or repair, but before it is physically destroyed or discarded it should be brought to the attention of the faculty members or subject matter specialists on the staff who can make an enlightened judgment on the basis of current curriculum and the shared knowledge of the discipline.

Because of the stress and emphasis now placed upon the economics of multimedia library operations, it is necessary for management to consider a growth policy as related to weeding. More and more in the literature today are found discussions of zero growth. Where this concept is found, for a variety of good reasons, there are serious implications for weeding. It becomes necessary in practice, under a zero growth policy, to weed out the same number of items in the collection as are to be added through the acquisitions process. And such a policy becomes more and more an imperative for some libraries, because of the tremendous cost involved in adding additional storage facilities. Now and in the future, it may be necessary for all libraries to give serious concern to a weeding policy and process which can implement zero growth, or at least carefully control the requirements of the collection process for storage and handling of materials. It is possible that technology will continue to take some of the pressure off by developing alternative storage methods, materials, and formats, as for example, microforms have done, which would reduce the need for increased storage space while permitting growth and expansion of the total collection. Finally, in developing a weeding process for whatever reasons, management must also be concerned with the costs involved.

Inventorying is the process by which the basic record or the shelflist of the multimedia library is actually checked against the shelves or stored materials to determine (1) whether the material is still actually available, and (2) what its condition is. The objective of inventorying, accordingly, is to assure accuracy of the records and related documents of the collection.

In the process of planning for an inventory, management must first make certain policy decisions. It must decide whether to inventory at all; whether to inventory the entire collection or only a part of it; and whether there is sufficient staff and funding available to do the inventory. A complete inventory can be costly and time consuming, but if it can be done in a relatively short period of time and within staff and budget constraints, there are many advantages to taking a complete annual inventory.

On the other hand, if an inventory procedure is going to seriously disrupt service to the patrons, for example, management should consider an alternative plan such as a partial inventory, a portion of the collection being inventoried perpetually so that over a period of time the complete collection is done.

A flowchart of the inventory process can be seen in Figure 40. Methods used will vary from library to library, but they are all similar in that the primary record used is the basic shelflist or similar record, which is checked against the actual shelves or storage areas and the discrepancies noted. If management does decide to weed and develops a policy and procedure for it, it is best to complement this with an inventory. The two processes can be very easily combined.

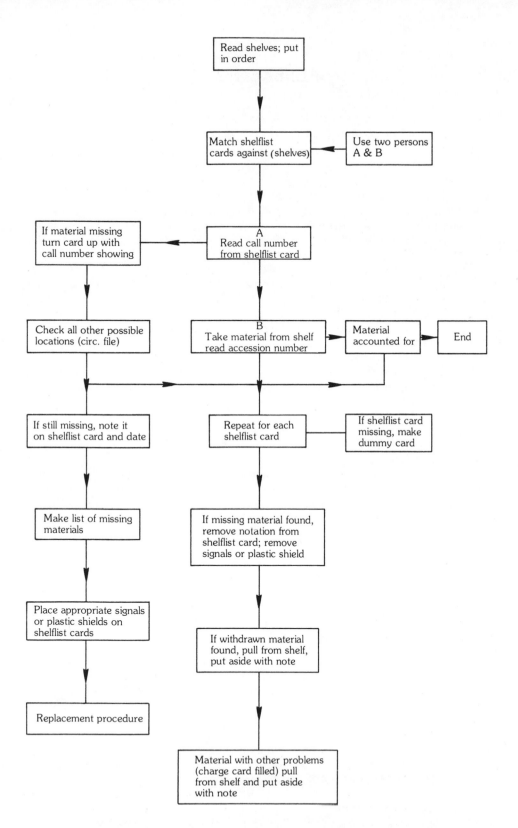

Figure 40. FLOWCHART OF THE INVENTORY PROCESS

REFERENCE

GOALS OF REFERENCE

The main goal of reference is to provide access for the patron to the information resources contained in the multimedia library. Note the terminology *information resources*, not reference collection. In filling a patron's request in a multimedia library, attention must be given to the informational distribution and transmission aspects of closed circuit television, dial retrieval systems, programmed materials, computer assisted reference service, and many media formats, such as filmstrips, slides, 8mm film loops, and microforms. At the present time there is some discussion in the profession as to whether the traditional reference service should not be called information service.

The use of the new, more comprehensive term is supported here. In the multimedia environment, informational services seems to be more descriptive than the traditional terminology. Most patrons think of reference services as being confined to those requests that can be filled by the so-called reference sources that are located in the reference area. In dealing with multimedia it is found, however, that the information needed to respond to requests is not limited to the traditional sources.

Providing information or reference service in any case is a critical responsibility of multimedia library management in meeting the needs not only of users but also of the prospective user. Management becomes responsible for coordinating all efforts to give the user access to all of the information resources available, both on-site and outside the walls of the local library. A trend that is going to affect reference and information services in any given multimedia library is that toward regional or national reference or information resource centers.

With the development of on-line computer capabilities, it is highly possible that even the smallest library will have informational access to resources far beyond the confines of its own walls. There are already many on-line applications of the computer and other devices which expand dramatically the informational resources available to patrons. With this capability it is to be anticipated that the tremendous bibliographic store of the nation, perhaps even the world, will become available to patron service.

Management is also going to have to give attention to machine-generated information and reference tools, from machine-readable national catalogs to locally developed reference tools. Thought is also going to have to be given to the use of programmed materials and teaching machines in meeting patrons' requests, as well as for use in teaching and orienting patrons to the informational sources available to them.

IMPACT OF THE SYSTEMS APPROACH   Of substantial effect upon the goals of reference is the introduction of systems concepts and the management aspects of systems in the multimedia library. The management concept as expounded in this book is rooted in the systems approach with its emphasis upon objectives, application of principles, and process evaluation and revision. The main impact of the systems approach as it bears upon reference is that it leads to an evolving process of management at several levels, which in turn provides for change and growth. Unlike the relatively static, traditional pattern of the reference desk, with its ponderous printed compendiums listing sources available for search, the systems approach provides a framework for reference service that is compatible with the considerably broader variety of informational sources that have become available as a result of the development of multimedia formats and techniques.

The advent of the systems approach, with its emphasis upon objectives, will also undoubtedly stimulate research in the area of reference and information services. In the past there was little research done in this phase of library activity because of the emphasis upon human and professional experience in reference work. The individual reference librarian was, in fact, a kind of authority, and a generally comprehensive knowledge of and skill in using the conventional tools of reference was the measure of service provided. Research was little used in this context. A systems approach, however, will necessitate attention to the research necessary to evaluate and revise stated objectives—the foundation of the whole concept.

At the present time, for example, there is a need to learn more about the users of informational services and what their needs are. Traditionally, reference librarians have been more concerned with how to answer a patron's request, than in determining why the request was made. Only research will provide the profession with the understanding of the needs of patrons that is required to provide a basis for the definition and statement of objectives that can make a systems approach work in the context of the contemporary multimedia library. Thus, bringing together of the computer and the systems approach creates both a responsibility and an opportunity for management to seek the answers necessary to make reference and information service more effective, efficient, and in keeping with contemporary information processing capabilities.

It follows, then, that the goal of management in reference is to apply the management process so as to provide the informational services necessary to satisfy a patron's request quickly and efficiently and in terms of a need for knowledge from all available sources. Management must give thought and attention to gearing all its resources—staff, facilities, and equipment—toward that end. Reference or informational services must be perceived as a central responsibility organized to insure the optimum availability of all resources to the patron, including machine readable data and the application of the computer to reference and information functions.

PLANNING THE REFERENCE PROCESS

Management of the reference process requires careful planning. Reference is a basic patron service in which management has the responsibility for assuring that patron requests are answered quickly, accurately, and efficiently.

Management will find it essential to plan even the selection of reference staff. Depending upon the type of library and patron, management's task is to select a staff having subject and library preparation to fit the reference requests and information required by patrons. Many libraries, such as the academic or special library, require subject background of their reference librarians.

The question of the use of paraprofessionals in reference is one that management can answer only with careful planning. The traditional process of having all reference desk inquiries answered only by professional librarians has come under serious question. With the development of trained paraprofessionals, it has become evident that directional questions and ready-reference questions could be handled by the library technician. This should not be thought of as a serious threat to the professional, however. Instead, it should be thought of as time saved to allow the graduate librarian the opportunity to spend more time on the professional aspects of the reference process. Many times the professional cannot spend sufficient time on a research question because of the press of directional questions. Professional time is also needed in the selection and evaluation of the collection.

It is only with planning that management can adequately determine the limits of reference service. In developing the reference process, it is imperative that policies limiting services be determined by forethought as to their consequences. It is not uncommon for public libraries to limit contest questions; for academic libraries to place limits on interlibrary loans, or to implement the concept of self-help by limiting the amount of time spent on any one patron's question.

In planning the reference process, the techniques utilized must be a primary concern of management. Any successful reference technique, for example, must be based on the approachability of the staff. Patrons will not approach and ask questions if staff members appear continually busy. Thus, the staff member who is assigned to handle patron requests should not be visibly involved in other tasks.

Additional reference techniques adding to the effectiveness of the reference process include the following: treat all questions as a private matter between the staff member and patron; place the patron at ease; be sure to listen carefully to the inquiry; and never consider any question as a "dumb" one.

The fiscal implications in planning the reference process relate to materials, staff, equipment, and facilities. It is absolutely essential to have an adequate, current, up-to-date reference collection. This requires planning for the evaluation of the collection, weeding, and selecting new materials. Funds must be anticipated.

Staffing is the most expensive item in the reference process, and management will have to plan carefully for staff. Decisions about needed staff will have to be made on the basis of policies of the reference service as they relate to the balance of professional, paraprofessional, clerical, and student aides assigned.

Specialized equipment, such as microform readers and printers, photocopy machines, and the like, will have to be planned for. In order to utilize all the formats in multimedia reference, filmstrip viewers, audiocassette players, motion picture projectors, and other equipment will have to be provided.

Reference facilities themselves must be well planned so that there is easy access for the patron. There must also be quick and easy access by staff to the reference and general collection, and to appropriate bibliographic tools such as the card catalog and indexes. Management must provide for a traffic flow pattern that will allow such access for staff and patrons.

The basic *need served by reference* is the interpretation of the collection in relation to patron inquiry and the need to know. This involves both helping the patron find information and providing guidance in the choice of materials. There is also a need to carry on instruction in the reference process, implementing the self-help concept.

Reference service is most satisfactory when an effort is made to enable the patron to help himself. This involves formal class instruction on the tools of the library, such as the card catalog and periodical indexes, as well as informal instruction of patrons on a one-to-one basis. In the multimedia environment there are many materials in technical formats which require some assistance for patron use, whether developed in-house or acquired from commercial sources. Instructional helps for use by patrons can be very useful in this regard. Slide-tape instructional programs, for example, for use by the individual patron will enable the patron to make better use of the collection.

A basic element in the reference process is the interview which is typically shared by the library patron and the reference librarian. The librarian needs to know what the patron is seeking. And in many instances, the patron needs to clarify what is being sought. The reference interview is the platform from which this understanding is attained, and fruitful service and search is begun. Thus, the reference process may be seen as an interactional system of relationships between the patron and the librarian, beginning with an understanding regarding a need for information, and culminating in the discovery and use of that information. Figure 41 describes this process.

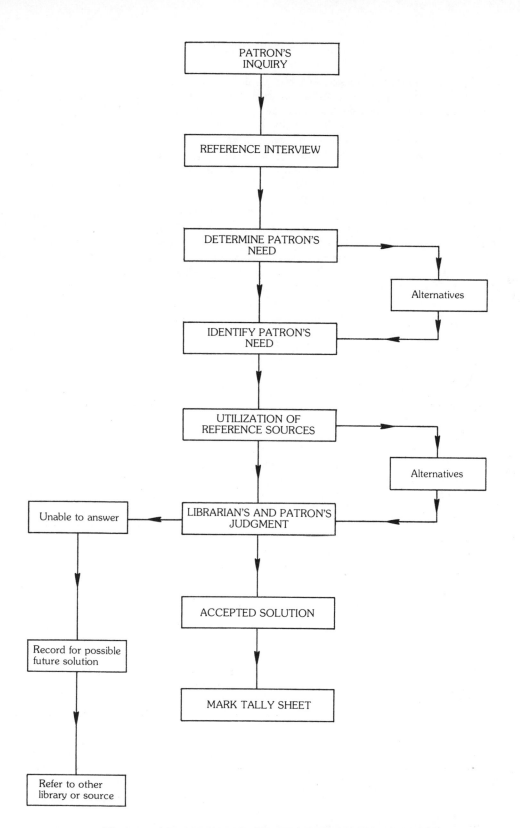

Figure 41. FLOWCHART OF THE REFERENCE PROCESS

In the reference process there are three ingredients: the patron, the librarian, and the collection. Reference tools are a bridging element among them. How well the reference librarian can use the tools of multimedia reference and how adequate these tools are will go far in determining the quality of information delivered.

The *parameters imposed on reference* are many. How adequately the reference process meets reference needs will depend largely upon the skills of the reference staff and the quality of the collection and tools. This, in turn, is affected by management decisions on the amount of fiscal resources assigned to the reference process and management judgments on the limits of the reference process.

As pointed out above, reference skills of the staff depend largely upon the techniques utilized. The approachability of the reference librarian, the skill utilized in the interview, and the judgment and knowledge of reference tools will determine the quality of service. The reference collection and other materials available determine the breadth and scope of information that can be utilized in answering patrons' inquiries. The fiscal support given by management will strongly affect the quality of the collection. Other factors in the quality of the collection are the skill and determination of the staff in reflecting patrons' needs in the selection of sources.

Fiscal realities, of course, affect materials, staff, equipment, and facilities. The reference process is costly in the multimedia library when viewed in the perspective of the number of formats available and the equipment, facilities, and staff needed to utilize all of these formats. Of course, the amount of information available is increased because the patron's need to both listen and view, as well as to perceive by other sensory means, can be fulfilled. To utilize all these different formats, costly, sophisticated equipment may be needed.

Good personnel balance is a vital ingredient in the reference process. The basic need of the reference area is to deal with the patron on a one-to-one basis, but it is most difficult to create "standard operating people." Flexibility and good individual judgment are a must in the reference function and suggest a need for adequate professional staff. Where tasks become routine, on the other hand, paraprofessionals or clerical staff can handle them.

There is indeed a unique and challenging opportunity for the librarian today in this highly specialized field, and in the part informational services management plays in the growing responsibility of the multimedia library to cope with the remarkable expansion of human knowledge in our time.

OBJECTIVES IN REFERENCE

POLICY   As in circulation, management must give attention to the development of policies according to the type of library and patron served. The type of library, for example, will determine to a large extent what policy is needed to provide for the amount of time, effort, and research that may go into answering any one patron's request. In traditional reference work, policy has specified few limitations on the extent of reference help. It is obvious, however, that limitations on staff time and even resources available may be needed to provide for such services, particularly as the volume of demand increases.

The so-called self-help policy has been mentioned. How far does the reference and informational services staff go in teaching patrons to use sources themselves? Obviously, the better users are able to do their own reference work, the fewer will be the number of questions handled by the reference staff. The policy challenge for management and staff in this matter is to decide on the *extent of services provided*; how far the librarians should go in providing answers and conducting searches themselves, and how far they should go in showing the patron how to do it.

A factor which is unique to the multimedia library in regard to this question is, of course, the specialized nature of the skills needed to use the resources available. Often the patron simply is not sufficiently familiar with the multimedia resources and equipment to utilize them properly.

Substantial thought will also be necessary by management in the area of involvement by individual libraries with *network systems*. Such involvement requires staff time, equipment, and strong financial support. Decisions on what to do about compensation for work done by the library for outside sources and participants in the network are also a part of this concern.

Finally a policy objective of central concern to management in the multimedia library environment is that statement which is needed to support *the multimedia approach itself,* and which makes it imperative that the traditional reference function give way to the more contemporary emphasis upon multimedia skills and sources.

In the context of this book, the new multimedia concept—the systems approach—and all that this reality implies for contemporary multimedia library professionals has been accepted and supported. A very real fact of life to recognize, however, is that this new position may not necessarily be taken in the real world of the library in which the traditional reference professional still holds forth. Policy, and a strenuous program for change, remain central management responsibilities.

Most reference people have traditionally been subject oriented, for example. This has grown from the idea that people who have subject backgrounds in history, science, art, and the like are best prepared to assist patrons in their search for answers in these areas; a point of view which is supported in many ways by experience, and probably will not change remarkably.

Nor is it necessarily proposed that it should. What is recognized is that, in the development of information and reference services in the multimedia library, it must be accepted that the sources to which a patron must go may be in any of several media formats, and that print sources are only one of them. The fifth grade student who asks the question: "How does a flower grow?" for example, is a case in point. The request could probably be best fulfilled by giving the student an 8mm time-lapse film in which the complete growth of a flower is shown from seed to full bloom, rather than by suggesting an encyclopedia or other print source only.

Perhaps another way to put this is that management has a responsibility and an obligation to work toward the audiovisualists' rediscovery of the book, and the print librarians' becoming knowledgeable in the use of other types of media.

GENERAL   In reference or information service, management's responsibility, as discussed in the previous section, is to provide the assistance necessary to fulfill the patron's requests quickly and efficiently. A basic management decision on accomplishing this objective has to do with the term "to provide." As discussed in the preceding section, does this mean that management sets a policy whereby the reference or information service staff spends unlimited time and resources in providing the information? Or does it mean that reference staff helps the patron locate the sources of information and then leaves the learning or the discovery of knowledge to the patron? In the educational environment the former is generally the case. In other types of libraries, some balance between the two alternatives is needed. Clearly stated objectives, based upon policy and applied in terms of procedures, are needed to provide a basis for consistent and thoroughgoing response to all patron requests. Such objectives also preclude too much interpretation by staff members and assure standard treatment for all.

Management objectives in the reference area which support this kind of service include those of (1) providing trained and capable staff to do the job of multimedia reference, (2) a collection adequate to anticipate demand, and (3) a budget which is sufficient to maintain current services and which will permit growth of the service.

The first of these requirements suggests that job descriptions, for example, need to be developed to make selection of personnel for the reference and information positions a more careful and effective process. The Appendix to this book provides illustrations of several job descriptions, which suggest that the training expected as a part of the application for a reference job be stringently examined, and that later on-the-job direction, guidance, and training be equally careful. They also suggest that the commitment to multimedia information sources on the part of the reference librarian in this context be complete and sincere and supported by experience and technical skill in the use of multimedia sources.

Secondly, the adequacy of the collection is an imperative. Every effort to provide sources in a variety of formats and as comprehensive a scope as possible should be made. Both print and nonprint formats must be maximized to the extent possible within budgetary constraints.

And finally, sufficient funds need to be provided and suitably distributed within the reference area to provide for the services and resources required of this area. Each of these points will be expanded in sections to follow.

REFERENCE COLLECTION   The basic objective that underlies management of the collection is to develop a selection policy that provides for an adequate collection in all media formats. Patron needs, sources both within and beyond the individual library's walls, cooperative acquisitions, reference and informational needs, and financial resources are all factors which must be considered in developing a collection which can fulfill this objective. Financial resources are of primary concern, particularly as related to the acquisition of the equipment necessary to use these several formats. Computer and color video informational distribution systems can be quite costly, for example, while major projection, recording and playback equipment is equally expensive.

A more specific objective that applies to collection development as related to patrons' needs is the need for diversity in formats and materials, in subjects and levels covered. The selection process was covered in the previous chapter. However, it is of importance here to reemphasize management's responsibility, particularly in planning and maintaining the collection, to provide for diversity. A good multimedia collection is first and foremost a diversified collection providing through a variety of presentational modes an opportunity to learn from the most appropriate and effective format. The best multimedia collection provides for an effective matching of kind of information with the needs of the patron in a format most likely to suit the individual patron's interests and abilities.

Other objectives of central interest to the reference and information staff, as related to the collection, include weeding, organization, and integration of reference materials with the general collection. In the weeding or replacement process, particularly, reference personnel must be directly and closely attuned to the condition and usefulness of materials so that repair and renewal are maintained at a constant level.

Another paramount management concern in the area of reference collection is organization. How is the material to be organized? Should the collection be centralized, or decentralized? A common practice is to subdivide the reference collection by subject, such as science or humanities; or by using more specific subdivisions such as physics, chemistry, or psychology. However it is done, a primary objective of collection management in the reference and information area is that one which is concerned with the organization of the collection itself.

A related question that is pertinent to the objectives of multimedia library organization is the location of the reference collection itself. In the print area, for example, standard reference sources have tended to be shelved together in a location that could indeed be labeled Reference.

The multimedia reference concept, however, involves the use not so much of standardized print reference sources, although there are many of these, but of the entire general collection, including nonprint materials. So the usual organizational pattern, in which the reference area consists of a separate print reference collection and a separate nonprint reference area, is unsuited to the kind of service recommended here.

Ideally, the nonprint reference collection should be adjacent to the general collection, with all media integrated together. Reference and information service staff may then utilize both print and nonprint reference sources and the general collection of all media.

REFERENCE SERVICE In viewing reference overall, management must give attention to developing a kind of reference service that meets the information needs and demands of all present and prospective patrons. A primary objective of the service aspect of reference, therefore, must be to meet these needs adequately and effectively. The basis for this kind of approach is in the conceptual framework out of which the service is designed; a philosophy, in other words, of reference service.

Historically there are at least two types of reference service: ivory tower or traditional reference service, and what may be called the *enterprising philosophy* of reference service.

In the ivory tower philosophy, the reference staff typically takes a somewhat passive attitude toward the user, looking upon their own responsibility as being that of acquiring the materials, organizing the collection, and developing procedures and processes by which the collection is made accessible to the patron. The rest is up to the patron, who may, if the rules are followed, approach the marvellous ivory tower and seek its insights and help.

The enterprising philosophy starts where the other leaves off. Staff selects, organizes, and provides procedures and techniques which make reference and information services accessible, but they do not stop there. They take positive steps to attract patrons, to interest them in using the service, and to help them learn the skills needed to use the service fruitfully. Hence the term, enterprising. Almost like the business world, the reference service has a product to sell—information—and staff members in this kind of reference environment take active steps to interest patrons in becoming customers in their shop.

Service objectives related to this philosophical basis for reference service have to do with management decisions on what *limitations* are to be placed upon the service, how far the professionals should go in providing assistance, what limitations are needed in the search or investigative phases of patron assistance, and the like. These limits for the most part have to be determined on the basis of staff and time availabilities, and factors relating to the type of library, kind of users, and so on.

Reference restrictions are also a management concern. Does the multimedia library answer telephone reference questions? Do they handle contest or cross-word puzzle questions?

Certain practical constraints in reference to questions like this, decided upon because of reasons relating to staff capability, appropriateness of the request, and so on, become restrictions on staff activity. They must be decided by management on the basis of objectives rooted in the philosophy of the service and the character of the individual library and its public.

An important and useful tool in connection with the service function is a manual which defines the services available and describes any limitations or restrictions which apply. At the same time surveys and other means need to be used to identify patrons who are not being served and why, with programs and special services developed on the basis of this information to draw those patrons into the reference and information area. This kind of effort is typical of the positive, enterprising philosophy of reference service. Evaluations and related activities following this can indicate how effective the program is, and suggest needed changes and revisions.

An interesting aspect of the enterprising approach is the instruction which needs to be provided in the use of multimedia library materials, equipment, and informational resources. This can include demonstrations by the reference librarian on how to use the card catalog, introduction of the user to the microfilm printer, or provision of opportunity for the patron to view a color videotape orientation to the multimedia library. With knowledge of the processes, materials, and equipment available and how to use them, the patron can provide his own guidance and direction in seeking information, thus freeing the reference staff to spend more time with those patrons who are not able to help themselves.

Management in reference service must also give substantial attention to a number of other questions involving policy and objectives. Cooperation, for example, with other information centers or agencies at local, regional, state, or even the national level is a valid and necessary function of reference. The decision, however, on how far to go in such cooperation, how far to go in referring local patrons' questions and needs to other sources and agencies, is an important one for management. Another question along these lines has to do with staffing, personnel, and hours of service. What hours will reference service be open? Should a professional be available all of those hours to give service to the patron? In the selection of staff, what emphasis should be placed upon specialties in formats or subject fields? What is management's responsibility for in-service training and professional development of the staff?

Up to this point the discussion has dealt with factors relating to direct reference services. Supplemental services which do not deal directly with the patron, but do implement and supplement the direct services, need to be considered as well. Supplemental reference services include the development of bibliographies, indexing, abstracting, selection, and local reference aids, for example. If a given reference service is involved in the use of the computer, a very time-consuming supplemental activity would be the development of programs and the preparation of data to be utilized by the computer.

In looking toward the future, it is reasonable to expect that reference services will have continuously growing access to machine-generated reference tools. Management will have the responsibility of generating appropriate policy statements, objectives, staff, and financial resources to keep abreast of such developments and relate them to the multimedia library user.

REFERENCE STATISTICS   The main objective in maintaining reference statistics is to provide management with the data needed on a regular basis to determine the effectiveness of reference service overall. Accordingly, statistics need to be developed on a systematic basis. Evaluation, policy decision reports, and budget preparation all rely heavily on statistical information; and the manager, to follow through on the different steps in the management process, must have available a measurement of reference services. It is true, of course, that reference services are probably one of the most difficult to measure, but the need is there, and the tabulation of quantitative information needs to be made to the best extent possible. Most reference departments take simple counts of a variety of quantitatively recorded events: requests for search assistance, requests for instruction, and the like. These figures are not entirely sufficient to assess the value of service to patrons, of course. Quantitative statistics cannot be directly utilized to determine qualitative achievements, but such counts do nevertheless assist greatly as indicators of the quality of service.

There is a trend also toward providing library managers with quantitative data so that accountability can be verified in the overall use of financial resources. Thus, the extent of the statistical record-keeping program would depend upon the type of library, patrons served, and the requirements of the individual situation. Some library managers might require very specific statistics that could be related to performance, while others might need only a more general kind of statistic.

It is pretty well agreed that the number, or volume, of patrons utilizing reference service is an important indicator of the quality of that aspect of reference service. If there is a high degree of use, and a significant number of returning patrons, for example, it can be judged that the service is satisfactory. If the statistics show a drop at certain times or when a certain staff member is working, management has a significant indicator to check out.

In the context of what is called the enterprising philosophy of reference service, the use of statistics is needed to provide a key to an appreciation of the market. No business would think of operating without statistics on transactions and volume of sales. Multimedia libraries, in order to validate their cost of operation, must be capable also of providing accountability in terms of patrons served, and dollar costs.

One of the principal items that management needs statistics on is the number of different types of questions being received and responded to at each service point. These figures should be kept by hours, or hourly periods, so that schedules and staff needs can be evaluated. An example of a form for recording different kinds of questions is found in Example 15.

There is a variety of activities for which statistics are developed in the multimedia library, and which are useful and necessary for good management as related to policy and statements of objectives. These include counts of a variety of kinds of questions, equipment requests and use counts, patron activity and behavior patterns as they can be recorded quantitatively, and percentage and comparative statistics on increases and decreases in demand or use.

The first of these—questions—takes a variety of forms, and some explanation should be useful here. *Information questions*, for example, are questions of a general

EXAMPLE 15
REFERENCE QUESTION TALLY SHEET

HICKS COLLEGE LIBRARY DAILY REFERENCE QUESTION TALLY SHEET							
Date:	**TIME**						
Type of Question	8–10	10–12	12–2	2–4	4–6	6–8	8–10
Information							
Reference							
Research							
Problem							
Machinery							

nature that can be responded to in a minute or less. *Reference questions*, on the other hand, are queries which can only be answered by a professional librarian, and may take up to 15 minutes. *Research questions*, also to be handled only by a professional, may take 15 minutes or longer and actually involve some research activity by the professional and the patron. A *problem question* as defined in the library field is a question which must be handled by a librarian, and which may take over a half hour to handle. The *machinery question* is one which involves the use and handling of a piece of equipment. By the use of these simple categories for recording purposes, records can be developed for each day's service which provide useful management insights into what is happening on the reference floor on any given day or evening.

Statistical data is also needed to provide a basis for budget requests and expenditures. Examples of these types of statistics include quantitative information on the use of new equipment and new materials, replacement of expendable parts, and other cost-related items, including figures which would justify the use of personnel to perform particular services and tasks which can be translated into cost figures.

Statistical data on patron activity and behavior is another important record-keeping area. Statistics are needed, as suggested above, on what types of questions the patrons are indeed asking, on types of questions which cannot be answered, and the like. These figures help answer other questions: What are the patrons' needs? What types of patrons are using reference services? Statistics of this kind would probably have to be obtained through surveys rather than on a day-to-day quantitative count, although daily records are possible even in this area.

Statistical data which reflect the growth and progress of the multimedia library are also useful, and can be presented in a comparative framework on a month-to-month or year-to-year basis. Percentage increases or decreases may be dramatized in this way and a comparative analysis made of all the different services which pertain to the reference area. Such figures are especially useful in the management process. The reader may wish to refer back to Example 4 in Chapter 3 which illustrates a statistical record.

And finally, internal management data is needed. A good example of this type of information is the development of work and budget objectives by each staff member, these objectives being evaluated periodically in terms of actual accomplishments. For example, a staff member is often required to prepare both an oral and written report quarterly on the fulfillment and evaluation of set objectives. These reports, in turn, can often be compared and evaluated against actual statistical records of services performed. This enables the manager to both monitor performance and obtain the internal communications necessary to keep in touch with the actual performance of staff people in the reference service. It must be emphasized that one of the most important aspects of the management process as related to objectives is the measurement of achievement and progress on the basis of statistically reported and validated performance.

It is worthy of note that statistics for any given period provide continuing guidance for succeeding periods, and lend useful insights for future planning.

SERVICE TO OTHER PROCESSES   Reference service, being one of the most vital functions of the multimedia library, must understand the relationship of all other processes and services to reference. Reference has a very strong relationship to selection and acquisitions, for example. Reference has the responsibility of informing acquisitions about gaps in the collections and suggestions for developing the collection.

In cataloging, there must be very close collaboration and cooperation with the reference service area. One of the most important tools of reference is the card catalog or catalog index. Cataloging has the primary responsibility for the development of this important tool so it is therefore absolutely necessary that management assure close cooperation between reference and cataloging.

There must be close cooperation also between circulation and reference. Both are public service activities and their policies and procedures must be closely correlated by management. Finally, management must keep in close touch with reference service for another important reason: in the planning and acquisition of new equipment and facilities, information on patrons' needs and interests are an important key to good planning.

SUMMARY

Reference and circulation services in the multimedia library are the areas in which direct public contact becomes most visible. Reference is that area which provides direct aid to the patron in finding and using the resources of the collection. Circulation is that area which handles the actual lending of materials to the patron, supervises and enforces procedures relating to their use, return, and reentry into the access system. Good management in these important multimedia library functions is essential to the fulfillment of the final and crucial goal of the library: the actual use of the library's resources for the enhancement of human life.

The need for management of reference and circulation activities is discussed; the goals of these areas of activity are described, and related concerns are discussed. Brought out are certain unique problems and concerns of reference and circulation in the multimedia library as contrasted with the strictly book environment to which the manager must give attention: differing formats and physical features which affect handling, use, and storage; the need for special equipment and specialized skills for viewing, listening, and accessing the materials in these formats; and the special problems in developing policies and applying procedures suitable to the maximum effective use and control of such materials. Security systems, both as a protective measure against theft and misuse and as a potential threat to the materials themselves, are given discussion. Magnetic devices, for example, which can protect print and other materials from theft or misuse, may also damage magnetically recorded audiotape and similar materials. It would be wise to check the security system to assure it will not damage recorded tapes.

Management aspects of the charging system and fines and related procedures are also discussed. It is pointed out that a good charging system must be accurate in detail, easy to implement, and within budget and personnel constraints and capabilities.

Management concerns in these areas of multimedia library operation are discussed in detail. Public relations aspects of circulation and the probable effect of the system of registration and charge-out procedures on activities of patrons are given some dialogue. Errors in the procedure are especially damaging to library-patron relationships, and the chapter strongly cautions against failure to handle these matters with care, both in the design and implementation of control and enforcement policies and procedures, and in the personnel assignments made to get these jobs done.

Weeding and inventory procedures are discussed in depth. This important process for keeping the collection current demands careful management attention. Weeding criteria include the following: (1) physical condition of the material; (2) age of the material; (3) dating of the material; and (4) suitability of the material to the curriculum or reading public served. Other factors: cost, space available for growth or no growth (zero growth), personnel available to do the job, and related factors. Inventory, the related job of determining what the collection actually contains, discovering losses, and assessing condition of materials, imposes similar management responsibilities. Weeding and inventory are major functions of collection management which can readily be combined.

Finally, in stressing the unique attributes of the multimedia library as contrasted with the primarily book oriented collection of the traditional library, the term *information resources* is suggested as a more appropriate label than reference collection. The traditional reference job has been related primarily to the use of so-called reference sources which in turn direct the patron to other sources of information and knowledge. The information needed in the multimedia environment, however, is not only not limited to such reference compendiums, but in fact involves direct use of the materials themselves and the special technologies needed to access them. These include informational distribution and transmission aspects of closed circuit television, audio and video dial retrieval programs and materials, computer access devices and program methods, and a variety of informational formats such as filmstrips, slides, 8mm loops, microforms, and the like.

Management is going to have more and more responsibility for providing for machine-generated information and reference tools, particularly in the multimedia library. Unlike the relatively static, traditional reference desk, with its ponderous printed compendiums listing sources available for search, the systems approach provides a framework for reference service that is compatible with the considerably broader variety of informational sources that have become available as a result of the development of multimedia formats and techniques. The reference librarian of today, in the multimedia context, is no longer the traditional authority but a specialist who needs to know not only how to answer a patron's request, but why the request was made.

The goal of management in the reference area thus becomes clear: to provide the informational services necessary to satisfy a patron's request in terms of the need for knowledge from all available sources. The sequential concerns of management-by-objectives are discussed in light of these factors in the specialized area of multimedia information resources management. Parameters are suggested or described in terms of such questions as *How much does the information-resources librarian do in assisting the patron?* and the like. Multimedia reference objectives are three: to provide trained and capable staff to handle informational needs; to maintain a collection adequate to anticipated demand; and to budget adequately to support the service needed. These, in turn, are interpreted in the context of specific reference collection and service objectives, and the related special objectives which can be discussed in the areas of reference statistics and processes.

Finally, the contemporary reference philosophy of the multimedia library, termed the *enterprising philosophy* of reference, is contrasted with the traditional view of reference in the book oriented environment—an ivory tower position. The enterprising philosophy starts where the other leaves off. The enterprising view is a dynamic, positive, patron oriented, outreaching service philosophy that contrasts sharply with the traditional, more passive stance of reference work. Almost like the business world, the reference service in the contemporary multimedia library has a product to sell, namely information, and staff members in this kind of reference environment take active steps to interest patrons in becoming customers in their shop. The management problem in this kind of shop is directly geared, from objectives through operational procedures, staffing, and budget foundation, to identifying the requirements needed to fulfill such a dynamic and action oriented task, and to do it in the best possible way, with the customer in mind.

CHAPTER 9

OVERVIEW AND DISCUSSION OF SOME FUTURE CONCERNS

Computer center feeds programs to labs, classrooms, and the learning center. (Courtesy of Los Medanos College.)

At the outset, the reader was enjoined to view the multimedia world as a very real one in which the new technologies of contemporary experience are accepted as a part of everyday life. The special challenges for management in the unique environment of contemporary multimedia with its formats, systems, and needed expertise, were dramatized. The librarian was seen as a professional keeping pace with our times and the multimedia library, the place where all this was happening. It was, we hope, an appropriate new starting point in conceptualizing the place of the multimedia library in today's society. Making man's accumulated knowledge available must certainly be one of the most challenging and demanding tasks to which the professional of our time can be dedicated.

The multimedia concept is based upon a core of fundamentals that are essential to the life of this new type of library. Successful implementation of multimedia services requires a dynamic management approach that systematically analyzes, structures, and evaluates, and thus perpetuates change and progress. The stated purpose of the book was to provide a guide for this kind of management, and to demonstrate practical day-to-day management techniques together with the principles needed to make them work. The central concept: management-by-objectives (MBO), the business of developing a management system based upon predetermined and carefully articulated outcomes toward which the whole effort of planning, operating, and dynamically reevaluating the policies and procedures for total multimedia resource services could be directed.

Management-by-objectives was first conceived and developed in a business environment. Its special application and usefulness in the multimedia library have been stressed, recognizing that this approach has had to be modified from the profit-motivated business environment to the environment of social and cultural service to the community. The new technologies which have provided a variety of access formats for human knowledge have been reviewed and their special applications in the multimedia library have been discussed. It is in the context of these factors that we have seen the unique role of the multimedia library in contemporary society and looked at the special concerns of management in that kind of library.

Chapter 1 discussed the multimedia library itself as a system, its goals and objectives, and the principles upon which its successful management must be built. Chapter 2 looked at the structure and organization of the multimedia library and dramatized the difference between the traditional and the contemporary management styles which characterize the identities of the print oriented collection and the diversified multimedia resource center. Chapter 3 defined management, discussed its purpose, philosophy, goals, and objectives, and provided a perspective on the management of multimedia by the MBO technique. Chapter 4 examined personnel management in light of its importance as a major tool for the effective control of library practice. Chapter 5 provided an overview of budget management and a detailed discussion of management responsibilities and techniques for the successful fiscal direction of a multimedia library program. Chapter 6 looked carefully at all aspects of management of selection of the resources of the multimedia library itself whereas Chapter 7 addressed the other supporting services related to resources. In Chapter 8, management of resources in the service of patron-related activities was discussed, with specific applications to the several areas of multimedia library practice.

What is the perspective within which the multimedia library manager must prepare for the future, anticipate the challenges and opportunities of the profession, and plan for tomorrow? The prospects are both exciting and startling. For example, it has been speculated that it will soon be possible to develop a brain–computer hook-up that would put the human brain in direct contact with a computer through electrodes implanted under the skull. This would give the average person the ability to understand anything and everything ever needed. Even though it is predicted that this system of information retrieval will not be available for 50 or 60 years, it indicates that the need for direct access to all kinds of information will continue to increase. This notion presupposes that all information already would be stored in the computer and would be organized for retrieval. Another assumption on the part of the scientist is that retrieval of information automatically begets understanding of information by the recipient; furthermore, that the information needs of the average person are extraordinarily comprehensive. These assumptions serve as a clue to possible future developments in the informational and educational functions of multimedia libraries which management will have to handle. One of these is networks.

NETWORKS

The multimedia library will undoubtedly be affected by the growth of networks which provide for widespread remote access to central computer facilities. Since the basis of the networking concept is cooperation, many of the resources and operations which are subsystems of the multimedia library system will also become subsystems of the network system. The cataloging process, for example, will become a network subsystem, contributing cataloged entries to the network data bank and receiving bibliographic data from it. This in turn has implications for the manager who must be aware of the psychological, production, personnel, monetary, and other problems which this process can engender, and be prepared to cope with them.

It is within the domain of the manager, who is the decision maker, to decide if the multimedia library will join a network in the first place. There may be various kinds of networks which may have to be considered, and the manager will have to become very well informed about them. The network jurisdiction or geographical area, product, and cost are some of the important factors which must be assessed. Given a particular multimedia library there are several questions to ask: What are the advantages and disadvantages of county, state, regional, and national networks? What would be the effect of an international network? How successful are these networks in producing what they have promised? What is their financial situation? What do the member libraries have to contribute now? Is it likely that this contribution will be considerably increased in the future? Is there conflict between county, state, regional, and national networks? If so, are these conflicts serious enough to threaten the service of the network? To what extent is the library's decision making taken over by the network? These and other questions will have to be explored before the manager comes to a decision.

In general, information may be considered the product of any network in which the multimedia library would be interested. There are, however, different kinds of information for different purposes. The manager, therefore, will have to examine very closely the kinds of information to which any particular network gives access, then evaluate the worth of this information on the basis of the goals of the library, its type, size, and variety of multimedia resources, its present and potential use by the library's clientele, and its effects on the coordination of various processes in the library system. For example, a network which indexes and abstracts articles from electrical and electronic periodicals and papers would probably improve the service of an electrical company's library, especially if the company's personnel were engaged in research projects. It is doubtful, however, that the specialized information from such a network would be of particular benefit to more than a few patrons of a medium-sized public library. On the other hand, a community information and referral center might be exactly the kind of network that would provide information sought by a majority of the clientele of the same type and size library.

Networks which furnish bibliographic data are the most well known to libraries in general. The Ohio College Library Center (OCLC), for example, when all phases of its design are completed, will provide on-line union catalog and shared cataloging, serials control, interlibrary loan communications, acquisitions, remote catalog access and circulation control, and retrieval by subject. The OCLC data base contains bibliographic records numbering well into the millions. Networks such as OCLC, and others which may be designed on a smaller scale and for a particular type of library such as a school media center, should always be subject to a thorough evaluation based on the criteria indicated in the preceding paragraphs.

At the present time the data bases of the majority of networks consist primarily of bibliographic records of print materials. In some instances there are networks for a specific type of media such as motion pictures. However, the slow recognition of the importance of integrating print and nonprint media, and the lack of standards for cataloging nonprint media have so far discouraged the building of multimedia bibliographic data bases. Considerable progress has been made, however, in formulating rules for the bibliographic description of nonprint media, both nationally and internationally, and it is anticipated that the number of nonprint media entries in bibliographic network data banks will continue to increase, so that eventually, a complete cataloging service can be offered to the multimedia library. Should a library decide to participate in a bibliographic network of this type, the manager should be prepared to modify the design of the acquisitions, cataloging, and physical processing processes of that library. Redesigning may involve new kinds of tasks, regrouping of tasks, training of personnel in different skills, and increasing the number of employees to whom responsibility is delegated. Whatever modifications must be made to implement such changes into the multimedia library system, the goals and objectives of the particular library must always take priority over those of the network in which it becomes a member.

Two very important concepts that seem to be emerging will undoubtedly influence the multimedia library's participation in networks. The first might be called the utility view of information. There is a shift in emphasis from the gathering of information to the organizing of information so that the user can assimilate it more quickly and easily. Those involved in information science are becoming more and more aware of the difference between the process of receiving information and the process of becoming informed. The measurement of information services will no longer be based only on the number of available entries in a data bank but will also take into consideration the value of the network's information to the user. The principal elements in assessing the worth of information will be the user's understanding of information and the use of it.

INDIVIDUALIZING INFORMATION

Growing out of this point of view is a second important concept which will affect multimedia libraries. Since the measurement of information will depend to a large extent upon the user, the goal of the information process will change. The focus will shift from information as a product to the effectiveness of the multimedia library in individualizing information. To adequately cover the information needs of all individuals will necessitate a broadening and enlarging of information sources to include a very wide variety of information in all formats and the combination of multimedia in many different packages. The successful accomplishment of this goal will necessitate more than a superficial survey of the needs of the information consumer. Although one of the goals of the multimedia library has always been to meet the needs of its clientele, these new concepts of information will require a more personal and individual knowledge of the library user in addition to the library's resources per se. The manager will have to be responsible for an ongoing, in-depth user study which, while utilizing many different methods of inquiry, will lean most heavily upon personal contact between users and staff members. The data gathered from such a study will be the most important element in the cost–benefit analysis that the manager will make in reaching a decision on the participation of the library in a network.

Individualization of information will result in a more conscious and concentrated effort to promote the educational function of the multimedia library. There is no transfer of information from the source to the recipient unless the latter understands it and makes it a part of a personal fund of useful knowledge. It is the task of the multimedia library to educate the user about the information system, how to find information, and how to understand it and use it for personal needs. This increased emphasis on learning will present a challenge to the multimedia library manager which may involve research, experimentation, innovation, and a more creative use of the skills and potential capabilities of the library staff.

EXPANSION OF PROGRAMS

Looking to the future, one can expect that the multimedia library will increase its efforts to educate the public not only in the techniques of information retrieval but also in the various other real and potential services which the library can provide. Fulfillment of the cultural and recreational functions of the multimedia library requires an awareness and analysis of social change which must lead to action. Planning, implementing, and evaluating such action will be the task of the manager. In the future, the manager will probably be more deeply involved in programs than in operational processes which, more and more, will be delegated to other members of the staff. These programs will bring the services of the multimedia library to the people and will be geared for cultural appreciation, recreational needs, or educational improvement suitable for each particular group or individual to whom the service is delivered. Outreach programs, neighborhood centers, satellite learning centers, media-mobiles, services to the aged, prisoners, handicapped, students, and the like, will continue to increase. These services can become more and more individualized if the manager recognizes how to make the best use of technology and media. For example, educational and cultural programs that are generated from the library could be received in the individual's home through facsimile delivery and other means; however, it is also realistic to project that programs will also be in effect to bring even more people into the library. These will involve well-planned public relations efforts and cooperation with community, institutional, regional, and state persons and agencies. By making the multimedia library a center for art and science exhibits, minimuseums, and recreational, arts and crafts, intercultural and continuing education programs, people will be encouraged to come out of their individual social and economic environments and be exposed to an even broader view of the world.

Exposure in itself is essentially passive, however. It must be followed up by efforts of the multimedia library staff to ascertain that such exposure has indeed accomplished this desired transfer of knowledge to the user, and that within the framework of personal understanding, the user has in fact benefited from the exposure. This is the enterprising philosophy of multimedia library management advocated by this text.

Programs such as these will be one of the principal challenges for the manager of the multimedia library in the future. Not only will it be necessary to justify them cost-wise. The manager will also have to devise methods of evaluation that will successfully measure services and benefits to the user. The manager will have to work very closely with staff in communicating an understanding of these kinds of program concepts, and in training staff in new skills that will be needed to make such programs work. The manager will have to promote staff participation in creative ideas and program planning, and will have to delegate responsibility to many more staff members in proportion to the number of special projects and programs that are put into effect.

INCREASED USE OF THE COMPUTER

Some discussion of what may be called the *technology of resources* is needed. This chapter has commented on the expected impact of networks, or the kinds of choices which can be expected to surface as major challenges to multimedia management, and on the necessity of adopting an enterprising operational philosophy of service in the environment of the new society to be served by the multimedia library. This chapter has discussed a variety of factors relating to new skills and appreciations which will be needed by the multimedia librarian in this future perspective. There remains for discussion the primary technological base from which these changes are generated: the computer, television, and a variety of special equipment devices which provide access to information in the many new formats common to multimedia collections.

It has been stressed that the computer and the automation of routine procedures in the multimedia library will have serious impact upon the multimedia library. Computer applications to routines such as ordering, cataloging, acquisitions, circulation, and periodical control, for example, have met with considerable success. Future generations of the digital computer, both in-house and in network systems, will undoubtedly provide even greater benefits in such areas as bibliographic access and reference information search, to name only two. Access to audio and video players, and an ever-growing capability to handle information from these sources are also enhanced by computer technology. Management must not be overawed by the computer, however, but must examine its use in light of the philosophy, objectives, and needs of the multimedia library in the new age.

Undoubtedly, the computer is the most powerful management tool to have been developed in the wake of contemporary technology. The computer is able to record, organize, classify, sort, and retrieve data very quickly. Its application to management is clear and its usefulness is unequaled in areas of both routine and nonroutine decision making. As technology and services become more complex, the computer promises to become even more useful and can be expected to significantly increase the manager's ability to handle complex problems. The complexity of decision making and the problems to be anticipated in the multimedia library of the future will certainly require a more elaborate and sophisticated information management system than now exists in most multimedia situations. The computer will undoubtedly increase the manager's capacity for dealing with such situations.

One application which is worthy of mention in this context is simulations. The computer can be programmed to sort, analyze, and report on the effects of a projected decision. It would, in effect, tell the manager what could be expected to happen in the practical everyday world if one or another decision were made, or action taken. The manager, in other words, could try out or test a decision before actually using it in an everyday situation. Of course, this application is one which needs to be seen in the perspective of human variables nonetheless. A computer can only arrive at decisions which are among the alternatives programmed into it in the first place.

An extension of this application that could have some impact upon media management is that a significant portion of planning and decision making could be done by specialists in computer and automatic technology. Such specialists would probably be located at a top administrative staff level. Decisions could be predicted, and media managers, who would be considered middle management, would find themselves in situations where their own tasks would become more structured and more routine. Obviously, such a development could require redefinition of the functions and responsibilities of middle management and could have considerable impact upon media managers' positions.

In forecasting the use of the computer in the multimedia library it is important to recognize that the trend is first toward computer applications in support of patron services, and secondly, toward the performance of routine operational tasks. One

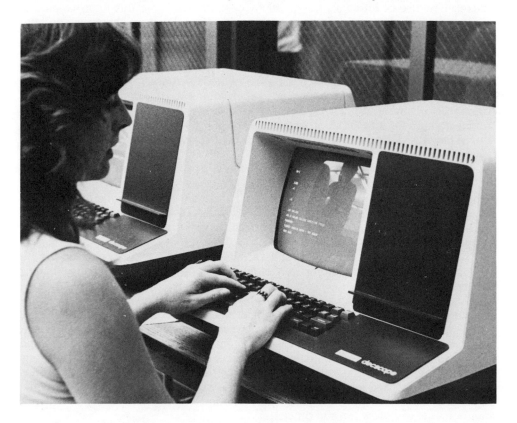

Students access CAI programs by means of terminals located in the learning laboratory. Programs cover areas such as math, science, art, history, and English. (Courtesy of Learning Resources Center, Solano Community College.)

fact that should be made clear is that computer use in libraries is not a futuristic idea. The computer goes back many years. General Electric, for example, had a computer indexing system in use in the 1950s.

In purely library terms, the greatest future use of the computer will be in storage, sorting, and retrieval of information. It may be only through the computer that it will be possible to both store and process all of human knowledge in an organized way, and provide access, quickly and efficiently, to this information. Yet this is the ultimate objective, as it always has been, of the library information mission. The practical question that management will have to answer is: how much of this information can be stored efficiently and economically, and how far is it possible to stretch fiscal resources in order to obtain access to that information?

It has already been noted that the typical large university library collection is fast approaching a volume of information items which may be beyond the memory storage capacity of present computers. Technology will of course find some manner of increasing this capacity; for instance by mating computer banks and microforms. The computer is recognized as the best method of storing information. Computer information can be recorded on microformats and then read back, and microforms can act as the data or memory bank of the computer.

In the area of reference, the computer will add a new dimension to service. As time goes on, reference librarians will see increasing numbers of computerized bibliographic information items made available by computerized catalogs and indexes. The use of terminals will greatly accelerate access to this information.

It will still be necessary for management to make decisions, however, on how much and what kind of information to store in relationship to the economics of direct access. Any computer application initiated is going to cost a lot of money before it is efficient and economical. A thorough analysis must be carried out by the media manager before justifying and obtaining the necessary funds for computer applications. It should go without saying that alternatives to the computer should be considered in preparing any justification for a computer proposal. The manager should expect to put together a combination of complex factors that may run over a five- to ten-year period in order to determine the economic advantages or disadvantages of computer utilization.

It is projected that where computer growth will probably continue for certain is in the realm of repetitive processes because the costs involved are much easier to justify. Almost any task that can be set up as a routine can readily be programmed for the computer. Increases in workload in such tasks may be expected to respond more economically to handling by standard programmed techniques than with manual methods.

Basically what management must ascertain is not that computers can do the job for less, but that the computer can offer better service for the money that is expended.

Another important factor which must be considered when looking to the future is the possible obsolescence of any system that is set up at any point in time. This is because, as time goes on, the tasks that need to be completed and the equipment required to accomplish such tasks will become more and more complex, more and more expensive, more and more demanding of a team of highly qualified specialists for design and implementation. There may even be less need for individual libraries to have computerized systems or computer specialists, on the one hand, while the demand for library-trained computer specialists in regional, multilibrary or network environments will grow, on the other.

Thus, the future of computer application to multimedia libraries does not lie in a one-only, or local library situation. Experience has shown that it is not generally economically feasible for any but very large libraries or library systems or networks to develop a computer-based system. As suggested earlier in this chapter, the future for local libraries will probably involve network or commercial applications of computer technology.

Automation, sometimes thought of as another term for computer technology, actually is not, but rather is an application of the systems idea. Automation can be, for all practical purposes, entirely nontechnical in character. It can, however it is implemented, be considered in the nontechnical sense as any system of planning, designing, supervising, controlling, and revising. It is possible to create automation by applying such a system and tying together processes and machinery to create optimum use of the productive resources available.

CABLE TELEVISION

A technology that has great potential for the future is cable television (CATV). Cable has the potential of delivering information directly to patrons in their homes, businesses, or places of employment. An important factor to consider in the utilization of CATV as an informational delivery system is that it can carry so many more signals, or channels, than can be made available by conventional or open broadcast. Another important factor is the technical capability of a cable hook-up to be two-way; information and messages can travel back and forth between the multimedia library and the patron. One of the greatest values of CATV may also be in the eventual connection of libraries so that resources can be passed from one library to another via the cable. This means, of course, that facsimiles of printed pages, microfilm, audio messages, and all kinds of visual materials could be passed from one library to another very quickly and efficiently.

In looking at CATV, it becomes apparent that it can be considerably more than simply an expansion of a conventional closed-circuit system. Cable television not only has the capability of additional channels, it also has the ability to serve whole geographical areas. It is also able to devote specific channels to particular uses or users. For the multimedia library of the future, it offers a new technology of promise for informational delivery and for continuing education. It is well to keep in mind that many experts believe that CATV will dominate the TV market of the future, and thus will create an informational system of great magnitude for libraries. It is suggested that the profession of librarianship, which is concerned with the selection, organization, and dissemination of information, will have to thoroughly investigate the possibilities of CATV as an informational delivery system.

Management will have to make decisions regarding these utilizations of television. It must be decided, for instance, whether a one-way system should be used or whether a two-way system should be provided for, permitting the library to send out information and then obtain feedback from the user, thus extending the reference-type service directly to the home. The possibilities for this type of service are immense.

Cable television offers the feasibility of transmitting images, such as pictures, diagrams, maps, and other information for display on the patron's television receiver, for example. The patron could even be equipped to record this transmission on a video recorder for additional or later use. Tied into the computer, CATV could assist the information-seeking patron by receiving a request via the cable, in-putting the request to the computer, and then printing out the response on the television screen in the patron's own living room or study.

OTHER COMMUNICATIONS TECHNOLOGY ADVANCES

Another important factor relating to television technology is the development of videotape players and recorders. The development of smaller and lighter video reproducers and the videocassette reproducer are also important parts of the new television technology. Cassette tapes are not only much easier for the library to prepare, they are easier for the library to distribute and circulate and for the patron to use.

The videocassette also looms as a very strong format for the multimedia library collection. The tapes are prerecorded and can be processed and made available to the patron much the same as a book. One of the important ancillary devices to this format is the video player. Until the library is able to supply countless patrons with video players, however, or until the average patron has one at home, the prerecorded videocassette will mainly be a library use only material. In education, many people see the videotape as the format of the future.

On the horizon is a new communications medium, the videodisc. Not yet on the market, but on the verge of introduction, the videodisc offers a bridge that could span information service from print to television. Its development will depend upon the producers' ability to standardize the form of the disc, and the hardware to reproduce the images on the disc.

Commercially the videodisc is primarily being designed for the home market. It will make educational programs, movies, and sports events available to patrons in the home on the family color TV set. Commercially, there are two videodisc systems on the way: a mechanical contact system, and an optical system utilizing the laser beam. The mechanical system is referred to as a capacitance system, used much like a phonograph with a stylus. The optical system uses a laser beam and a complex arrangement of lenses.

The challenge in videodiscs is not going to be so much in the hardware as in the development of software that can be utilized by videodisc players. Commercially, this has possibilities for a huge market. For the multimedia library, it offers tremendous possibilities as well. It would be possible for the multimedia library to have videodiscs with all types of media from print to visuals which could be sold, distributed or circulated to the patron. The large problem would be in obtaining videodiscs with the type of information needed by the multimedia library. Commercially, most of the material reproduced on videodiscs would have typical consumer applications, such as full-length movies and sports events. It would be possible, on the other hand, for the videodisc to make a strong contribution to self-learning and programmed instruction.

The important fact to emphasize here is that the videodisc makes it possible to present all types of media on one format. It has the potential of offering to the multimedia library what may prove to be the best and most efficient method of information delivery so far available.

With the development of audio and video capability for multimedia library use, management will have to make many decisions on whether to place emphasis on individual access or to utilize remote access information systems. In connection with the computer, there are tremendous developments already in progress which would facilitate the utilization of video and audio materials through a remote access system. Remote access is also especially adaptable to a decentralized system as is often found in resource centers in educational systems. A most impressive potential of the random access system is found in the possible connection of both video and audio hardware with a random access computer base. This is an application for instructional programs that can be utilized at all levels of education. It is in the educational field where growth or use of random access systems will probably find its place in the future.

An already established and rapidly growing technology is that of microforms. In the future, management will be especially interested in this format because of its storage advantages. With the ease of use of cartridge microfilm in both 16mm and 35mm sizes, the microfiche, and ultra-microfiche, there are money- and space-saving formats to meet every need.

One of the great breakthroughs in technology in the area of microforms will come in the near future with the development of an easy to use reading device, the so-called lap reader, that has been under consideration for many years. When this device is on the market it is expected to be so convenient to use that it can be handled by the patron in much the same way as reading a book held in a lap. The quality of microforms will undoubtedly improve along with this development, and both images and color are anticipated.

With the coming of the new copyright law, changes in policies affecting the manner of publication of microforms may also be anticipated. As the equipment becomes easier to use, the quality increases, and more uses are made of this valuable format, there will be more patron enthusiasm about utilizing these types of materials.

A final technology that must be given serious consideration by management is reprography. This capability is becoming significantly more visible and useful in the transfer of information and knowledge because of the relative ease of making inexpensive copies of printed matter. Reprography is, of course, very closely affected by copyright laws. Publishers, understandably, consider this technology as a threat to their livelihood. The photocopy machine has made it possible to make duplicates instead of borrowing or buying materials.

Reproduction of periodical articles for interlibrary loan has just about replaced the traditional exchange of the actual publications.

The most serious problem of reprography lies in the education field where students and faculty members want material duplicated that is copyrighted. Continuing discussion can be expected on what the educational fair use of materials is, and how it is defined.

Offset duplicating masters, another reprographic technique, now permit easy duplication of untold numbers of printed materials. There will be a tremendous expansion in the future of the multimedia library's ability to reproduce materials through such photocopying and offset printing methods. How far the multimedia library goes into duplication of such materials will be a serious matter of concern to management in the future.

Within the sphere of reprography is the process of facsimile transfer. This is really a combination of electronic transmission and the photocopy technique or offset press duplication. It is possible to transmit a facsimile copy, prepare a master, and duplicate almost anything or present it on a television screen for a patron who, in turn, could then copy and reproduce the facsimile desired.

Worthy of mention here is a final item: programmed learning. Not a technology, it is a learning technique and presentational method implemented by the new technologies. Programmed learning is the basic design and format for independent study or individualized study, and is a fast growing area of materials utilization which promises to have continued emphasis in the multimedia library of the future. What programmed learning has to suggest for the future of the multimedia library is a basic change in the philosophical approach of the library from service to instruction, an approach which can only be dealt with effectively by the dynamic kind of librarianship suggested in the new, enterprising approach to library service.

FISCAL AND PERSONNEL OUTLOOK

A few comments would be appropriate here about concerns of the multimedia library manager in the future as related to fiscal and personnel resources. Management will always have to face the question of finances. The library will always have to be staffed. Technological developments will constantly create areas for decision making. Leadership in these vital areas will always be the media manager's most immediate challenge—particularly in the system which is managed on the basis of the MBO concepts as expressed in this book.

Collective bargaining, unions, and participatory management techniques will result in other challenging problem areas for the multimedia manager. These concerns should be primary for those who expect to manage. There are no easy solutions to the challenges either. In looking at the financial implications for management in the future, for example, the media manager will find that it is premature to look at technology as a means for reducing cost, or at least it is an area in which, though there may eventually be a dollar advantage in terms of services to the patron, there is no easy panacea at hand. Development of new technology in terms of the development process itself, its use, research, capital outlay requirements, and the like, will in fact increase the fiscal requirements of the multimedia library.

In looking at the financial picture as a whole, however, there are more signs of optimism than pessimism. The national experience suggests that over the last few years, most libraries have held their own or have had aid increased. Inflation and recession are realities to be dealt with and will probably be important continuing factors in the fiscal life of the library. The continuing problem of a lag in increases, despite larger budgets year after year, which keeps the multimedia library behind the increases in cost for materials, equipment, and personnel, does not appear to be going away. But the lag is getting closer—smaller if you will. Federal funds, although not at the level of the 1960s and early 1970s, will still be available to many libraries. Local funding sources are becoming continuously more aware of the needs and opportunities for the library. The demand for greater accountability suggested in earlier chapters of this book is an indicator of this awareness. Media management, in responding to this adequately, can expect at the same time to discover stronger support from the community served when good accounting demonstrates real need. It is obvious that management has a tremendous job to do in creating sufficient confidence in the collective minds of those who control its fiscal resources to stimulate adequate support in terms of dollars. One reason the MBO budget procedure is so emphasized in this book is that if budgets are adequately presented, justified, and communicated to fiscal decision makers, the multimedia library will stand a better chance of maintaining adequate funding for its program.

Another type of decision that management will have to face in the future is in the area of fees charged for services. As multimedia formats become more sophisticated, and the library offers services such as computerized reference, cable television delivery, college-level instruction through programmed materials, and materials on videocassette and discs for example, there is going to be pressure on the patron to share some of the cost of this technology. The fee system is already used in the case of the interlibrary loan, for example, where many libraries are charging the requestor a fee for a photocopy instead of sending the material requested.

Personnel management is another large area of concern with fiscal implications for the media manager. Salaries and benefits are costing more, and will continue to rise. It seems probable that in the late 1970s and into the 1980s there will be an increase in unions, collective bargaining activity, and staff participation in decision making. Since staffing is the largest part of any multimedia budget, costs for staff can be expected to increase.

In looking toward these staffing concerns for the future, serious consideration must be given especially to the trend toward collective bargaining. There is, at the present time, an oversupply of trained, professional librarians. Those who have positions are very much concerned about job security, and many feel it is necessary and advisable to take collective action rather than to rely upon individual action and negotiation. Historically it has been observed that union and collective bargaining programs draw strength and grow during periods of unemployment. Accordingly, there are serious implications for the future multimedia librarian in the experience of the present day.

Whether professional librarians will utilize their professional organizations for collective bargaining, or turn to traditional labor unions, for example, is a question as yet unresolved. Two of our largest states, New York in 1968 and California in 1975, have already provided legislation which assures public employees of their right to collective bargaining. These laws give public employees the right to join, or not to join, a collective bargaining unit. They give public employees the right to organize, to be represented by an employee organization, and to negotiate collectively. They require the public agency to negotiate and enter written agreements, and establish procedures for grievances, disputes, and the like. They prohibit strikes by public employees.

While unions have gained some members from professional librarians' ranks, the trend for the future seems to point to management working with professional organizations which become involved in collective bargaining. For the next few years competition between professional organizations and unions for the membership and participation of professional librarians may be expected. It may be well for librarians to give strong consideration to the retention of their professional status and affiliations.

Among staff members other than the professionals, management in the multimedia library must certainly expect to see considerable union activity. Managers will need to be concerned and knowledgeable about day-to-day operations under a formal union contract.

Another interesting trend that is developing in the multimedia library is that, with the development of the new technologies such as computers and other methods of information handling, there is more and more utilization of nonlibrarians in library management. The use of skilled specialists in television and computers, among others, can drastically change the overall picture of whether professional library organizations or unions should represent the professional staff. It may be well for professional schools to include training in these technologies as part of their professional requirements.

There is also the distinct possibility under the MBO approach that the professional library staff may become designated management. In this context, they would not come under collective bargaining laws, and the organization speaking for them professionally would be the traditional professional organization rather than a union. It must be emphasized that job security is going to become very important as the supply of librarians increases and the number of positions available decreases. Management must, therefore, be very concerned about methods and techniques that provide for adequate employment security.

Finally, it is necessary to mention the Library Technical Assistant (LTA), a paraprofessional trained in the community college and graduate of a two-year associate in arts degree program. Media managers are faced with a unique challenge in deciding how to utilize LTAs. These paraprofessionals are trained to be familiar with enough library procedures and techniques to step in between the clerical and the professional staff. They are often placed in supervisory positions and may relieve professional librarians in many capacities, releasing the professional for duties requiring other kinds of specialized education and training. With the development of this paraprofessional level in multimedia library organization and the sophistication of contemporary library technology, the professional librarian may well be placed in a management role, with the LTAs as skilled specialists, in which case the professional may eventually be clearly designated as management, and thus in a noncollective bargaining role.

In the years to come, collective bargaining and the status of union activity in the library environment are going to be in a state of flux, and the manager must be prepared to understand the issues and work with the various interests and needs that arise during such a period. In academic libraries, for example, a key side issue relating to unions and collective bargaining will be the question of faculty status. Academic librarians have traditionally placed high value on faculty status. Factors in contemporary experience may change that point of view. The media manager must be prepared to deal with it.

These are but a few of the concerns, opportunities, and management realities which must be considered as the multimedia library manager looks toward the future. Certainly there is much to do and much to anticipate as the library of today looks toward its role in the future, a role in which remarkable advances in technology will certainly result in new definitions of contemporary practice, and in which the philosophy and operational dynamics of the profession will be experienced in a much different light than ever before.

BIBLIOGRAPHY

GENERAL

Adams, Charles W. "The School Media Program: A Position Statement." *School Media Quarterly* 2:127–143 (Winter 1974).

American Library Association. Public Library Association. Audiovisual Committee. *Guidelines for Audiovisual Materials and Services for Large Public Libraries.* Chicago: American Library Association, 1975.

————. *Recommendations for Audiovisual Materials and Services for Small and Medium Sized Public Libraries.* Chicago: American Library Association, 1975.

Anderson, Dorothy. "A Tiger Is a Tiger (Rather Than a Non-Lion)." *Media Manpower for Schools and Libraries* 3:10 (Oct. 1971).

A-V Task Force Survey. Final Report. Special Summary Prepared for the Audio-Visual Committee, American Library Association. Pittsburgh, Pa.: University of Pittsburgh Libraries, 1969.

Becker, Joseph. *The First Book of Information Science.* Washington, D.C.: U.S. Atomic Energy Commission, Office of Information Services, 1973.

Belland, John C. "Educational Media: Why Bother?" *School Media Quarterly* 3:219–236 (Spring 1975).

Blasingame, Ralph. "Libraries in a Changing Society." *Library Journal* 97:1667–1671 (1 May 1972).

Bretz, Rudy. *A Taxonomy of Communication Media.* Englewood Cliffs, N.J.: Educational Technology Publications, 1971.

Brown, James W. *Educational Media Yearbook, 1973.* New York: Bowker, 1973– (Annual).

———— and others. *Administering Educational Media: Instructional Technology and Library Services.* 2nd ed. New York: McGraw-Hill, 1972.

————. *AV Instruction: Technology, Media and Methods.* 4th ed. New York: McGraw-Hill, 1973.

Burr, R. L. "Library Goals and Library Behavior." *College and Research Libraries* 36:27–32 (Jan. 1975).

Busha, Charles H. "Sins of Omission—Or Commission? A Look at New School and Public Library Standards." *The Southeastern Librarian* 20:19–26 (Spring 1970).

Campbell, John C., and others. *Managerial Behavior, Performance, and Effectiveness.* New York: McGraw-Hill, 1970.

Church, John G. *Administration of Instructional Materials Organizations; Analysis and Evaluative Criteria for Materials Centers.* Belmont, Calif.: Fearon Publishers, 1970.

Clark, Geraldine. "Secondary School Libraries, Problems, Problems, Problems." *Library Journal* 98:972–973 (15 Mar. 1973).

Currall, Henry F. J., ed. *Phonograph Record Libraries: Their Organization and Practice.* 2nd ed. Hamden, Conn.: Shoe String, 1970.

Cyr, Helen W. "Why Not the Instant Media Center." *School Libraries* 20:21–23 (Spring 1971).

Davies, Ruth Ann. *The School Library Media Center; A Force for Educational Excellence.* 2nd ed. New York: Bowker, 1974.

DeMont, Billie C., and DeMont, Roger A. "A Practical Approach to Accountability." *Educational Technology* 13:40–45 (Dec. 1973).

Dougherty, Richard M., and Heinritz, Fred J. *Scientific Management of Library Operations.* New York: Scarecrow, 1966.

Erickson, Carlton W. H. *Administering Instructional Media Programs.* New York: Macmillan, 1968.

Estes, Glenn. "The School Library, Revision of a Statement of the School Library Development Project of the American Association of School Librarians." *School Libraries* 21:45–46 (Winter 1972).

"Evaluating Learning Resources Programs." *Audiovisual Instruction* 19:4–38 (Sept. 1974).

Evans, Edward, and others. "Review of Criteria Used To Measure Library Effectiveness." *California Librarian* 33:72–83 (Apr. 1972).

Every Librarian a Manager: Proceedings of a Conference Sponsored by Indiana Chapter, Special Libraries Association and Purdue University Libraries and Audio-Visual Center, Sept. 27–28, 1974. West Lafayette, Ind.: Purdue University, 1975.

Ewing, David W., ed. *Technological Change and Management.* Cambridge: Harvard University Press, 1970.

Eyre, John, and Tonks, Peter. *Computers and Systems: An Introduction for Librarians.* London: Clive Bingley, 1971.

Fast, Elizabeth T. "Blueprint for Action." *School Media Quarterly* 2:194–199 (Spring 1974).

Fleischer, Eugene. "Decks, Cassettes, Dials or Buffers: Systems for Individual Study." *Library Journal* 96:695–698 (15 Feb. 1971).

Fox, June. "Library Planning and Evaluation Institute: Helping State Libraries Write Effective Long-Term Programs." *American Libraries* 3:501–505 (May 1972).

Gaver, Mary V. *Services of Secondary School Media Centers.* ALA Studies in Librarianship, no. 2. Chicago: American Library Association, 1971.

Gerlach, Vernon S., and Ely, Donald P. *Teaching and Media: A Systematic Approach.* Englewood Cliffs, N.J.: Prentice-Hall, 1971.

Gillespie, John T., and Spirt, Diana L. *Creating a School Media Program.* New York: Bowker, 1973.

Giondomenica, W. T., and Sullivan, T. "What Makes a Good Media Center?" *Instructor* 85:64 (Nov. 1975).

Gunselman, M. "Community College Learning Resources Center: More Than a Library." *Peabody Journal of Education* 51:84–89 (19 Jan. 1974).

Heiliger, Edward M., and Henderson, Paul B. *Library Automation: Experience, Methodology, and Technology of the Library as an Information System.* New York: McGraw-Hill, 1971.

Heyel, Carl, ed. *The Encyclopedia of Management.* 2nd ed. New York: Van Nostrand, 1973.

Hicks, Warren B., and Tillin, Alma M. *Developing Multi-Media Libraries.* New York: Bowker, 1970.

Holroyd, Gileon, ed. *Studies in Library Management.* vol. 2. Hamden, Conn.: Linnet Books, 1975.

Hug, William E. "Thoughts on Media Programs: District and School." *School Media Quarterly* 3:109–114 (Winter 1975).

An Instrument for the Qualitative Evaluation of Media Programs in California. Prepared by a committee representing the Bureau of Audio-Visual and School Library Education, the California Association for Educational Media and Technology, and the California Association of School Librarians. Sacramento, Calif.: California State Department of Education, 1972.

Kast, Fremont E. "Planning the Strategies in Complex Organizations," in his *Education, Administration, and Change: The Redeployment of Resources*, pp. 104–133. New York: Harper, 1970.

Kipp, Laurence J. "Management Literature for Librarians." *Library Journal* 97:158–160 (15 Jan. 1972).

Lifton, Walter M., ed. *Educating for Tomorrow; The Role of Media, Career Development, and Society.* New York: Wiley, 1970.

Lincoln, Joanne. "Library Automation Arrives in the Atlanta Public Schools." *The Georgia Librarian* 8:3–11 (Oct. 1972).

Lucio, William H., and McNeil, John C. *Supervision: A Synthesis of Thought and Action.* 2nd ed. New York: McGraw-Hill, 1969.

Lyle, Guy R. *Administration of the College Library.* 4th ed. New York: Wilson, 1975.

Mason, Ellsworth. "Along the Academic Way." *Library Journal* 96:1671–1676 (15 May 1971).

Media Manpower for the 70's. A Report of the Leadership Training Institute on the Activities of the Media Specialist Program of the Bureau of Educational Personnel Development. Washington, D.C.: Media Manpower, 1971.

Miller, Hannah Elsas. "A Working Media Center: An All-Media Approach to Learning." *Audiovisual Instruction* 19:59–60 (Feb. 1974).

Neville, S. H., and Clark, A. S. "How Can a University Library Support Educational Needs in a Period of Change?" *Educational Technology* 15:48–55 (Sept. 1975).

"News Report—1973 (A Year of Rude Shocks Marred Real Progress Toward the Goals That Libraries Have Set Themselves for the Decade)." *Library Journal* 99:21–35 (1 Jan. 1974).

North, Gwendolyn J. "A Place to Read, Relax and Think—Developing Library Programs for Teachers." *Canadian Library Journal* 30:20–25 (Jan. 1973).

Penland, Patrick R. *Communication for Librarians*, preliminary ed. Pittsburgh, Pa.: University of Pittsburgh, 1971.

———. *Communications Management of Human Resources for Librarians.* Pittsburgh, Pa.: University of Pittsburgh, 1971.

Ponder, John, ed. *Management in Libraries.* Melbourne, Australia: Ormond Book & Educational Supplies Pty. Ltd., 1971.

P.P.B.S. and the Library: Goals, Objectives, Program. A Report of a Librarian's Workshop. Santa Barbara, Calif.: Santa Barbara High School District, 1971.

Prostano, Emanuel T. *School Media Programs: Case Studies in Management.* Metuchen, N.J.: Scarecrow, 1970.

——— and Prostano, Joyce S. *The School Library Media Center.* Littleton, Colo.: Libraries Unlimited, Inc., 1971.

Redfern, Brian, ed. *Studies in Library Management.* Vol. 1. Hamden, Conn.: Linnet Books, 1972.

Rees, Alan, ed. *Contemporary Problems in Technical Library and Information*

Center Management: A State-of-the-Art. Washington, D.C.: American Society for Information Science, 1974.

Rogers, Rutherford D., and Weber, David C. *University Library Administration.* New York: Wilson, 1971.

Romine, Ben H. "Field Development: A Procedure for Change in Educational Systems." *Learning Today* 4:54–59 (Fall 1971).

Rosoff, Martin. *The School Library and Educational Change.* P.O. Box 263, Littleton, Colo.: Libraries Unlimited, Inc., 1971.

Ross, Johanna C. "Scientific Management in Libraries." *California Librarian* 33:83–87 (Apr. 1972).

Solberg, R., and Whiting, R. "Individualizing Learning Through Media: An ESEA Project in La Crosse." *Wisconsin Library Bulletin* 67:411–415 (Nov. 1971).

Stone, C. Walter. "An A-V Report Card for Librarianship." *Wilson Library Bulletin* 14:290–293 (Nov. 1969).

Strabel, Edward G., ed. *A Model for Management—Special Libraries: A Guide for Management.* rev. ed. New York: Special Libraries Association, 1975.

Sullivan, L. "The Media Center in Today's Curriculum." *Catholic Library World* 44:24–27 (July 1972).

Sullivan, Peggy. *Problems in School Media Management.* New York: Bowker, 1971.

Tracey, William R. *Managing Training and Development Systems.* New York: American Management Association, 1974.

Umans, Shirley. *The Management of Education.* Garden City, N.Y.: Doubleday, 1970.

Vagianos, Louis. "Information Science: A House Built on Sand." *Library Journal* 97:153–157 (15 Jan. 1972).

Ward, Pearl L., and Beacon, Robert, comps. *The School Media Center; A Book of Readings.* Metuchen, N.J.: Scarecrow, 1973.

Wasserman, Paul. *The New Librarianship: A Challenge for Change.* New York: Bowker, 1972.

—— and Bundy, Mary Lee, eds. *Reader in Library Administration.* Washington, D.C.: Microcard Editions, 1968.

Weaver, Donald C. "Contributing to Relevance in School Programs." *School Libraries* 20:15–20 (Summer 1971).

Webster, Duane E. *Library Policies: Analysis, Formulation and Use in Academic Institutions.* Office of University Library Management Studies, Washington, D.C.: Association of Research Libraries, 1972.

Zachert, Martha Jane K. *Simulation Teaching of Library Administration.* New York: Bowker, 1975.

CHAPTER 1

Adams, Charles W. "The School Media Program: A Position Statement." *School Media Quarterly* 2:127–132; 141–143 (Winter 1974).

American Library Association. Subcommittee of the Public Library Association. *Interim Standards for Small Public Libraries: Guidelines Toward Achieving the Goals of Public Library Service.* Chicago: American Library Association, 1967.

——. Public Library Association. *Performance Measures for Public Libraries.* Chicago: American Library Association, 1973.

Banathy, Bela H. *Instructional Systems.* Palo Alto, Calif.: Fearon Publishers, 1968.

Blake, Fay, and Perlmutter, Edith. "Libraries in the Marketplace." *Library Journal* 99:108–111 (15 Jan. 1974).

Boguslaw, Robert. *The New Utopians; A Study of System Design and Social Change.* Englewood Cliffs, N.J.: Prentice-Hall, 1965.

Bone, Larry Earl. "Study in Renewal: A Library in Search of Itself." *Library Journal* 97:844–847 (1 Mar. 1972).

Bromberg, Erik. *Simplified PPBS for the Librarian.* Prepared for the Dollar Decision Pre-Conference Institute. Library Administration Division, Dallas, Texas: American Library Association, 1971.

Burr, Robert L. "Library Goals and Library Behavior." *College and Research Libraries* 36:27–32 (Jan. 1975).

California Library Association. "Master Plan for Total Library Service." *California Librarian* 31:108–109 (April 1970).

Churchman, C. West. *The Systems Approach.* New York: Delacorte Press, 1968.

Citizens for the 21st Century; Long-Range Considerations for California Elementary and Secondary Education; A Report from the State Committee on Public Education to the California State Board of Education. Sacramento, Calif.: State Printing Office, 1969.

Cleland, David I., and King, William R. *Systems Analysis and Project Management.* New York: McGraw-Hill, 1968.

Conant, Ralph W., ed. *The Public Library and the City.* Cambridge, Mass: MIT Press, 1965.

Cox, Carl T. "A Total System View of the School Library." *School Media Quarterly* 1:36–40 (Fall 1972).

Dane, Chase. "The New Standards." *California School Libraries* 41:9–13 (Fall 1970).

Darling, Richard L. "Accountability: Notes Toward a Definition." *Library Journal* 96:3805–3808 (15 Nov. 1971).

———. "The Emerging School Media Center." *Wisconsin Library Bulletin* 65:279–285 (July 1969).

Decaigny, T. "The Media Resources Centre—a New Myth." *Educational Media International* 2:4–8 (1973).

Dougherty, Richard M. "The Unserved—Academic Library Style." *American Libraries* 2:1055–1058 (Nov. 1971).

Drucker, Peter F. *The Practice of Management.* New York: Harper, 1954.

Elstein, Herman. "Standards, Selection, and the Media Center: Where Are We Now?" *Audiovisual Instruction* 17:35–39 (Dec. 1970).

Emery, Richard. "Philosophy, Purpose and Function in Librarianship." *Library Association Record* 73:127–129 (July 1971).

The Formulation and Use of Goals and Objectives in Academic and Research Libraries. Occasional Paper No. 3. Office of University Library Management Studies, Washington, D.C.: Association of Research Libraries, 1972.

Frederick, Franz J. "Overview of Current Learning Theories for Media Centers." *Library Trends* 19:401–409 (Apr. 1971).

Freedman, Morris. "Integrated School Resource Programs: A Conceptual Framework and Description." *Audiovisual Instruction* 20:5–9 (Sept. 1975).

Geller, Evelyn. "This Matter of Media." *Library Journal* 96:2048–2053 (15 June 1971).

Haro, Robert P. "The Floating Academic Librarian." *American Libraries* 2:1169–1173 (Dec. 1971).

Hartley, Harry J. "Limitations of Systems Analysis." *Phi Delta Kappan* 50:515–519 (May 1969).

Hayman, John L "The Systems Approach: Alternative to Impotence in ITV Research, Part 2." *Educational and Industrial Television* 3:24 (Apr. 1971).

Kaser, David. "Modernizing the University Library Structure." *College and Research Libraries* 31:227–231 (July 1970).

King, Donald W., and Bryant, Edward C. *The Evaluation of Information Services and Products.* Washington, D.C.: Information Resources Press, 1971.

Lavisky, Saul. "A Systems Approach." *Educational Screen and AV Guide* 49:18–19 (Jan. 1970).

LeBreton, Preston P. "A Planning Philosophy for Librarians." *Mountain Plains Library Quarterly* 15:3–10 (Spring 1970).

Leopold, Carolyn. "School Librarians: Are We for Real?" *Library Journal* 96:1424–1428 (15 Apr. 1971).

Liesener, J. W. "Development of a Planning Process for Media Programs." *School Media Quarterly* 1:278–287 (Summer 1973).

Lott, Richard W. *Basic Systems Analysis.* San Francisco: Canfield Press, 1971.

Lowrie, Jean Elizabeth. "Somebody Has to Build Suspension Bridges: The Creative Innovative Librarian." *South Dakota Library Bulletin* 57:225–230 (1971).

McBeath, Ron J. "Program Planning and Management in Audiovisual Services for Higher Education." *Audiovisual Instruction* 16:62–67 (Oct. 1971).

Martin, Allie Beth. "Decision in Tulsa: An Issue of Censorship." *American Libraries* 3:370–374 (April 1971).

Media Programs: District and School. Prepared jointly by the American Association of School Librarians, American Library Association, and Association for Educational Communications and Technology. Chicago: ALA; Washington, D.C.: AECT, 1975.

Miller, Nancy. "Learning Resources Center—Its Role in Education." *Audiovisual Instruction* 16:48 (May 1971).

Nelson, Ervin N. "The Media Industry: Its Growth, Structure, and Role in Education." *School Library Journal* 16:101–103 (Mar. 1970).

Orne, Jerrold. "The Undergraduate Library." *Library Journal* 95:2230–2233 (15 June 1970).

Paetro, Madeline E. "Getting a Head Start." *School Library Journal* 18:44–45 (Sept. 1971).

Penland, Patrick R. "Discovery Management for Librarians: An Institute in Pittsburgh for Libraries Serving Underprivileged Neighborhoods." *Media Manpower for Schools and Libraries* 3:11 (Oct. 1971).

Perkins, John W., and others. *Library Objectives, Goals, and Activities.* Inglewood, Calif.: Inglewood Public Library, 1973.

Peterson, Gary T. "Conceptualizing the Learning Center." *Audiovisual Instruction* 18:67 (Mar. 1973).

Peterson, I. "Libraries Widen Activities Sparking Debate on Goals." *New York Times,* p. 41 (25 Oct. 1974).

Pfeiffer, John. *New Look at Education: Systems Analysis in Our Schools and Colleges.* New York: Odyssey, 1968.

Rowell, John. *Interpreting the Standards: People Problems in School Activities and the Library.* Chicago: American Library Association, 1972.

Shera, Jesse H. *Libraries and the Organization of Knowledge.* ed. by D. J. Fosket. Hamden, Conn.: Archon Books, 1965.

Stone, C. Walter. "Some Thoughts on Administering Media Services." *Media Manpower for Schools and Libraries* 3:12–13 (Oct. 1971).

Stowe, Richard A. "Research and the Systems Approach as Methodologies for Education." *AV Communication Review* 21:165–175 (Summer 1973).

Strauss, Lucille J., and others. *Scientific and Technical Libraries: Their Organization and Administration.* New York: Wiley, 1964.

Summers, F. William. "State Library Standards Revised: A Critique." *Library Journal* 96:1191–1192 (1 Apr. 1971).

"Systems Design and Analysis for Libraries." Issue ed. by F. Wilfrid Lancaster. *Library Trends* 21: (April 1973).

Thiagarajan, Sivasailam. "Good Objectives and Bad: A Checklist for Behavioral Objectives." *Educational Technology* 13:23–28 (Aug. 1973).

Thomas, J. Alan. *The Productive School: A Systems Analysis Approach to Educational Administration.* New York: Wiley, 1971.

Van Gigch, John P., and Hill, Richard E. *Using Systems Analysis to Implement Cost-Effectiveness and Program Budgeting in Education.* Englewood Cliffs, N.J.: Educational Technology Publications, 1971.

Ward, Pearl. "Facts Versus Values." *California School Libraries* 44:37–38 (Fall 1972).

———. "Monuments in Footprints; The School Library in the Decade of the Seventies." *California Librarian* 3:32–35 (Jan. 1970).

Wasserman, Paul. "Toward a Methodology for the Formulation of Objectives in Public Libraries: An Empirical Analysis." Unpublished Ph.D. dissertation, University of Michigan, 1960.

Weaver, Donald C. "Contributing to Relevance in School Programs." *School Libraries* 20:15–20 (Summer 1971).

Wehmeyer, Lillian W. "The Student-Centered Media Center." *California School Libraries* 45:19–24 (Summer 1974).

White, F. J. "Observational Learning of Indirect Verbal Behavior Through the Medium of Audio-Tapes." *Journal of Education Research* 65:417–419 (May/June 1972).

CHAPTER 2

Allen, Louis A. *Management and Organization.* New York: McGraw-Hill, 1958.

Bundy, Mary Lee. "Conflict in Libraries." *College and Research Libraries* 27:253–262 (July 1966).

Cain, Carolyn L. "To Meet the Needs of a Certain Subject." *Wisconsin Library Bulletin* 68:101–104 (Mar./Apr. 1972).

Emery, Richard. *Staff Communication in Libraries.* Hamden, Conn.: Linnet Books, 1975.

Jacobs, James W. "Organization of Instructional Materials Services at the System Level." *American Library Association Bulletin* 62:149–153 (Feb. 1968).

Kingsbury, M. E. "Plan by Increments." *Library Journal* 97:465–468 (Feb. 1972).

Lowrie, Jean E. "Organization and Operation of School Library Materials Centers." *Library Trends* 16:211–227 (Oct. 1967).

Shapiro, Lillian. "Bureaucracy and the School Libraries." *Library Journal* 98:1346 (15 Apr. 1973).

Waddington, Charles. "Some Principles of Administration in Libraries." *Journal of Education for Librarianship* 10:138–143 (Fall 1969).

CHAPTER 3

Anderson, John. "Aspects of Main Library Administration and Management." *Library Trends* 20:654–661 (Apr. 1972).

Bryant, David. "MBO." *New Library World* 73:286 (May 1972).

Buginas, Scott J., and Crow, Neil B. "The Computerized File Management System—A Tool for the Reference Librarian." *Special Libraries* 64:48 (Jan. 1973).

Conley, W. D., and Miller, F. W. "MBO, Pay and Productivity." *Personnel* 50:21–25 (Jan./Feb. 1973).

DeProspo, Earnest R., and Altman, Ellen. "Library Measurement: A Management Tool." *Library Journal* 98:3605–3607 (15 Dec. 1973).

Dickinson, Fidelia. "Participative Management: A Left Fielder's View." *California Librarian* 34:24–33 (Apr. 1973).

Donnelly, James H., and others. *Fundamentals of Management*. Dallas: Business Publications, 1975.

Flener, Jane G. "Staff Participation in Management in Large Libraries." *College and Research Libraries* 34:275–279 (July 1973).

Guy, Leonard C. "The Management of Libraries." *Library Association Record* 70:91–95 (Apr. 1968).

Hacker, Thorne. "Management by Objectives for Schools." *Administrator's Notebook* 20:1–4 (Nov. 1971).

Hamburg, Morris, and others. *Library Planning and Decision-Making Systems*. Cambridge, Mass.: Massachusetts Institute of Technology Press, 1974.

Handy, H. W., and Hiatt, Peter. *Dynamic Library Management Seminar: Management-By-Objectives for Library Leaders*. Boulder, Colo.: Western Interstate Commission for Higher Education, 1973.

Hetland, Richard R. "MBO: Let's Set Managing Objectives." *Supervisory Management* 18:2–10 (Feb. 1973).

Hicks, Herbert G., and Gullett, C. Ray. *Modern Business Management*. New York: McGraw-Hill, 1974.

Hoye, Robert E. "Systems Management: The Media Program." *Audiovisual Instruction* 20:6–7 (Oct. 1975).

Humble, John W. *How To Manage by Objectives*. New York: American Management Association, 1973.

Ingraham, William W., and Keefe, John E. "Values of Management by Objectives." *School Management* 16:28–30 (June 1972).

Kingsbury, M. E. "Plan by Increments." *Library Journal* 97:465–467 (1 Feb. 1972).

Kleber, Thomas. "The Six Hardest Areas to Manage by Objectives." *Personnel Journal* 51:571–575 (Aug. 1972).

Knezevich, S. J. "MBO: Its Meaning and Application to Educational Administration." *Education* 93:12–21 (Sept./Oct. 1972).

Lasanga, John. "Make Your MBO Pragmatic." *Harvard Business Review* 49:64–69 (Dec. 1971).

Longenecker, Justin. *Principles of Management and Organizational Behavior.* 3rd ed. Columbus, Ohio: Charles E. Merrill, 1973.

McConkey, Dale D. "Applying Management by Objectives to Non-Profit Organizations." *Advanced Management Journal* 38:10–19 (Jan. 1973).

————. "20 Ways to Kill Management by Objectives." *Management Review* 61:4–13 (Oct. 1972).

MacKenzie, A. Graham. "Systems Analysis as a Decision-Making Tool for the Library Manager." *Library Trends* 21:493–504 (Apr. 1973).

Mahler, Walter R. "Management by Objectives: A Consultant's Viewpoint." *Training and Development Journal* 26:16–19 (Apr. 1972).

Marchant, M. P. "Participative Management as Related to Personnel Development." *Library Trends* 20:48–59 (July 1971).

Marks, Rose. "What You Always Wanted to Do in Your Library but Were Afraid to Try." *Kansas Library Bulletin* 41:14–16 (Jan. 1972).

Mattleman, Marciene S., and Kean, Michael H. "Project Management to Improve Reading Instruction." *Educational Technology* 13:13–14 (Spring 1973).

Miller, T. E. "Media-Management Grid: A Tool for Introspection." *Audiovisual Instruction* 19:45 (Apr. 1974).

National Education Association. *Is MBO the Way to Go? A Teacher's Guide to Management by Objectives.* Washington, D.C.: National Education Association, 1975.

Ordiorne, George. *Management by Objectives: A System of Managerial Leadership.* New York: Pitman, 1965.

"Publicity With a Purpose . . . For Libraries on a Shoestring." *Library Journal* 99:862–863 (15 Mar. 1974).

Raia, Anthony P. *Management by Objectives.* Glenview, Ill.: Scott, Foresman, 1974.

Riggs, Robert O. "Management by Objectives: Its Utilization in the Management of Administrative Performance." *Contemporary Education* 43:129–132 (Jan. 1972).

Ross, Johanna C. "Scientific Management in Libraries." *California Librarian* 33:83–87 (Apr. 1972).

Ross, Kenton E. *Management by Objectives.* Cleveland: Association for Systems Management, 1971.

Saunders, Helen E. *The Modern School Library: Its Administration as a Materials Center.* Metuchen, N.J.: Scarecrow, 1968.

Seaman, Scott K. "Administration of a Learning Resources Center." *Educational Broadcasting* 8:25–27 (Oct. 1975).

Sheparovych, Zenon B. "MBO at the LRC." *Community and Junior College Journal* 44:26–27 (Oct. 1973).

Stockman, Cal. "Media Management by Objectives: A Balance Between Administrative and Leadership Roles." *Audiovisual Instruction* 19:10–12 (Apr. 1974).

Sullivan, Peggy. *Problems in School Media Management. Problem-Centered Approaches to Librarianship.* New York: Bowker, 1971.

Thomas, P. A., and Ward, Valerie A. "Librarians and the Management of Library Systems." *ASLIB Proceedings* 24:229–232 (Apr. 1972).

Tosti, Donald T., and Harmon, N. Paul. "The Management of Instruction." *AV Communication Review* 21:31–43 (Spring 1973).

Varney, Glenn H. *Management by Objectives.* Chicago: Dartnell Corp., 1971.

Wadia, Maneck S. "The Operational School of Management: An Analysis." *Advanced Management Journal*: 26–33 (July 1967).

Waller, Salvador B. "Thoughts on MBO: A Review of the Literature." *The Journal of Navy Civilian Manpower Management* 1:14–27 (Spring 1975).

Wohlking, Wallace. "Management by Objectives: A Critical View." *Training and Development Journal* 26:2 (Apr. 1972).

CHAPTER 4

Aaron, Shirley Louise. "The Making of a Differentiated Staffing Model 1973." *School Media Quarterly* 2:36–40, 57–59 (Fall 1973).

American Library Association. Library Administration Division. *Personnel Organization and Procedure: A Manual Suggested for Use in Public Libraries.* 2nd ed. Chicago: American Library Association, 1968.

Barton, Grant E. "Designing Competency Statements." *Audiovisual Instruction* 17:16–18 (Feb. 1972).

Brandwein, Larry. "Developing a Service Rating Program." *Library Journal* 100:267–269 (1 Feb. 1975).

Burton, Hilary D. "Personal Information Systems—Implications for Libraries." *Special Libraries* 64:7–10 (Jan. 1973).

Campbell, Rosalind. "The Library Technical Assistant." *North Carolina Libraries* 31:15–19 (Spring 1973).

Capri, Walt. "How One School Added a Media Specialist to Its Teaching Team—At No Extra Cost." *California School Libraries* 43:6–8 (Winter 1972).

Case, Robert N. "Who Should Do What In the Media Center." *Wilson Library Bulletin* 45:852–855 (May 1971).

Cooprider, David. "Does School Media Require Professionals?" *Illinois Libraries* 53:481–482 (Sept. 1971).

Denov, Charles C. *Establishing a Training Function: A Guide for Management.* Englewood Cliffs, N.J.: Educational Technology Publications, 1971.

DeProspo, Ernest R. "Personnel Evaluation as an Impetus to Growth." *Library Trends* 20:60–70 (July 1971).

Elliott, Ann B. "Volunteers are Vital." *California School Libraries* 45:14–18 (Summer 1974).

Emerson, William L. "Try It, You'll Like It." *Wilson Library Bulletin* 46:326 (Dec. 1972).

Famularo, J. J. *Supervisors In Action.* New York: McGraw-Hill, 1961.

Flippo, Edwin B. *Principles of Personnel Management.* 3rd ed. New York: McGraw-Hill, 1971.

Goodman, Charles H. "Employee Motivation." *Library Trends* 20:39–47 (July 1971).

Greenlaw, Paul S., and Smith, Robert D. *Personnel Management: A Management Science Approach.* Scranton, Pa.: International Textbook Co., 1970.

"Guidelines for Using Volunteers in Libraries." *American Libraries* 2:407–408 (Apr. 1971).

Jenkins, Harold. "Volunteers In the Future of Libraries." *Library Journal* 97:1399–1403 (15 Apr. 1972).

Jucius, Michael. *Personnel Management.* 6th ed. Homewood, Ill.: Richard D. Irwin, 1967.

Lowrey, Anna Mary. "School Library Manpower Project Launches Phase II." *Audiovisual Instruction* 17:26–28 (Jan. 1972).

Myers, M. Scott. *Every Employee a Manager.* New York: McGraw-Hill, 1970.

Newcomb, Ruth Becker. "Role Expectations of the School Library Supervisor as a Function of the Distance Between Expected and Perceived Fulfillment." *Educational Leadership* 4:637–640 (Mar. 1971).

O'Bruba, William, and Mika, Joseph. "The Para and the Pro." *Learning Today* 6:22–24 (Summer 1973).

Occupational Definitions for School Library Media Personnel. Chicago: American Library Association, 1971.

Peele, David. "Evaluating Library Employees." *Library Journal* 97:2803–2807 (15 Sept. 1972).

Pigors, Paul, and Myers, Charles A. *Personnel Administration.* 5th ed. New York: McGraw-Hill, 1965.

Ricking, Myrl, and Booth, Robert E. *Personnel Utilization in Libraries: A Systems Approach.* Chicago: American Library Association, 1974.

Rudnik, Sister Mary Chrysantha. "What Every Librarian Should Know About Library Technical Assistants." *Wilson Library Bulletin* 46:67 (Sept. 1971).

Schultzenberg, Antony, and Burlingame, Dwight. "Bringing it All Together." *Learning Today* 6:68–71 (Summer 1973).

Scott, M. S., "Competency-Based Evaluation For Media Personnel." *Audiovisual Instruction* 19:45 (June 1974).

Scott, Walter Dill, and others. *Personnel Management.* New York: McGraw-Hill, 1961.

Silver, Carole K. "The Librarian and the AV Specialist: Less Talk of 'either/or' More of Both." *Library Trends* 19:352–355 (Apr. 1971).

Simon, Barry. "Preventing Discriminating Employment Practice." *American Libraries* 3:1207–1209 (Dec. 1972).

"The Staffing of Secondary School Libraries." *The School Librarian* 19:10–14 (Mar. 1971).

Stebbins, Kathleen B. *Personnel Administration in Libraries.* 2nd rev. ed. by Foster E. Mohrhardt. New York: Scarecrow, 1966.

Stone, Elizabeth W. "Administrators Fiddle While Employees Burn—or Flee." *ALA Bulletin* 63:181–187 (Feb. 1969).

Tanzman, Jack. "What You Need to Build an Instructional Materials Center." *School Management* 15:62–63 (Jan. 1971).

"Task Analysis Study in Illinois: Phase I of a Cooperative Project." *American Libraries* 2:312–314 (Mar. 1971).

Tucker, Marjorie P. "Volunteers For the Library." *California School Libraries* 44:21–22 (Winter 1973).

Wallington, Clinton James. "Act II of JIMS." *Audiovisual Instruction* 17:29–32 (Jan.1972).

CHAPTER 5

Baumol, William J., and others. "The Costs of Library and Information Services," in Douglas M. Knight and E. Shepley Nourse. *Libraries at Large*, pp. 168–227. New York: Bowker, 1969.

Brong, Gerald. *Audiovisual Center Allocation Formula*. The Author, 1972.

Costs of Public Library Services: 1971. Chicago: American Library Association, 1971.

Dougherty, Richard M. *Management and Costs of Technical Processes: A Bibliographical Review, 1876–1969*. Metuchen, N.J.: Scarecrow, 1970.

Fulton, W. R. *Criteria Relating to Educational Media Programs in Colleges and Universities*. Norman, Okla.: University of Oklahoma Press, 1972.

Gelfand, Morris. "Budget Preparation and Presentation." *American Libraries* 3:496–500 (May 1972).

Gerstenberg, Charles W. *Financial Organization and Management of Business*. 4th rev. ed. Englewood Cliffs, N.J.: Prentice-Hall, 1959.

Gulko, Warren W. *Program Classification Structure*. P.O. Drawer P, Boulder, Colo.: Planning and Management Systems Division, Western Interstate Commerce for Higher Education, 1972.

Hall, Clem. "Writing Project Applications for Funding." *American Libraries* 1:779–780 (Sept. 1970).

Hellum, Bertha D., and others. "Financing Library Construction." *California Librarian* 34:52–57 (Jan. 1970).

Holland, Elsie D. "The Initials PPBS Stand For Planning, Programming, Budgeting System." *California School Libraries* 41:143–144 (May 1970).

Howard, Edward N. "Toward PPBS in the Public Library." *American Libraries* 2:386–393 (Apr. 1971).

Howard, Lore. "A Better Look at Budgets." *Library Journal* 96:1081–1082 (15 Mar. 1971).

Jenkins, Harold R. "The ABC's of PPB: An Explanation of How Planning-Programming-Budgeting Can Be Used to Improve the Management of Libraries." *Library Journal* 96:3089–3093 (1 Oct. 1971).

Jordan, Roy. "Clarifying an AV Budget." *Audiovisual Instruction* 15:69–71 (May 1970).

Kilgour, Frederick. "Evolving, Computerizing, Personalizing." *American Libraries* 3:143–147 (Feb. 1972).

Kountz, John. "Library Cost Analysis: A Recipe." *Library Journal* 97:459–464 (1 Feb. 1972).

Little, Robert D. "Budgeting for Instructional Resources." *Wisconsin Library Bulletin* 68:327–331 (Sept./Oct. 1971).

Louderback, Joseph G., and Dominiak, Geraldine F. *Managerial Accounting*. Belmont, Calif.: Wadsworth, 1975.

Meyers, Judith, and Barber, Raymond. "McNamara, Media and You." *Library Journal* 96:1079–1081 (15 Mar. 1971).

Miller, Evelyn R. "Dollars Are a Year-Round Job." *Wisconsin Library Bulletin* 69:89–91 (Mar./Apr. 1973).

A Model Budget Analysis System for Program 05 Libraries. Interinstitutional Committee of Business Officers, c/o J. Curry, Director, Olympia, Wash. (98501): Evergreen State College, 1972.

Morris, Barry. "Budgeting to Meet the New Standards," in Pearl L. Ward and Robert Beacon, comps. *The School Media Center: A Book of Readings*, pp. 76–81. Metuchen, N.J.: Scarecrow, 1973.

"Revenue Sharing Roundup: Reports from the Field." *Library Journal* 98:2033–2035 (July 1973).

"School Book Allowances: Financial Needs of the Schools." *School Librarian* 19:291–293 (Dec. 1971).

Summers, William. "A Change in Budgetary Thinking." *American Libraries* 2:1169–1173 (Dec. 1971).

Thomson, S. K. *Learning Resource Centers in Community Colleges: A Survey of Budgets and Services*. Chicago: American Library Association, 1975.

Wedgeworth, Robert. "Budgeting for School Media Centers." *School Libraries* 20:29–36 (Spring 1971).

Wilkins, Henry Theodore. "How to Shake the Money Tree: A Look at Some Ways of Securing Support for the Educational Media Discipline." *Audiovisual Instruction* 18:31–34 (Apr. 1973).

CHAPTER 6

Alexander, Elenora. "The School Libraries." *Library Resources and Technical Services* 12:148–152 (Spring 1968).

American Library Association. Public Library Association. Audiovisual Committee. *Guidelines for Audiovisual Materials and Services for Large Public Libraries*. Chicago: American Library Association, 1975.

———. Public Library Association. Audiovisual Committee. *Recommendations for Audiovisual Materials and Services for Small and Medium-Sized Public Libraries*. Chicago: American Library Association, 1975.

———. Public Library Association. Standards Committee. *Minimum Standards for Public Library Systems, 1966*. Chicago: American Library Association, 1967.

Asheim, Lester, and Fenwick, Sara I., eds. *Differentiating the Media*. Proceedings of the 37th annual conference of the University of Chicago Graduate Library School, Aug. 5–6, 1974. Studies in Library Science, Chicago: University of Chicago Press, 1975.

Ball, Howard G. "A Model for Program Planning in Media." *California Librarian* 36:16–21 (July 1975).

Billings, Jane. "Selecting for the Instructional Materials Center." *Wisconsin Library Bulletin* 64:9–12 (Jan. 1968).

Boucher, Brian G., and others. *Handbook and Catalog for Instructional Media Selection*. Englewood Cliffs, N.J.: Educational Technology Publications, 1973.

Boyer, Calvin J., and Eaton, Nancy L., eds. *Book Selection Policies in American Libraries: An Anthology of Policies from College, Public, and School Libraries*. Box 8131, University of Texas Station, Austin, Tex. (78712): Armadillo Press, 1971.

Broadus, Robert N. *Selecting Materials for Libraries*. New York: Wilson, 1973.

Bukalski, Peter J. "Collecting Classic Films." *American Libraries* 3:475–479 (May 1971).

Bundy, Mary Lee. "Decision Making in Libraries." *Illinois Libraries* 43:780–793 (Dec. 1961).

Carter, M. D. *Building Library Collections*. 4th ed. Metuchen, N.J.: Scarecrow, 1974.

Coon, Christa K. "Protective Book Selection," with reply by Regina Minudri. *Library Journal* 97:1162 (15 Mar. 1972).

———. "Precensorship: Round 2," with letter as a rebuttal, answered by Regina Minudri. *Library Journal* 97:2226 (15 June 1972).

Cyrs, Thomas E., and Lwenthal, Rita. "A Model for Curriculum Design Using a Systems Approach." *Audiovisual Instruction* 15:16–18 (Jan. 1970).

Della-Peana, Gabriel M., and others. "A Scheme for Maximizing Program Effectiveness." *Educational Product Report* 2:6–9 (Mar. 1969).

Denova, Charles C. *Establishing a Training Function: A Guide for Management*. Englewood Cliffs, N.J.: Educational Technology Publications, 1971.

Douglas, Jeanne Masson. "Media/Library Integration in Practice." *Audiovisual Instruction* 18:83–84 (Mar. 1973).

Eash, Maurice J. "Evaluating Instructional Materials." *Audiovisual Instruction* 17:12–13 (Dec. 1972).

Elliott, Paul H. "The Logistics Function in Instructional Technology." *Audiovisual Instruction* 18:74–76 (Mar. 1973).

"Evaluation and Selection of Media." *Audiovisual Instruction* 20:4–45 (Apr. 1975).

Evaluation Practices Used In the Selection of Educational Materials and Equipment: A Report Prepared by the Educational Products Information Exchange Institute. Albany, N.Y.: New York State Education Department, 1969.

Evaluative Criteria for the Evaluation and Selection of Instructional Materials and Equipment in the Montgomery County Public Schools. Rockville, Md.: Montgomery County Public Schools, 1974.

French, Janet. "The Evaluation Gap: The State of the Art in A/V Reviewing, with Special Emphasis on Filmstrips." *School Library Journal* 16:104–109 (Mar. 1970).

Goldman, Leonard C., and Goldman, Nancy C. "Problem-Solving in the Classroom: A Model for Sharing Learning Responsibility." *Educational Technology* 14:53–58 (Sept. 1974).

Guidelines for Two-Year College Learning Resources Programs. Prepared by the Association of College and Research Libraries, American Library Association, the American Association of Community and Junior Colleges, and the Association for Educational Communications and Technology. Washington, D.C.: AECT, 1972.

Higginson, George M., and Love, Reeve. "Planning Without Peril: Long Range Planning for Educational Development." *Educational Technology* 13:22 (Dec. 1973).

Hug, William E. *Instructional Design and the Media Program*. Chicago: American Library Association, 1975.

Improving Materials Selection Procedures: A Basic "How To" Handbook. EPIE Educational Product Report 54 (June 1973). New York: Educational Products Information Exchange Institute, 1973.

Jones, Harry, and Lawson, Ray. "Intellectual Freedom and Material Selection." *School Media Quarterly* 1:113–116 (Winter 1973).

Kelly, Edward F. "Extending the Countenance: A Comment for Evaluators." *Audiovisual Instruction* 17:23–24 (Dec. 1972).

Kemp, Jerrold E. "Which Medium?" *Audiovisual Instruction* 16:32–38 (Dec. 1971).

Leisener, James W. *A Systematic Process for Planning Media Programs.* Chicago: American Library Association, 1976.

Levitan, Karen. "The School Library as an Instructional Information System." *School Media Quarterly* 3, No. 3:194–203 (Spring 1975).

The Library Association. *School Library Resource Centres; Recommended Standards for Policy and Provision.* London: The Association, 1970.

Mali, Paul. *Managing By Objectives: An Operating Guide to Faster and More Profitable Results.* New York: Wiley, 1972.

Miller, Thomas E. "The Media-Management Grid—A Tool For Introspection." *Audiovisual Instruction* 19:7–9 (Apr. 1974).

Nickel, Mildred L. *Steps to Service: A Handbook of Procedures for the School Library Media Center.* Chicago: American Library Association, 1975.

Ott, Jack M., and others. "Taxonomy of Administrative Information Needs: An Aid to Educational Planning and Evaluation." *Educational Technology* 13:29–31 (May 1973).

Romiszowski, A. J. *The Selection and Use of Instructional Media: A Systems Approach.* New York: Halsted Press, 1974.

Rowell, John. "Interpreting the Standards: People Problems." *School Activities and the Library,* pp. 3–4. Chicago: American Library Association, 1970.

Schad, Jasper G., and Tanis, Norman E. *Problems in Developing Academic Library Collections.* New York: Bowker, 1974.

Sheahan, Drake, and Dougall, Stewart. *Management and Planning.* New York: Association of New York Libraries for Technical Services, 1969.

Shoner, Johnny M. "Selecting Initial Media Equipment for New Facilities." *School Media Quarterly* 2:227–233 (Spring 1974).

Spirt, Diana L. "Criteria, Choices, and Other Concerns About Filmstrips." *Previews* 1:5 (Jan. 1973).

Spotlight: Media Solution; Handbook for Media Specialists. Comp. by the Audio-Visual Committee, 1972–73, Ohio Association of School Librarians. Columbus, Ohio: The Association, 1973.

Standards for Secondary School Libraries. Prepared by the Commonwealth Secondary Schools Libraries Committee. Canberra, Australia: Australian Government Publishing Service, 1971.

Standards for the Development of School Media Programs in California. Prepared by a Joint Committee of California Association of School Librarians and Audio-Visual Education Association of California. Burlingame, Calif.: California Association of School Librarians, 1970.

Stockman, Cal. "Media Management by Objectives: A Balance Between Administrative and Leadership Roles." *Audiovisual Instruction* 19:10–12 (Apr. 1974).

Topper, Louis. "Back to Basics: Some Problems and Pointers for Those Introducing AV Materials Into the Library." *Wilson Library Bulletin* 47:42 (Sept. 1972).

———. "Evaluating Audio-Visual Material." *Educational Technology* 13:19–20 (May 1973).

Vagianos, Louis. "Scaling the Library Collection." *Library Journal* 98:712–715 (1 Mar. 1973).

Woolls, Blanche. "Who Previews What. . . ." *AV Guide* 51:4–7 (July 1972).

CHAPTER 7

American Library Association. Resources and Technical Services Division. Acquisi-tions Section, Bookdealer-Library Relations Committee. *Guidelines for Han-dling Library Orders for In-Print Monographic Publications.* Chicago: American Library Association, 1973.

———. Resources and Technical Services Division. Resources Section. Bookdealer-Library Relations Committee. *Guidelines for Handling Library Orders for Serials and Periodicals.* Acquisitions Guidelines No. 2. Chicago: American Library Association, 1974.

Anglo-American Cataloging Rules, North American Text. ed. by Sumner Spaulding. Chicago: American Library Association, 1967.

———. Chapter 6, *Separately Published Monographs.* rev. to accord with the International Standard Bibliographic Description (Monographs). Chicago: American Library Association, 1974.

———. Chapter 12, revised: *Audiovisual Media and Special Instructional Materials.* Chicago: American Library Association, 1975.

Applebaum, Edmond L., ed. *Reader in Technical Services.* Washington, D.C.: Microcard Editions, 1973.

Badten, Jean, and Motomatzu, Nance. "Commercial Media Cataloging—What's Holding Us Up?" *School Library Journal* 15:34–35 (Nov. 1968).

Bookstein, Abraham. "Effect of Uneven Card Distribution on a Card Catalog." *Library Resources and Technical Services* 19:19–23 (Winter 1975).

Carter, Ruth C. "Automation of Acquisitions at Parkland College." *Journal of Library Automation* 5:118–136 (June 1972P.

Case, Robert N. *Behavioral Requirements Analysis Checklist: A Compilation of Competency-Based Job Functions and Task Statements for School Library Media Personnel.* Chicago: American Library Association, 1973.

Chapman, Edward A., and others. *Library Systems Analysis Guidelines.* New York: Wiley-Interscience, 1970.

Cohen, Jackson B. "Science Acquisitions and Book Output Statistics." *Library Resources and Technical Services* 19:370–379 (Fall 1975).

Daily, Jay E. *Cataloging Phonorecordings.* Practical Library and Information Science Series, vol. 1. New York: Marcel Dekker, 1975.

DeVolder, Arthur. "Why Continue an Approval Plan." *Mountain-Plains Library Quarterly* 17:11–16 (Summer 1972).

Doiron, Peter M. "The Anatomy of Acquisitions." *Library Journal* 98:2981 (15 Oct. 1973).

Dougherty, Richard M., and Leonard, Lawrence E. *Management and Costs of Technical Processes: A Bibliographical Review, 1876–1969.* Metuchen, N.J.: Scarecrow, 1970.

Ford, Stephen. *The Acquisition of Library Materials.* Chicago: American Library Association, 1973.

Geller, Evelyn. "A Media Troika and Marc: A Progress Report on A/V Cataloging Standards and Services." *Library Journal* 97:249–253 (15 Jan. 1972).

Gore, Daniel. "In Hot Pursuit of FASTCAT." *Library Journal* 97:2693–2695 (1 Sept. 1972).

———. "Zero Growth for the College Library." *College Management* 9:12–14 (Aug. 1974).

Goyal, S. K. "A Systematic Method for Reducing Overordering Copies of Books." *Library Resources and Technical Services* 16:26–32 (Winter 1972).

Gregory, Roma. "Afternoon of an Acquisitions Librarian, or How to Hurry Up and Rush." *Publishers Weekly* 201:45 (10 Jan. 1972).

Hensel, Evelyn, and Veillette, Peter D. *Purchasing Library Materials in Public and School Libraries: A Study of Purchasing Procedures and the Relationships Between Libraries and Purchasing Agencies and Dealers.* Chicago: American Library Association, 1969.

Hickey, Doralyn J. *Problems in Organizing Library Collections.* New York; Bowker, 1972.

International Federation of Library Associations. *ISBD (M)—International Standard Bibliographic Description for Monographic Publications.* 1st std. ed. London: International Federation of Library Associations Committee on Cataloging, 1974.

Kountz, John. "Library Cost Analysis: A Recipe." *Library Journal* 97:459–464 (1 Feb. 1972).

Lennox, Tom. "Slides Acquisition, a Media Librarians Problem." *Library Journal: School Library Journal Previews* 1:5–11 (Nov. 1972).

"Libraries Look to the State Agency." *American Libraries* 2:735–742 (July/Aug. 1971).

Little, Helen Welch. "Library-Book Trade Relations." *Library Trends* 18:398–409 (Jan. 1973).

McGrath, William E. "A Pragmatic Book Allocation Formula for Academic and Public Libraries With a Test for Its Effectiveness." *Library Resources and Technical Services* 19:356–369 (Fall 1975).

Massonneau, Suzanne. "Bibliographic Control and Cataloging Cost Control: Interlocking Problems." *Library Journal* 98:1890–1893 (15 June 1973).

———. "Cataloging Nonbook Materials: Mountain or Molehill?" *Library Resources and Technical Services* 16: 294–304 (Summer 1972).

———. "Which Code For the Multi-Media Catalog?" *School Media Quarterly* 2:116–122 (Winter 1974).

Melcher, Daniel. *Melcher on Acquisition.* Chicago: American Library Association, 1971.

Mitchell, Betty J. "A Systematic Approach to Performance Evaluation of Out-of-Print Book Dealers: The San Fernando Valley State College Experience." *Library Resources & Technical Services* 15:215–222 (Spring 1971).

Morey, Thomas J. "Many Benefits From Centralized Library Service: Xerox Corporation's Information Product Activities." *Special Libraries* 63:245–247 (May/June 1972).

Nickel, Mildred L. "Acquisition of Materials in the School Media Center," in Pearl L. Ward and Robert Beacon, comps., *The School Media Center: A Book of Readings*, pp. 144–151. Metuchen, N.J.: Scarecrow, 1973.

O'Beirne-Ranelagh, Elaine. "A Librarian Makes a Case for Ordering Direct." *Publishers Weekly* 205:84 (14 Jan. 1974).

Parker, Thomas F. "Resource Sharing From the Inside Out: Reflections On the Organizational Nature of Library Networks." *Library Resources & Technical Services* 19:349–355 (Fall 1975).

Perez, Ernest R. "Acquisitions of Out-Of-Print Materials." *Library Resources & Technical Services* 17:42–59 (Winter 1973).

Perkins, John W., and others. *Library Technical Processes Procedures.* 2nd ed. Inglewood, Calif.: Inglewood Public Library, 1972.

Ross, Robert F. "You and the Common Sense of PPBS." *Educational Technology* 13:57–59 (Dec. 1973).

Seymour, Carol A., and Schofield, J. L. "Measuring Reader Failure at the Catalogue." *Library Resources & Technical Services* 17:6–23 (Winter 1973).

Stein, Rose. "A Systems Approach to Improved Efficiency in Cataloging." *Library Resources & Technical Services* 16:521–525 (Fall 1972).

Tillin, Alma M. *School Library Media Center Procedures.* Madison, Wis.: Demco Educational Corporation, 1973.

———, and Quinly, William J. *Standards for Cataloging Nonprint Materials, Fourth Edition: An Interpretation and Practical Application.* Washington, D.C.: Association for Educational Communications and Technology, 1976.

Walker, Nancy C. "Automation and Acquisitions." *Drexel Library Quarterly* 5:80–83 (Apr. 1969).

Wynar, Bohdan S. *Library Acquisitions: A Classified Bibliographic Guide to the Literature and Reference Tools.* 2nd ed. Littleton, Colo.: Libraries Unlimited, 1971.

CHAPTER 8

Bommer, M. R. W., and Ford, B. "Cost-Benefit Analysis for Determining the Value of an Electronic Security System." *College and Research Libraries* 35:270–279 (July 1974).

Childers, Thomas. "Managing the Quality of Reference/Information Service." *Library Quarterly* 42:212–217 (Apr. 1972).

Davis, D. G. "Security Problems in College and University Libraries: Student Violence." *College and Research Libraries* 32:15–22 (Jan. 1971).

Fuller, Donald F. "Santa Clara Public Library's Computerized Circulation System." *News Notes of California Libraries* 67:283–286 (Spring 1972).

Holler, Frederick. "Toward a Reference Theory." *RQ* 14:301–309 (Summer 1975).

Joy, H. L. "Surveillance Systems for School Media Centers." *Wilson Library Bulletin* 48:529–530 (Mar. 1974).

"Library Security: Book Thefts Are Up." *Library Journal* 100:352 (15 Feb. 1975).

"Library Security Roundup: Reports From the Field." *Library Journal* 98:1533–1534 (15 May 1973).

Morgan, Candace. "The Reference Librarian's Need For Measures of Reference." *RQ* 14:11–13 (Fall 1974).

"New Book Detection System For Small Library Use." *Library Scene* 3:35 (Dec. 1974).

Pierson, Robert M. "Thoughts On Circulation: 'Sorry—It's Charged Out.'" *Wilson Library Bulletin* 44:951–956 (May 1970).

Pritchard, Hugh. "Sensitivity at the Reference Desk." *RQ* 11:49–50 (Fall 1971).

Revill, D. H. "Theft Problem in Libraries." *New Library World* 76:123–124 (June 1974).

Runyon, Robert S. "The Library Administrator's Need For Measures of Reference." *RQ* 14:9–11 (Fall 1974).

Schefrin, R. A. "Barriers To and Barriers Of Library Security." *Wilson Library Bulletin* 45:870–878 (May 1971).

Scott, M. S. "Automedia: Automated Techniques in the Management of Resources." *Audiovisual Instruction* 19:63 (June 1973).

Shifrin, Malcolm. *Information in the School Library*. Hamden, Conn.: Linnet Books and Clive Bingley, 1973.

"Stop Thief." *Library Scene* 4:28–29 (June 1975).

Stowers, M. P. "AV Services Prove Their Worth by Computer: University of Nevada." *College and University Business* 56: 49–52 (Feb. 1974).

"Theft Detection Systems for Libraries: A Survey." *Library Technical Reports* 10:1–98, Section U (May 1974).

Veihman, Robert A. "Some Thoughts On Intershelving." *Audiovisual Instruction* 18:87–88 (Mar. 1973).

Wilkinson, Billy R. *Reference Services for Undergraduate Students: Four Case Studies*. Metuchen, N.J.: Scarecrow, 1972.

CHAPTER 9

Becker, Joseph, ed. *Interlibrary Communications and Information Networks*. Chicago: American Library Association, 1972.

Bender, David R. "Cooperative Planning for Media Program Development." *School Media Quarterly* 3:115–120 (Winter 1975).

Beswick, Norman W. "Corner Shop or Supermarket? Future of Resource Centres." *Times Educational Supplement* 3135:31 (4 July 1975).

Biblarz, Dora, and others. "Professional Associations and Unions: Future Impact On Today's Decisions." *College and Research Libraries* 36:121–128 (Mar. 1975).

Bock, D. Joleen. "Community Colleges: Much More." *Audiovisual Instruction* 18:91 (Mar. 1973).

Bork, Alfred M. "Videodiscs—The Ultimate Computer Input Device?" *Creative Computing* 2:44–45 (Mar./Apr. 1976).

Bowden, Virginia M. "MARVICE: A Cooperative Automated Library System." *Journal of Library Automation* 7:183–200 (Sept. 1974).

The Bowker Annual of Library and Book Trade Information. 20th ed.; ed. and comp. by Madeline Miele and Sarah Prakken. New York: Bowker, 1975.

Brose, F. K. "Collective Bargaining: Can We Adjust To It?" *California Librarian* 36:37–47 (Apr. 1975).

Butler, Brett. "State of the Nation In Networking." *Journal of Library Automation* 8:200–220 (Sept. 1975).

Clark, Alice S. "Subject Access To a Data Base Of Library Holdings." *Journal of Library Automation* 7:267–274 (Dec. 1974).

Commerton, Anne. "Union Or Professional Organization? A Librarian's Dilemma." *College and Research Libraries* 36:129–135 (Mar. 1975).

"Computerized Collection." *Nation's Schools and Colleges* 1:15–19 (Dec. 1974).

"Current Issues and Future Concerns in Libraries and Educational Technology." *Media Manpower Supplement* 3: supp. no. 3, 1–14 (Mar. 1972).

DeGennaro, Richard. "Library Automation: Second Decade." *Journal of Library Automation* 8:3–4 (Mar. 1975).

————. "Public Notice: We, the Librarians, Are No Longer Responsible For the Debts of Our Former Suitors." *American Libraries* 6:456–457 (Sept. 1975).

Donohue, Joseph C., and Kochen, Manfred, eds. *Information For the Community.* Chicago: American Library Association, 1976.

Edwards, B. A. "What Equipment and Systems Can We Expect in the 1970's and Beyond." *Aslib Proceedings* 24:11–21 (Jan. 1972).

Galvin, Thomas J. "The Education of the New Reference Librarian." *Library Journal* 100:727–730 (15 Apr. 1975).

Haro, Robert P. "Change in Academic Libraries." *College and Research Libraries* 33:97–103 (Mar. 1972).

Harrelson, Larry E. "Cable Television and Libraries: The Promise, the Present, and Some Problems." *RQ* 14:321–333 (Summer 1975).

Hock, Randolph E. "Providing Access to Externally Available Bibliographic Data Bases in an Academic Library." *College and Research Libraries* 36:208–215 (May 1975).

Holler, Frederick. "Toward a Reference Theory." *RQ* 14:301–319 (Summer 1975).

Hueckel, Glenn. "A Historical Approach to Future Economic Growth." *Science* 187:925–931 (14 Mar. 1975).

Kingsbury, M. E. "Future of School Media Centers." *School Media Quarterly* 4:19–26 (Fall 1975).

Kirkland, Jean. "Reference Service and the Computer: An Experiment at the Georgia Tech Library." *RQ* 14:211–223 (Spring 1975).

Knight, Douglas M., and Nourse, E. Shepley, eds. *Libraries at Large.* New York: Bowker, 1969.

Kohut, Joseph J. "Allocating the Book Budget: A Model." *College and Research Libraries* 35:192–199 (May 1974).

Kountz, John C. "Library Support Through Automation: The California State University and College Plan For Library Automation." *Journal of Library Automation* 8:98–114 (June 1975).

Levitan, Karen. "The School Library as an Instructional Information System." *School Media Quarterly* 3:194–203 (Spring 1975).

Licklider, J. C. R. *Libraries of the Future.* Cambridge, Mass.: Massachusetts Institute of Technology Press, 1965.

Lukenbill, Willis Bernard. "The School Library Media Center: Implications for Its Future Development in a Technological Age." *Louisiana Library Association Bulletin* 35:23–28 (Spring 1972).

McShean, Gordon. "Switchboard . . . A Threat to Libraries?" *California Librarian* 34:47–59 (Jan. 1973).

Martell, Charles. "Administration: Which Way—Traditional Practice or Modern Theory?" *College and Research Libraries* 33:104–112 (Mar. 1972).

Mason, Ellsworth. "Contemporary Education: A Double View." *School Library Journal* 16:35–40 (Nov. 1969).

————. "The Sobering Seventies: Prospects for Change." *Library Journal* 97:3115–3119 (1 Oct. 1972).

Maxwell, Monty M. "Unconventional Photographic Systems: How Will They Change Your Library?" *Wilson Library Bulletin* 17:518–524 (Feb. 1972).

Myers, Alpha S. "Media Centers and Innovation." *Audiovisual Instruction* 18:77–80 (Mar. 1973).

Myers, Charles A. *Computers in Knowledge-Based Fields*. Cambridge, Mass.: Massachusetts Institute of Technology Press, 1970.

"1976, The Year To Be Cautious." *Business Week* 2413:45–46 (29 Dec. 1975).

Parker, Thomas F. "Resource Sharing From the Inside Out: Reflections On the Organizational Nature of Library Networks." *Library Resources and Technical Services* 19:349–355 (Fall 1975).

Pratt, Allan D. "Libraries, Economics, and Information: Recent Trends in Information Science Literature." *College & Research Libraries* 36:33–38 (Jan. 1975).

Prostano, Emanuel T. *Audiovisual Media and Libraries: Selected Readings*. Littleton, Colo.: Libraries Unlimited, 1972.

Reed, Mary Jane Pobst. "The Washington Library Network's Computerized Bibliographic System." *Journal of Library Automation* 8:174–199 (Sept. 1975).

Ruark, Henry C. "Learning Media: Year 2000." *AV Guide* 51:2–15 (July 1972).

Saffady, William. "A Computer Output Microfilm Serials List For Patron Use." *Journal of Library Automation* 7:263–266 (Dec. 1974).

Sauage, Noel. "News Report 1975." *Library Journal* 101:579–593 (15 Feb. 1976).

Sheets, Kenneth R. "As the Future Closes In On Us." *U.S. News and World Report* 79:88 (3 Nov. 1975).

Simonds, Michael J. "Work Attitudes and Union Membership." *College and Research Libraries* 36:136–142 (Mar. 1975).

Spang, Lothar. "Collective Bargaining and University Librarians." *College and Research Libraries* 36:106–114 (Mar. 1975).

Stone, Walter C., comp. *Academic Change and the Library Function*. Pittsburgh, Pa.: Pennsylvania Library Association, 1970.

Toombs, Kenneth F. "Light-Pen Technology at the University of South Carolina—the South Carolina Circulation System." *Journal of Library Automation* 7:226–227 (Sept. 1974).

Vagianos, Louis. "Scaling the Library Collection; a Simplified Method for Weighing the Variables." *Library Journal* 98:712–715 (1 Mar. 1973).

Vail, Walter J. "District-Wide Closed-Circuit Television." *Audiovisual Instruction* 19:45–48 (May 1974).

"Videodiscs, The Expensive Race To Be First." *Business Week* 2398:58–66 (15 Sept. 1975).

Vollbrecht, John. "Will Future Media Centers Be Built Around Computers?" *Audiovisual Instruction* 19:42–44 (May 1974).

Waters, Harry F., and others. "Video's New Frontier." *Newsweek* 86:52–57 (8 Dec. 1975).

Wheelbarger, Johnny J. "The Learning Resource Center at the Four-Year College Level." *Audiovisual Instruction* 18:92 (Mar. 1973).

Yamada, K. "Impact: A College Library and Educational Technology." *Audiovisual Instruction* 18:12–13 (Dec. 1973).

Youngs, Gordon W. "Collective Bargaining and the Para-Professional." *California Librarian* 37:46–48 (Jan. 1976).

APPENDIX: JOB DESCRIPTIONS

REFERENCE LIBRARIAN

I. *Objectives*
   A. To give direct, personal aid to students and faculty in searching for information and materials
   B. To instruct students in the use of the library and its materials; to encourage the use of the library as an independent study center
   C. To select suitable materials for the reference, circulating, and periodical collections
   D. To assist in the maintenance and evaluation of the collection
   E. To create such files and/or indexes, etc., as are necessary for the efficient retrieval of information

II. *Description of Duties*
   A. Answering reference and research queries. These may be of a short answer variety, or may involve searches of thirty minutes depending on the nature of the problem
   B. Scanning lists, bibliographies, and other selection tools for suitable additions to the collections
   C. Ordering and indexing vertical file materials
   D. Ordering and indexing vocational file materials
   E. Supervising the organization and maintenance of special files, such as the drama file, vocational file
   F. Scheduling of library orientation talks
   G. Giving library orientation talks
   H. Instructing students in the proper use of indexes, card catalogs, etc., on an individual basis
   I. Instructing students in the use of library equipment
   J. Pursuing such special projects or assignments as may be deemed necessary by the director
   K. Supervising maintenance of library equipment. Troubleshooting minor mechanical problems as necessary
   L. Maintaining a quiet atmosphere in the library, taking disciplinary measures when necessary
   M. Scanning daily newspaper for items to be clipped and filed in the vertical file
   N. Indexing certain magazines not covered by *Readers' Guide* or other indexes
   O. Arranging for art exhibits and other community interest displays
   P. Assisting in and supervising the handling of art exhibits
   Q. Selection of and supervising the ordering and claiming of periodicals
   R. Selection of and supervising the ordering and claiming of microforms

    S. Weeding of the reference collections

    T. Compiling bibliographies and special collections of materials to assist students and faculty

    U. Handling interlibrary loans

    V. Abstracting printed materials

    W. Informing faculty and students about materials relating to their special interests

III. *Responsibilities and Authority*

    A. Supervising all reference desk activities

    B. Recommending reference policies and the rules and regulations to implement established policies. Making reports on same

    C. Assisting the circulation area in maintaining an orderly collection in the stack area and in the browsing collection

LIBRARY MEDIA TECHNICIAN I, II, III

I. *Definition*

Under general supervision, to perform a variety of responsible and complex technical tasks related to (a) the acquisition, preparation and utilization of library materials; or (b) the installation, operation, maintenance, and utilization of assigned media equipment; and to do related work as required.

II. *Distinguishing Characteristics*

All media technician positions require the independent and responsible application of paraprofessional knowledge and skills derived from specialized training and intensive experience in library technology, art, photography, and electronics or television production. Practical knowledge may be required of library functions and services and ability to apply standard library tools, methods, and procedures. The positions typically involve responsibility for the full operations of a basic library service unit, working under general supervision. Such positions are designed to relieve the professional librarians for higher level responsibilities, or to provide advanced technical skills in specialized library media such as television, electronics, or graphics. Most positions involve the supervision of student assistants and may include the supervision of media clerks and technicians of a lower classification.

    A. Job Areas. Library media technicians may have responsibilities in one or more of the following job areas, each of which requires specific technical knowledge and proficiency.

        1. Working supervisor responsible for the full operations of a basic library service or production unit which is under the overall direction of a library administrator (e.g., acquisitions, circulation/reference and other public services, assistance with independent study and materials, or audiovisual)

        2. Preparation of graphic materials involving skilled art work and knowledge of the technical processes or photography and camera operation

        3. Operation of television studio and equipment, and serving as production technician

        4. Installation, operation, maintenance, repair, and utilization of electronics/mechanical audiovisual equipment used in instruction

    B. Position Levels. Library Media Technician I, II, and III are differentiated on the basis of such factors as size and scope of operating service unit, availability of written procedures, amount of independent judgment and action required, variety and complexity of technical processes and equipment, extent of public contact and types of assistance provided, complaints and discrepancies handled, the technical knowledge and skills required, and the degree of supervisory responsibility.

1. Library Media Technician I. Works within well-defined verbal and written procedures, performing responsible and difficult paraprofessional library work which requires skills and knowledge of phases of library activities which exceed those normally expected in clerical positions; typically has full accountability for operations in a technical library service of moderate size not under the direct supervision of a professional librarian; may perform skilled work in the preparation of materials, operation, repair, and maintenance of audiovisual equipment; or television procedures, but working with problems of limited scope and complexity.

2. Library Media Technician II. Operates within general policies and procedures as a working supervisor or skilled technician providing technical library services; may have full accountability under general direction of a library administrator for operations in a moderate to large size campus or district library service unit; may have more direct responsibilities in assisting students or dealing with the adjustment of important complaints and discrepancies; responsibility extends to carrying through relatively independently on a complete set of library activities or technical procedures necessary to maintain a basic library function; possesses the full range of journeyman level skills required in the assigned area and is able to solve most problems of average difficulty; varies from Library Media Technician I in the added size of the service unit, greater independence of operation, more accountability and overall responsibility, more variety of functions, and/or greater degree of specialization.

3. Library Media Technician III. Works within general policies and procedures and may initiate procedures to guide other employed personnel; performs as a working supervisor with full accountability for the technical operations of a large and complex campus or district service unit under the general direction of a library administrator; prepares evaluation materials on the effectiveness of operations and makes recommendations for improvement; may be expected to apply specific paraprofessional library skills and knowledge as well as a comprehensive knowledge of the practices and procedures of a basic library function; or, applies advanced technical skills and theory that require special college or technical training to such areas as electronics-mechanics, telecommunications, or television; must use initiative in developing methods, techniques, and procedures and be responsible for providing technical and quasi-professional information on a wide variety of topics; may be distinguished from professional librarian positions on the basis of the intensive knowledge of certain areas obtained through coursework in library technology and through experience as contrasted with the knowledge of theories and fundamentals of library science acquired by professionals who hold advanced degrees.

4. Special Note on Library Media Technician IV. Positions in this class are limited to the full range performance of campus wide or district-wide services involving either (a) complex electronics equipment installation, repair and maintenance, and including all types of instructional audiovisual equipment, or (b) the more complex technical and production techniques of closed circuit and cable television, including color.

III. *Examples of Duties*

Trains, supervises, and evaluates student assistants and other assigned library personnel; serves as working supervisor of assigned service area or as skilled technician; assists in preparing budget requests and maintaining budget control; initiates correspondence and memoranda; plans and conducts inventories; maintains safety standards; provides for security of facilities and equipment; writes and updates operating procedures; maintains data and prepares annual report of service area; evaluates effectiveness of assigned service unit and makes recommendations for improvements.

And

Directs full operations of a library service unit; may supervise circulation desk work; revises and files catalog cards, cross reference, add new serials; plans and prepares displays; checks bibliographies; assists in preparing lists of instructional materials on specific subjects; processes full range of orders for library materials; prepares statistics; maintains files of special materials; assists in preparation and utilization of instructional materials, and so on.

Or

Prepares, distributes, and stores individual study materials; assists students as instructional aides; plans and implements system for filing, issuing, receiving, and recalling library materials; plans new instructional modules to suit student needs; researches for available programmed materials; prepares displays, written and graphic materials.

Or

Prepares lettering, illustrations, art work and photography for materials to be reproduced, videotaped or used in signs or displays; designs, makes layouts, and translates features of written subject matter into graphic terms; exposes and develops film; enlarges, reduces, and intensifies prints; provides guidance on graphic technology; uses a variety of still cameras and related equipment.

Or

Disassembles and repairs electronics/mechanical audiovisual equipment; uses electronics measuring and testing devices; works from blueprints; organizes shop area; operates power tools; maintains television equipment and public address systems; implements preventive maintenance program.

Or

Sets up, adjusts, and operates television equipment in a variety of locations; provides technical assistance to faculty; prepares schedules of television use; edits and dubs video and audio recording tapes; maintains videotape library; serves as floorman and cameraman during recording sessions.

IV. *Desirable Qualifications*

A. Knowledge of
   1. materials, equipment, terminology and standard practices, and techniques used in the assigned area of library technology
   2. basic electrical, electronics, and mechanical principles as applied to audiovisual, television, and other instructional equipment in assigned area; tools, equipment, and supplies used in the technology
   3. standard office methods, practices and machines
   4. proper English usage, grammar, spelling and vocabulary

B. Ability to
1. supervise and evaluate assigned library personnel
2. take initiative and make independent judgments
3. maintain a service-oriented attitude, remaining poised under pressure
4. learn technical terminology, methods, and techniques and remain current with trends in library technology
5. skillfully use the tools and instruments in the assigned area and properly instruct others in the safe use of tools and equipment
6. perform skilled work in the repair, maintenance, and adjustment of assigned audiovisual equipment, including television
7. operate and perform skilled production work with any assigned television equipment
8. maintain assigned spaces in safe, secure, and orderly condition
9. enforce safety regulations
10. maintain stock records and inventories
11. speak, write, and explain clearly
12. type at a speed necessary for effective performance in the assigned area
13. establish and maintain cooperative and effective working relationships and meet the public with courtesy and tact

V. *Preferred Experience and Education*
   A. Library Media Technician I. Equivalent to completion of the twelfth grade and two years experience as a library media clerk; or equivalent to completion of the first year of the major in library technology as offered in a community college, or in technical training related to assignment
   B. Library Media Technician II. Equivalent to completion of the twelfth grade and two years experience as a Library Media Technician I; or equivalent to completion of all required major courses in library technology as offered in a community college, or equivalent technical training in the assigned area
   C. Library Media Technician III. Equivalent to completion of the twelfth grade and two years experience as Library Media Technician II; *or* equivalent to completion of the associate in arts degree with a major in library technology or subject related to assignment and two years of related experience

LIBRARY MEDIA CLERK I, II, III

I. *Definition*

Under supervision, to perform a variety of specialized library clerical work related to one or more of the following areas: (1) acquisitions, circulation, public services, and reference materials; (2) audiovisual processes; (3) operation of office machines, duplication and offset reproduction equipment and supporting processes; and to do related work as required.

II. *Distinguishing Characteristics*

All media clerk positions provide general and specialized clerical support services to a basic library unit. The work involves typing, filing, posting, matching and verifying, sorting, checking out books and materials, taking counts and inventories, handling mail and processing orders, meeting and assisting the public, operating office machines and reproduction equipment, and training and supervising student assistants. Specific library routines and procedures are performed under well-defined guidelines usually contained in a written manual. Special orientation is required to the library program, practices, and terminology.

   A. Library Media Clerk I. Performs the more routine clerical or manual library work of average difficulty; applies library procedures within specific guidelines usually contained in an operating manual; the work is limited in variety and scope; close supervision is provided by a professional librarian or by a media clerk or technician; may supervise a few student assistants.

   B. Library Media Clerk II. Performs a variety of the more responsible and specialized clerical tasks following verbal or written procedures; may be responsible for the efficient operations of a small service area or portions of a large basic service unit under readily available supervision; recommends improvements in service; may operate duplicating and offset reproduction equipment and perform specialized services within a central production or other laboratory; may supervise student assistants and Library Media Clerks I.

   C. Library Media Clerk III. Performs a greater variety and/or considerably more complex tasks, or has responsibility for a large number of student assistants; often works in a large service area where some independent action and initiative is required within defined guidelines and written procedures; recommends and implements improvements in service; may assist with routine complaints; may supervise Media Clerks I or II.

III. *Examples of Duties*

Processes orders and receives library materials and equipment; works at circulation desk in such routines as charging, discharging, or renewing materials, reserving books, collecting fines and following up on overdue materials; searches shelves and arranges materials; books delivery and care of audiovisual equipment and materials; types a variety of statistical, accounting and general library, and correspondence materials; may operate duplicating and offset reproduction equipment and provide other services in a central production laboratory (applies chemical agents and dampening solutions such as inks and protective coatings, installs sensitized metal printing plates or master copy of plastic coated paper; adjusts roller, feed, inking and paper guides; cleans, oils, and makes minor repairs to equipment); assists in public service areas and provides directions and factual information; maintains both specialized and general files; operates microfilm and other general and specialized machines; maintains statistical records and makes reports; participates in inventories; revises bibliographies and periodical lists and prepares acquisitions lists for circulation; does minor book and periodical repair; assigns accession numbers and assists in precataloging procedures; serves as receptionist; trains and supervises student assistants.

IV. *Desirable Qualifications*

   A. Knowledge of
      1. proper English usage, grammar, spelling and vocabulary
      2. standard office methods, practices, and procedures
      3. basic library terminology and practices

   B. Ability to
      1. learn and act correctly according to library policies and regulations
      2. demonstrate a service attitude in contacts with students, faculty, and the general public
      3. type at a speed of not less than 50 words per minute from legible copy
      4. learn to operate specialized reproduction equipment and general office equipment in area assigned
      5. maintain poise and calm under pressure
      6. supervise student assistants and other assigned personnel

       7. understand and follow oral and written directions accurately
       8. establish and maintain cooperative and effective working relationships and meet the public with courtesy and tact

C. Experience
       1. Library Media Clerk I. Six months of general clerical experience, preferably in a library
       2. Library Media Clerk II. One year of general library experience; or of specialized experience with comparable equipment to that used in major assignment
       3. Library Media Clerk III. Two years of experience equivalent to a Library Media Clerk II; or of specialized experience with comparable equipment to that used in major assignment

D. Preferred Education
       1. Library Media Clerk I. Equivalent to completion of the twelfth grade
       2. Library Media Clerk II. Equivalent to completion of the twelfth grade and with course work in library procedures/technology; or special training on equipment used in major area of assignment
       3. Library Media Clerk III. Equivalent to the completion of the first-year course in library technology as offered in a community college

Note: Courtesy of the Office of the Dean of Administrative Services, Chabot College, Hayward, California.

INDEX